The Imitation of Christ

✦ THE BARNES & NOBLE LIBRARY OF ESSENTIAL READING ✦

THE IMITATION OF CHRIST
Four Books

THOMAS À KEMPIS

INTRODUCTION BY JOHN R. TYSON

BARNES & NOBLE
NEW YORK

THE BARNES & NOBLE
LIBRARY OF ESSENTIAL READING

Originally published in 1418

This 2004 edition published by Barnes & Noble, Inc.

Barnes & Noble, Inc.
122 Fifth Avenue
New York, NY 10011

ISBN-13: 978-0-7607-5591-4
ISBN-10: 0-7607-5591-4

Printed and bound in the United States of America

7 9 10 8

CONTENTS

THE SECOND BOOK
ADMONITIONS PERTAINING TO INWARD THINGS

THE THIRD BOOK
OF INTERNAL CONSOLATION

THE FOURTH BOOK
A DEVOUT EXHORTATION TO THE HOLY COMMUNION

Introduction

Walter Elwell recently described *The Imitation of Christ* as "Religion's second-best seller"; it is second only to the Bible in sales and popularity among religious readers. Through its realistic delineation of the complexities of human existence, and in its soul-building optimism about the benefits of aspiring to a Christ-shaped life *The Imitation* clearly deserves the accolade of "Spiritual Classic." Although they were written early in the fifteenth century, the number of short meditations that comprise this work remain strikingly fresh and relevant for modern readers. Hence, Olive Wyon rightly asserted that, "*The Imitation* is unique. Its appeal is universal and it is never out of date."

Thomas à Kempis (1380–1471) or Thomas Hammerken was born at a place called Kempen, near Dusseldorf, Germany. His parents were people from the artisan class; their family name Haemerken (or Haemerlein) is derived from "little hammer." Thomas left home at the age of thirteen and traveled to Deventer, in the Netherlands, where Geert Groote had established the schools of the Brethren of the Common Life (1376). His service among the Brethren provided both the impetus and the shape for this, his most famous work. It was penned or compiled as a result of the years Thomas spent as a teacher and "Master of Novices" among the Brethren. For this reason, then, *The Imitation of Christ,* which was born in the practical piety of its author and his movement, breathes that same spirit into the reader. Surviving personal recollections of Thomas à Kempis are few indeed;

but those that are extant demonstrate this deep inner connection between the man and his work. The Carthusian Prior at Nürnberg, for example, remembered Thomas as a "most wise, most sweet and most religious man." Thomas' earliest biographer could detect no gap or distinction between his writing and à Kempis' living witness: "As he taught others, so he lived; he fulfilled in very deed, or verified in himself what he recommended in his discourses should be done."

In 1406 Thomas professed a call to religious life, and in 1413 he entered the priesthood, at the age of thirty-three. He spent the balance of his life as a Canon of St. Augustine (member of the Augustinian Order), at the monastery of St. Agnes in Zwolle. À Kempis seems to reflect upon his monastic life in the *Imitation*; for example, addressing God, he wrote: "You have given grace and friendship beyond all my deserts. What return can I make to You for this grace? For it is not granted to all men to forsake everything, to renounce the world, and to enter the life of religion."(Bk. III: 10). Among Thomas' duties were those typical of a monastic priest: preaching, study, writing, giving spiritual counsel, and copying manuscripts. Primary among his responsibilities, however, was the cultivation of his own spiritual life and Christian discipleship and if we were are to judge the success of this later responsibility by the power and popularity of his literary work *Imitation of Christ* we would be forced to conclude that à Kempis wrote from a deep well spring of spiritual practice and practical insight.

In the late-medieval period popular spirituality seemed to be at low ebb. For much of the populace Christianity had degenerated into a sort of "arithmetical piety" that sought to add up enough "good deeds" to counter balance one's sins; it attached greater significance to rote repetition of prayers and sacraments than to introspection or personal reflection. In his classic text, R.W. Southern observed: "The vast majority of people remained firmly attached to the religious aids offered by the institutional church. To put it bluntly, Europe had sunk too much intellectual, emotional, and material capital in these aids to resign them lightly. Masses and prayers for the dead, indulgences, good works, and pious donations for the remission of purgatorial pains, have never been so widely and even wildly popular as they were in the fourteenth and fifteenth centuries." Yet there was also a sparkling resurgence of lay-spirituality towards the end of the fifteenth century that was linked to the emergence of lay brother and sisterhoods (confraternities) as well as with the popularity of lay devotional aids like *The Imitation of Christ.*

Springing from the efforts of Master Geert Groote (1340–84) of Deventer, Holland, the Brethren or "the New Devout" formed themselves into "houses" or communities of priests and laymen who resolved to renounce worldliness to live in the world by the power of God. The congregations of the New Devout were formed, in part, in reaction against the growing wealth and power of the established religious orders. Unlike their contemporaries they neither begged for alms nor collected rents; rather, like the tent-maker Saint Paul and ancient monks of the desert, the Brethren sustained themselves by working with their hands. Since they did not intend to found a new religious order, the Brethren took no formal vows that bound them to the movement. They sought to live, as described by the title of one of Master Groote's founding documents, by *Resolutions and Intentions, But Not Vows.* In it he wrote: "I intend to order my life to the glory, honor, and service of God and to the salvation of my soul; to put no temporal good of body, position, fortune, or learning ahead of my soul's salvation; and to pursue the *imitation* of God in every way consonant with learning and discernment and with my own body, and estate, which predispose certain forms of *imitation.*" They intended to be devout, but not "religious" in the technical sense in which the late Middle Ages reserved that term for members of the established religious orders.

The spirituality of the Brethren of the Common Life was strongly Christocentric. It intended, as suggested by the title of this—the most significant work that comes from this movement—to imitate Jesus Christ; that is to say, they intended to live according to the injunctions and examples of Christ, and in so doing they intended to live "in Christ" and to have Christ live in them. To this end, the reverent reading of Holy Scripture especially the gospels—formed a critical portion of their pious regimen. Their interest in the Bible had an ethical edge to it, since the Brethren were studying it to cultivate moral sanctity.

And, finally, the imitation of Christ affected the inner person, and the New Devout were concerned about the "training of the heart" so that one's fallen nature might be subdued and purged out and replaced by a renewing, affectionate devotion to Christ.

Scholars have debated whether Thomas à Kempis actually wrote *The Imitation of Christ,* though there is ample evidence to suggest that he did. But Thomas probably did not create the teaching contained in the book; it is more likely that he complied, organized, and set the Deventer devotional tradition into a fixed form. There seems to be a strong correlation between the authorship of the book and Thomas' work as "Master of the Novices," a post he held from 1425 until his death in 1471.

The Imitation comprises four subsections, or "Books": (1) Counsels on the Spiritual Life, (2) Counsel on the Inner Life, (3) On Inward Consolation, and (4) On the Blessed Sacrament. Each section is made up of a series of short meditations that lead the novice deeper and deeper into union with Christ. Unity with Christ was to be realized not only through contemplation, but also through inward and outward imitation of Christ, as well as sacramental oneness with him. These four books circulated separately prior to being circulated as a unified work. The *sequela Christi* (following, imitating Christ) is the unifying theme of the entire work; but this is not a merely external or ethical modeling reminiscent of the recent "What Would Jesus Do?" slogan and jewelry. À Kempis aims at utter transformation of the reader's inner person. By meditating upon Christ's life and teaching, the author intends that we would make Christ's virtues our own and that we would conform our inner attitudes to His.

The aims of this work strongly dictated its shape and the resources used to develop it.

The chapters amount to short meditations offered in a length entirely suitable for a morning or evening devotional reading; yet, the meditations are seasoned with nuggets of spiritual wisdom that are worth pondering over the course of a long life. While there is an occasional quote from classical Greek or Roman writers, or a passing allusion to a familiar saying from one of the Church Fathers, the preponderance of sources applied by our author are—by far—drawn from the Bible. Fr. Bernard Sappen has given this matter careful study and concluded: "The books most often quoted" are the Psalms (140 times, notably the Penitential Psalms), the Wisdom books (60 times), the Prophets (42 times), Job (24 times), and etc. In the New Testament Saint Paul is utilized more than the four Evangelists (120 times against 100). Hence, Walter Elwell rightly observed: "the power of the Scripture surges through its pages."

The work does not fall neatly into any of the categories of classical Christian Spirituality, rather it represents a composite approach that includes the purgative (purging out), illuminative (receiving wisdom) and unitive ways (union with God through Christ). These three approaches receive successive emphasis in the first three books of the *Imitation.*

Numerous themes drawn from classical Christian Spirituality are intertwined in the book. Among these are: (1) Union with Christ: "Christ will come to you, and impart his consolations to you, if you prepare a worthy dwelling for Him in your heart. All true glory and beauty is within, and there He delights to dwell. He often visits the spiritual man, and holds sweet discourse with him, granting him refreshing grace, great peace, and friendship exceeding all expectation" (Bk. II: 1). Hence, ". . . you will never know peace until you become inwardly united to Christ." (2) Self-negation and humility: "Had you but once entered perfectly into the Heart of Jesus, and tasted something of His burning love, you would care nothing for your own gain or loss; for the love of Jesus causes a man to regard himself very humbly" (Bk. II: 1). (3) Purity or simplicity of heart: "There are two wings that raise a man above earthly things—simplicity and purity. Simplicity must inspire his purpose, and purity his affection. Simplicity reaches out after God; purity discovers and enjoys Him" (Bk. II: 4). (4) Divine Illumination and consolation through Christian wisdom: "Were you inwardly good and pure, you would see and understand all things clearly and without difficulty. A pure heart penetrates both heaven and hell. As each man is in himself, so does he judge outward things. If there is any joy to be had in this world, the pure in heart most surely possess it; and if there is trouble and distress anywhere, the evil conscience most readily experiences it. Just as iron, when plunged into fire, loses its rust and becomes bright and glowing, so the man who turns himself wholly to God loses his sloth and becomes transformed into a new creature" (Bk. II: 4). (5) Liberation through Detachment: "Keep yourself free from all worldly entanglement, and you will make good progress; but if you set great value on any worldly things, it will prove a great obstacle. Let nothing be great, pleasant, or desirable to you save God alone, and whatever comes from God" (Bk. II: 5). (6) Cultivation of true humility: "Set yourself always in the lowest place, and you shall be awarded the highest, for the highest cannot stand without the lowest. The Saints stand highest in God's eyes who are lowest in their own; and the more glorious they are, the more humble is their spirit" (Bk. II: 10). (7) The Way of the Cross: "Jesus has many who love His Kingdom in Heaven, but few who bear His Cross. He has many who desire comfort, but few who desire suffering. He finds many to share His feast, but few His fasting. All desire to rejoice with Him, but few are willing to suffer for His sake" (Bk. II: 11).

The piety of the New Devout paved the way for the Sixteenth Century Reformations; Protestant and Roman Catholic alike. Martin Luther encountered it in the Brethren's school at Magdeberg and through his acquaintance with the *Theologica Germanica.* John Calvin, Desiderius Erasmus, and Ignatius of Loyola each lived in the Brethren's house in Paris, though at different times, and each bore the imprint of the practical piety found in the *Imitation of Christ.* The Anabaptists embraced the theme of imitation of Christ, whether or not they embraced à Kempis' book. John Wesley, the founder of Methodism, was deeply affected by the book; both before and after his "Aldersgate experience," of May 1738, he read the work of "pious Kempis" with great appreciation. Wesley wrote: "one day I light on Thomas à Kempis. The more I read, the more I liked it. I bought one of the books, and read it over and over. I was more convinced of sin that ever, and had more power against it."

The artist Vincent van Gogh was also influenced by reading *The Imitation.* As Kathleen Erickson noted: "Vincent took from the *Imitation of Christ* the notion that the earthly life is one of trial and ordeal, a kind of journey through perils and pitfalls of earthy existence to the ultimate of glorious reunion with the Lord in heaven."

This influence is discernable in van Gogh's masterpiece entitled "Starry Night."

Former Secretary General of the United Nations, Dag Hammarskjold, was known the world over as a just, fair, and deeply spiritual man. What was less well known about Hammarskjold was the significant role that *Imitation of Christ* played in his own spiritual pilgrimage. Henry P. Van Dusen recalls seeing a French language copy of the *Imitation* at the bedside of the General Secretary's New York apartment; the same book was found next to his bed, in Leopoldville, Congo, where Hammarskjold spent his last fateful night in 1963. Tucked inside the *Imitation,* written on an index card, was the General Secretary's oath of office. *The Imitation of Christ* and the opportunity to serve the world merged to form an indissoluble whole in the life of the man who cherished them both. Hammarskjold's devotional journal was published under the title *Vägmärken* (*Markings,* 1964) soon after his death. It is clear from *Markings* that Hammarskjold turned to *The Imitation of Christ* at crucial periods of his life for spiritual reflection and direction. One such entry appeared in 1953 when, at the peak of his career as a Swedish diplomat, he had just been elected General Secretary of the U.N. Amidst phone calls, telegrams, and cables of congratulations Hammarskjold turned to the words of Thomas à Kempis as he wrote in his journal: "'Not I, but God in me. . . . I am the vessel.' The drink is God's. And God is the thirsty One."

John R. Tyson, Ph.D. is professor of Theology at Houghton College in Houghton, NY, and professor of Church History at United Theological Seminary in West Seneca, NY. He earned a Ph.D. in Theological and Religious Studies at Drew University and is the author and editor of several books and numerous articles on topics in Church History and Christian Spirituality.

Prefatory Note

Although there are a multitude of English editions of *The Imitation of Christ*, the great majority follow a certain set tradition both in arrangement, phraseology, and index; the differences consisting chiefly in type and binding.

The present edition possesses the following new features:

1. The translation is absolutely faithful to the original Latin of Thomas à Kempis. No word or phrase has been altered in the interests of any school or party.
2. The traditional arrangement into *verses* which rested on no authority whatsoever and dated only from the seventeenth century, has been abandoned in favour of an arrangement according to the original paragraphs of the MS of Thomas à Kempis, as distinguished in Hirsche's edition.
3. All direct quotations from Holy Scripture are printed in *italics*; marginal references are given not only for these, but for all allusions to or indirect quotations from the Bible.
4. The traditional index of subjects printed with some editions, which was very imperfect, has been much enlarged, and will be found extremely useful.
5. Indexes have also been added of direct Scriptural quotations, and of quotations from other books than the Bible.

October 1900

THE FIRST BOOK

ADMONITIONS, USEFUL FOR A SPIRITUAL LIFE

→ CHAPTER ONE ←

OF THE IMITATION OF CHRIST, AND CONTEMPT OF ALL THE VANITIES OF THE WORLD

He *that followeth Me, walketh not in darkness*,[1] saith the Lord. These are the words of Christ, by which we are admonished, how we ought to imitate His life and manners, if we would truly be enlightened, and delivered from all blindness of heart. Let therefore our chiefest endeavour be, to meditate upon the life of Jesus Christ.

The doctrine of Christ exceedeth all the doctrines of holy men; and he that hath the Spirit, will find therein *the hidden manna*.[2] But it falleth out, that many who often hear the Gospel of Christ, feel little desire after it, because they *have not the Spirit of Christ*.[3] But whosoever will fully and with relish understand the words of Christ, must endeavour to conform his life wholly to the life of Christ.

2. What doth it avail thee to discourse profoundly of the Trinity, if thou be void of humility, and art thereby displeasing to the Trinity? Surely profound words do not make a man holy and just; but a virtuous life maketh him dear to God. I had rather feel contrition, than know the definition thereof. If thou didst know the whole Bible by heart, and the sayings of all the philosophers, what would all that profit thee without the love of God,[4] and without His grace?

Vanity of vanities, and all is vanity,[5] except to love God, and to serve Him only. This is the highest wisdom, by contempt of the world to press forward towards heavenly kingdoms.

Vanity therefore it is, to seek after perishing riches, and to trust in them. Vanity also it is to hunt after honours, and to climb to high degree. Vanity it is to follow the desires of the flesh, and to long after that for which thou must afterwards suffer grievous punishment. Vanity it is, to wish to live long, and to be careless to live well. Vanity it is to mind only this present life, and not to foresee those things which are to come. Vanity it is to set thy love on that which speedily passeth away, and not to hasten thither where everlasting joy abideth.

Call often to mind that proverb, *The eye is not satisfied with seeing, nor the ear filled with hearing*.[6] Endeavour therefore to withdraw thy heart from the love of visible things, and to turn thyself to things invisible. For they that follow their own sensuality, defile their conscience, and lose the grace of God.

→ CHAPTER TWO ←

OF THE HUMBLE CONCEIT OF OURSELVES

EVERY MAN NATURALLY DESIRETH TO KNOW;[1] BUT WHAT AVAILETH knowledge without the fear of God? Better, surely, is an humble rustic that serveth God, than a proud philosopher that, neglecting himself, studieth the course of the heavens.[2] Whoso knoweth himself well, groweth mean in his own conceit, and delighteth not in the praises of men. If I understood all things in the world, and were not in charity,[3] what would that help me in the sight of God, who will judge me according to my deeds?

Cease from an inordinate desire of knowing, for therein is found much distraction and deceit. The learned are well pleased to seem so to others, and to be accounted wise. There be many things, which to know doth little or nothing profit the soul: and he is very unwise, who is intent upon anythings save those which avail for his salvation. Many words do not satisfy the soul; but a good life comforteth the mind, and a pure conscience giveth great confidence towards God.

How much the more and the better thou knowest, so much the more rigorously shalt thou therefore be judged, unless thy life hath been the more holy. Be not therefore lifted up for any art or science, but rather fear for the knowledge that is given thee.

2. If thou thinkest that thou knowest many things and understandest them very well; know also that there be far more things which thou knowest not. *Be not high-minded*,[4] but rather acknowledge thine own ignorance. Why wilt thou prefer thyself before another, since there be

found many more learned, and more skilful in the Law than thou art? If thou wilt know or learn anything profitably, love to be unknown, and to be esteemed as naught.

The deepest and the most profitable reading is this, the true knowledge and contempt of ourselves. It is great wisdom and high perfection to esteem nothing of ourselves, and to think always well and highly of others. If thou shouldst see another openly sin, or commit some heinous offence, thou oughtest not to esteem the better of thyself; for thou knowest not how long thou shalt be able to remain in good estate. All of us are frail,[5] but thou oughtest to esteem none more frail than thyself.

CHAPTER THREE

OF THE DOCTRINE OF TRUTH

HAPPY IS HE WHOM THE TRUTH BY ITSELF DOTH TEACH,[1] NOT BY figures and words that pass away; but as it is in itself. Our own opinion and our own sense do often deceive us, and they discern but little.

What availeth a great cavilling and disputing about dark and hidden things;[2] concerning which we shall not be reproved in the Judgment because we knew them not? It is a great folly to neglect the things that are profitable and necessary, and give our minds to things curious and hurtful: *having eyes, see we not*?[3] And what have we to do with *genus* and *species*? He to whom the Eternal Word speaketh, is set free from many opinions. From that one Word are all things, and that one all things speak; and this is *the Beginning, which also speaketh unto us*.[4] No man without that understandeth or judgeth rightly. He to whom all things are one, and who draweth all things to one, and seeth all things in one, can be steadfast in heart, and remain peaceable in God.

O God, who art the truth, make me one with Thee in continual charity. I am weary often to read and hear many things: in Thee is all that I desire and long for. Let all doctors hold their peace; let all creatures be silent in Thy sight; speak unto me Thou alone.

2. The more a man is at one within himself, and becometh single in heart, so much the more and higher things doth he without labour understand; for that he receiveth the light of the understanding from above.[5] A pure, sincere, and stable spirit is not distracted in a multitude of works; for that it worketh all to the honour of God, and

inwardly striveth to be at rest from all self-seeking. Who hindereth and troubleth thee more than the unmortified affections of thine own heart? A good and devout man disposeth within himself beforehand his works which he is to do before the world. Neither do they draw him according to the desires of a sinful inclination, but he himself ordereth them according to the decision of right reason. Who hath a harder struggle than he that laboureth to conquer himself? This ought to be our endeavour, to conquer ourselves, and daily to wax stronger than ourselves, and to make some progress for good.

3. All perfection in this life hath some imperfection bound up with it; and no knowledge of ours is without some darkness. An humble knowledge of thyself is a surer way to God than a deep search after learning; yet learning is not to be blamed, nor the mere knowledge of anything whatsoever, for knowledge is good, considered in itself, and ordained by God; but a good conscience and a virtuous life are always to be preferred before it. But because many endeavour rather to know than to live well; therefore they are often deceived, and reap either none, or scanty fruit.

O, if men bestowed as much labour in the rooting out of vices, and planting of virtues, as they do in moving of questions, there would neither be so great evils and scandals in the world, nor so much looseness in religious houses.

Truly, when the day of judgment cometh, we shall not be examined what we have read, but what we have done;[6] not how well we have spoken, but how religiously we have lived.

Tell me, where are now all those Masters and Doctors, with whom thou wast well acquainted whilst they lived and flourished in learning? Now others possess their livings, and perhaps do scarce ever think of them. In their lifetime they seemed to be somewhat, but now they are not spoken of. O, how quickly passeth away the glory of the world![7]

O that their life had been answerable to their learning? Then had their study and reading been to good purpose. How many perish by reason of vain learning[8] in this world, who take little care of the serving of God: and because they rather choose to be great than humble, therefore they come to naught in their imaginations.[9]

He is truly great, that is great in charity. He is truly great, that is little in himself, and that maketh no account of any height of honour.[10] He is truly wise, that accounteth all earthly things as dung, that he may gain Christ.[11] And he is truly very learned, that doeth the will of God, and forsaketh his own will.

CHAPTER FOUR

OF FORETHOUGHT IN OUR ACTIONS

We ought not to believe every saying or suggestion,[1] but ought warily and patiently to ponder the matter with reference to God. But alas! Such is our weakness, that we often rather believe and speak evil of others than good. Those that are perfect men do not easily give credit to every tale; for they know that human infirmity is prone to evil,[2] and very subject to slip in words.[3]

2. It is great wisdom not to be rash in thy actions,[4] nor to stand obstinately in thine own conceits; it belongeth also to this same wisdom not to believe everything which thou hearest, nor presently to pour into the ears of others[5] what thou hast heard or believed. Consult with a man that is wise and conscientious, and seek to be instructed by a better than thyself, rather than to follow thine own inventions.[6]

A good life maketh a man wise according to God,[7] and giveth him experience in many things.[8] The more humble a man is in himself, and the more resigned unto God; so much the more prudent shall he be in all things, and the more at peace.

→ CHAPTER FIVE ←

OF THE READING OF HOLY SCRIPTURES

TRUTH IS TO BE SOUGHT FOR IN THE HOLY SCRIPTURES, NOT ELOQUENCE; every Holy Scripture ought to be read with the same Spirit wherewith it was written.[1] We should rather search after profit in the Scriptures, than subtilty of speech.

2. We ought to read devout and simple books as willingly as the high and profound. Let not the authority of the writer offend thee, whether he be of great or small learning; but let the love of pure truth draw thee to read.[2] Search not who spoke this or that, but mark what is spoken. Men pass away, but *the truth of the Lord remaineth forever.*[3] God speaketh unto us in sundry ways, without respect of persons.[4]

3. Our own curiosity often hindereth us in reading of the Scriptures, when we desire to understand and discuss that which we should rather without more ado pass over. If thou desire to reap profit, read with humility, simplicity, and faithfulness; nor ever desire the reputation of learning. Enquire willingly, and hear with silence the words of holy men: let not the proverbs of the elders displease thee, for they are not recounted without cause.[5]

→ CHAPTER SIX ←

OF INORDINATE AFFECTIONS

WHENSOEVER A MAN DESIRETH ANYTHING INORDINATELY, HE IS forthwith disquieted in himself. The proud and covetous are never at rest. The poor and humble in spirit dwell in the multitude of peace.[1]

2. The man that is not yet perfectly dead to himself, is quickly tempted; and he is overcome in small and trifling things. The weak in spirit, and he that is yet in a manner carnal and prone to things of sense, can hardly withdraw himself altogether from earthly desires: and therefore he hath often sadness, when he withdraweth himself from them; and easily falleth into indignation, if anyone resisteth him. And if he hath attained that which he lusteth after, he is forthwith burdened with remorse of conscience; for that he followed his own passion, which profiteth him nothing to the obtaining of the peace he sought for.

3. True peace of heart therefore is found by resisting our passions, not by obeying them. There is then no peace in the heart of a carnal man, nor in him that is given up to outward things, but in the fervent and spiritual man.

CHAPTER SEVEN

OF FLYING VAIN HOPE AND PRIDE

VAIN IS HE THAT SETTETH HIS HOPE IN MAN,[1] OR IN CREATURES. BE not thou ashamed to serve others for the love of Jesus Christ; nor to be esteemed poor in this world.

Presume not upon thyself, but place thy hope in God.[2] Do what lieth in thee, and God will assist thy goodwill.

Trust not in thine own knowledge,[3] nor in the subtilty of any living creature; but rather in the grace of God, who helpeth the humble, and humbleth those that are self-presuming.[4]

2. Glory not in wealth if thou have it, nor in friends because they are powerful; but in God who giveth all things, and above all desireth to give thee Himself.

Extol not thyself for the height of thy stature, or beauty of thy person, which is disfigured and destroyed by a little sickness.

Take not pleasure in thy natural gifts, or talent, lest thereby thou displease God, whose is all the good, whatsoever thou hast by nature.

Esteem not thyself better than others,[5] lest perhaps in the sight of God, who knoweth what is in man, thou be accounted worse than they. Be not proud of good works;[6] for the judgments of God are different from the judgments of men, and that often offendeth Him which pleaseth men. If there be any good in thee, believe better things of others, that so thou mayest preserve humility. It doth no hurt to thee to set thyself lower than all men, but it hurteth thee exceedingly if thou set thyself before even one man. Continual peace is with the humble; but in the heart of the proud is envy and frequent indignation.

CHAPTER EIGHT

THAT TOO MUCH FAMILIARITY IS TO BE SHUNNED

Lay not thy heart open to every man;[1] BUT TREAT OF THY AFFAIRS WITH the wise and him that feareth God. Converse not much with young people and strangers.[2] Flatter not the rich: and before great personages appear thou not willingly. Keep company with the humble and the simple, with the devout and the virtuous; and confer with them of those things that may edify. Be not familiar with any woman; but in general commend all good women to God.

2. Desire to be familiar with God alone and His Angels, and avoid the acquaintance of men. We must have charity towards all, but familiarity with all is not expedient. Sometimes it falleth out, that a person unknown to us waxeth bright from the good report of others; yet his presence darkeneth the eyes of the beholders. We think sometimes to please others by our company, and we begin rather to displease them with the wickedness which they discover in us.

CHAPTER NINE

OF OBEDIENCE AND SUBJECTION

It is a very great matter to stand in obedience; to live under a superior; and not to be at our own disposing. It is much safer to stand in subjection, than in authority.

Many are under obedience, rather for necessity than for charity; such are discontented, and do easily murmur. Neither can they attain to freedom of mind, unless with their whole heart they put themselves under obedience for the love of God. Run hither and thither, thou shalt find no rest, but in humble subjection under the rule of a superior. Fancy and continual changing of places have deceived many.

2. True it is, that everyone willingly doeth that which agreeth with his own mind; and is apt to affect those most that are like-minded with him. But if God is amongst us, we must sometimes leave even our own mind to gain the blessing of peace.

Who is so wise that he can fully know all things? Be not therefore too confident in thine own mind; but be willing to hear the mind of others.

If that which thou thinkest is good, and yet thou partest with this very thing for God, and followest another, it shall be better for thee. I have often heard, that it is safer to hear and to take counsel, than to give it.

It may also fall out, that each one's opinion may be good; but to refuse to yield to others when reason or a special cause requireth it, is a sign of pride and obstinacy.

CHAPTER TEN

OF AVOIDING SUPERFLUITY IN WORDS

FLY THE TUMULT OF MEN AS MUCH AS THOU CANST;[1] FOR THE TALK OF worldly affairs is a great hindrance, although they be discoursed of with sincere intention; for we are quickly defiled, and enthralled with vanity. Oftentimes I could wish that I had held my peace; and that I had not been among men.

2. But why do we so willingly speak and talk one with another, when notwithstanding we seldom return to silence without hurt of conscience?[2] The cause why we so willingly talk, is because by discoursing one with another, we seek to receive comfort one of another, and desire to ease a heart overwearied with conflicting thoughts: and we very willingly talk and think of those things which we most love or desire; or of those which we feel are contrary unto us. But alas, oftentimes in vain, and to no end; for this outward comfort is the cause of no small loss of inward and divine comfort.

3. Therefore we must *watch and pray*,[3] lest our time pass away idly. If it be lawful and expedient for thee to speak, speak those things that may edify. An evil custom and neglect of our own good often maketh us to set no watch before our mouth.[4] Yet devout discourses of spiritual things do greatly further our spiritual growth, especially when persons of one mind and spirit be gathered together in God.[5]

CHAPTER ELEVEN

OF THE OBTAINING OF PEACE, AND ZEALOUS DESIRE OF PROGRESS IN GRACE

We might enjoy much peace, if we would not busy ourselves with the words and deeds of other men, which appertain nothing to our care. How can he abide long in peace, who thrusteth himself into the cares of others, who seeketh occasions abroad, who little or seldom recollecteth himself within his own breast?

Blessed are the single-hearted; for they shall enjoy much peace.

Why were some of the Saints so perfect and contemplative? Because they studied to mortify themselves wholly to all earthly desires; and therefore they could from their very heart's core fix themselves upon God, and be free to retire within themselves.

We are too much holden by our own passions, and too much troubled about transitory things. We seldom overcome even one vice perfectly, and are not set on fire to grow better everyday; and therefore we remain cold and lukewarm. If we were perfectly dead unto ourselves, and not entangled within our own breasts, then should we be able to relish things divine, and to know something of heavenly contemplation.

The greatest, and indeed the whole impediment is, that we are not disentangled from our passions and lusts, neither do we endeavour to enter into the perfect path of the Saints. When any small adversity meeteth us, we are too quickly cast down, and turn to human comforts.

2. If we would endeavour like brave men to stand in the battle, surely we should behold above us the help of God from Heaven. For He

Himself who giveth us occasions to fight, to the end we may get the victory, is ready to succour those who strive, and trust in His grace.

If we esteem our progress in religious life to consist only in some outward observances, our devotion will quickly have an end. But let us *lay the axe to the root*,[1] that being freed from passions, we may possess our soul in peace.

If every year we would root out one vice, we should soon become perfect men. But now oftentimes we perceive it goeth contrary, and that we were better and purer at the beginning of our entrance into the religious life, than after many years of our profession.

Our fervour and profiting should increase daily: but now it is accounted a great matter, if a man can retain but some part of his first zeal.

If we would use some little violence at the beginning, then afterwards should we be able to perform all things with ease and delight. It is a hard matter to leave off that to which we are accustomed, but it is harder to go against our own wills. But if thou dost not overcome little and easy things, how wilt thou overcome harder things? Resist thy inclination in the very beginning, and unlearn an evil habit, lest perhaps by little and little it draw thee into greater difficulty.

O if thou didst but consider how much peace unto thyself, and joy unto others, thou shouldst procure by demeaning thyself well, I trow thou wouldest be more careful for thy spiritual progress!

CHAPTER TWELVE

OF THE PROFIT OF ADVERSITY

IT IS GOOD FOR US THAT WE SOMETIMES HAVE SOME WEARINESSES AND crosses; for they often call a man back to his own heart; that he may know that he is here in banishment, and may not set his trust in any worldly thing.

It is good that we sometimes endure contradictions; and that men think ill or meanly of us; and this, although we do and intend well. These things help often to humility, and defend us from vain glory: for then we the more seek God for our inward witness, when outwardly we are contemned by men, and when no good is believed of us.

And therefore a man should settle himself so fully in God, that he need not to seek many comforts of men.

2. When *a man of goodwill*[1] is afflicted, tempted, or troubled with evil thoughts; then he understandeth better the great need he hath of God, without whom he perceiveth he can do nothing that is good.

Then also he sorroweth, lamenteth, and prayeth, by reason of the miseries he suffereth. Then he is weary of living longer, and wisheth that death would come, that he might *be dissolved and be with Christ*.[2] Then also he well perceiveth, that perfect security and full peace cannot exist in this world.

→ CHAPTER THIRTEEN ←

OF RESISTING TEMPTATIONS

SO LONG AS WE LIVE IN THE WORLD WE CANNOT BE WITHOUT TRIBULATION and temptation. Accordingly it is written in Job, *The life of man upon earth is temptation*.[1] Everyone therefore ought to be full of care about his own temptations, and to watch in prayer, lest the devil find an advantage to deceive him; who never sleepeth, but ever *goeth about seeking whom he may devour*.[2] No man is so perfect and holy, but he hath sometimes temptations; and altogether without them we cannot be.

2. Nevertheless temptations are often very profitable to a man, though they be troublesome and grievous; for in them a man is humbled, and purified, and instructed.

All the Saints passed through many tribulations and temptations, and profited thereby. And they that could not bear temptations, became reprobate, and fell away.

3. There is no order so holy, nor place so secret, where there be not temptations, or adversities. There is no man that is altogether safe from temptations whilst he liveth on earth; for in ourselves is the root of temptation, in that we are born in the desire of evil.[3] When one temptation or tribulation goeth away, another cometh; and we shall ever have something to suffer, because we have lost the blessing of our first happiness.[4]

4. Many seek to fly temptations, and do fall more grievously into them. By flight alone we cannot overcome, but by patience and true humility we are made stronger than all our enemies.

He that only avoideth them outwardly, and doth not pluck them up by the roots, shall profit little; yea temptations will the sooner return unto him, and he shall feel himself in a worse case than before.

By little and little, and by patience with long suffering, (through God's help) thou shalt more easily overcome, than with violence and thine own importunity. Often take counsel in temptation, and deal not roughly with him that is tempted; but give him comfort as thou wouldest wish to be done to thyself.

The beginning of all evil temptations is inconstancy of mind, and small confidence in God. For as a ship without a helm is tossed to and fro with the waves; so the man who is careless, and apt to leave his purpose, is many ways tempted.[5]

5. Fire proveth iron, and temptation a just man. We know not oftentimes what we are able to do, but temptation sheweth us what we are.

Yet we must be watchful, especially in the beginning of the temptation; for the enemy is then more easily overcome, if he be not suffered in any wise to enter the door of our hearts, but be resisted without the gate at his first knock. Wherefore one said,

Beginnings check, too late is physic sought.[6]

For first there cometh to the mind a bare thought of evil, then a strong imagination thereof, afterwards delight, and an evil motion, and then consent. And so by little and little our wicked enemy getteth complete entrance, whilst he is not resisted in the beginning. And the longer a man is slow to resist, so much the weaker doth he become daily in himself, and the enemy stronger against him.

6. Some suffer heavier temptations in the beginning of their religious life, others in the end. Others again are much troubled almost through the whole time of their life. Some are very lightly tempted, according to the wisdom and equity of the Divine appointment, which weigheth the states and deserts of men, and ordaineth all things for the welfare of His own chosen ones.

We ought not therefore to despair when we are tempted, but so much the more fervently to implore God, that He will vouchsafe to help us in every tribulation; who surely, according to the word of S. Paul, *will give with the temptation such issue, that we may be able to bear it*.[7]

Humble we therefore our souls under the hand of God[8] in all temptation and tribulation, for He will save and exalt the humble in spirit. In temptations and tribulations, a man is proved how much he hath profited; and his reward is thereby the greater, and his virtue the better made clear. Neither is it a great thing if a man be devout and fervent, when he feeleth no affliction; but if in time of adversity he bear himself patiently, there is hope then of great progress.

Some are guarded from great temptations, and in little daily ones are often overcome; to the end that being humbled, they may never presume on themselves in great matters, who are made weak in so small things.

⇢ CHAPTER FOURTEEN ⇠

OF AVOIDING RASH JUDGMENT

TURN THINE EYES UPON THINE OWN SELF, AND BEWARE THOU JUDGE not the deeds of other men.[1] In judging of others a man laboureth in vain, often erreth, and easily sinneth;[2] but in judging and examining himself, he always laboureth fruitfully.

2. We often judge of a thing according as we fancy it; for through private affection we easily lose true judgment. If God were always the pure intention of our desire, we should not be so easily troubled, through the repugnance of our own feelings. But oftentimes something lurketh within, or else meeteth us from without, which draweth us after it.

Many secretly seek themselves in what they do, and know it not. They seem also to live in good peace of mind, when things are done according to their will and feeling; but if things happen otherwise than they desire, they are straightway moved and made sad.

3. From diversity of feelings and opinions arise oftentimes dissensions between friends and countrymen; between religious and devout persons.[3] An old habit is with difficulty abandoned,[4] and no man is willing to be led farther than himself can see. If thou dost more rely upon thine own reason or industry, than upon that power which bringeth thee under the obedience of Jesus Christ, seldom and slowly shall thou be a man illuminated, because God willeth us to be perfectly subject to Him, and by the fire of love to transcend all human reason.

CHAPTER FIFTEEN

OF WORKS DONE FOR CHARITY

FOR NO WORLDLY THING, NOR FOR THE LOVE OF ANY MAN, IS ANY EVIL to be done;[1] but yet, for the profit of one that standeth in need, a good work is sometimes without any scruple to be left undone, or rather changed for a better. For by doing this, a good work is not lost, but changed into a better. Without charity the outward work profiteth nothing;[2] but whatsoever is done of charity, be it never so little and contemptible in the sight of the world, it becometh wholly fruitful. For God weigheth more the love out of which a man worketh, than the work which he doeth. He doeth much that loveth much. He doeth much that doeth a thing well. He doeth well that serveth the community rather than his own will.[3]

2. Oftentimes there seemeth to be charity, and it is rather a fleshly mind; because natural inclination, self-will, hope of reward, and desire of our own interest, will seldom be away.

He that hath true and perfect charity, seeketh himself in nothing:[4] but only desireth in all things the glory of God.

He also envieth none; because he is in love with no private joy, neither willeth he to rejoice in himself; but wisheth above all good things to be made happy in the enjoyment of God.[5] He attributeth nothing that is good to any man, but wholly referreth it unto God, from whom as from the fountain all things proceed; in whom finally all the Saints do rest in fruition.

O whoso had but one spark of true charity, would surely feel that all earthly things will be full of vanity!

➔ CHAPTER SIXTEEN ⬅

OF BEARING WITH THE DEFECTS OF OTHERS

THOSE THINGS THAT A MAN AVAILETH NOT TO AMEND IN HIMSELF OR in others, he ought to suffer patiently, until God order things otherwise. Think that perhaps it is better so, for thy trial and patience, without which all our good deeds are not much to be esteemed. Thou oughtest to pray notwithstanding when thou hast such hindrances, that God would vouchsafe to help thee, and that thou mayest bear them contentedly.[1]

If one that is once or twice warned will not stay, contend not with him: but commit all to God, that His will may be done,[2] and He be honoured in all His servants, who well knoweth how to turn evil into good.

2. Endeavour to be patient in bearing with the defects and infirmities of others, of what sort soever they be; for that thyself also hast many failings which must be borne with by others.[3] If thou canst not make thyself such an one as thou wouldest, how wilt thou be able to have another in all things to thy liking?

We would willingly have others perfect, and yet we amend not our own faults. We will have others severely corrected, and will not be corrected ourselves. The large liberty of others displeaseth us, and yet we will not have our own desires denied us. We will have others bound down by ordinances, and in no sort do we ourselves endure further restraint.

And thus it appeareth, how seldom we weigh our neighbour in the same balance with ourselves.

3. If all men were perfect, what should we then have to suffer of others for God's sake? But now God hath thus ordered it, that we may learn to *bear one another's burdens*;[4] for no man is without fault, no man without his burden, no man sufficient of himself, no man wise enough of himself; but we ought to bear with one another, comfort one another, help, instruct, and admonish one another.[5]

Occasions of adversity best discover how great virtue each one hath. For occasions do not make a man frail, but they shew of what sort he is.

→ CHAPTER SEVENTEEN ←

OF THE MONASTIC LIFE

THOU MUST LEARN TO BREAK DOWN THINE OWN SELF IN MANY THINGS, if thou wilt have peace and concord with others.[1] It is no small matter to dwell in religious communities or in a congregation, to converse therein without complaint, and to persevere therein faithfully unto death.[2] Blessed is he that hath there lived well, and ended happily.

If thou wilt stand fast as thou oughtest, and grow in grace, esteem thyself as an exile and a stranger upon earth.[3] Thou must be *made a fool for Christ's sake*,[4] if thou desire to lead a religious life. The wearing of a religious habit, and the shaving of the crown, do little profit; but change of manners, and perfect mortification of passions, make a true religious man.

2. He that seeketh anything else but merely God, and the welfare of his own soul, shall find nothing but tribulation and sorrow.[5] Neither can he stand long in peace, that laboureth not to be the least, and subject unto all.

Thou camest to serve, not to rule.[6] Know that thou wast called to suffer and to labour, not to be idle, and spend thy time in talk. Here therefore men are proved as gold in the furnace. Here no man can stand, unless he be willing to humble himself with his whole heart for the love of God.

CHAPTER EIGHTEEN

OF THE EXAMPLES OF THE HOLY FATHERS

GAZE UPON THE LIVELY EXAMPLES OF THE HOLY FATHERS, IN WHOM true perfection and religion shined;[1] and thou shalt see how little it is, and almost nothing, which we do now in these days. Alas! What is our life, if it be compared with them!

The Saints and friends of Christ served the Lord in hunger and thirst, in cold and nakedness, in labour and weariness, in watchings and fastings, in prayers and holy meditations, in many persecutions and reproaches.[2]

2. O how many and grievous tribulations did the Apostles, Martyrs, Confessors, Virgins, and all the rest suffer, that willed to follow the steps of Christ! For they *hated their lives in this world,* that they might *keep them unto life eternal*.[3]

O how strict and self-renouncing a life did those holy Fathers lead in the wilderness![4] How long and grievous temptations suffered they! How often were they assaulted by the enemy! What frequent and fervent prayers offered they to God! What rigorous abstinences did they fulfill! How great zeal and ardour had they for their spiritual progress! How fierce a war they waged for the taming of their faults! How pure and upright an intention kept they towards God!

Through the day they laboured, and in the nights they attended to continual prayer: although when they laboured, they ceased not from mental prayer. All their time they spent with profit; every hour seemed short for the service of God; and by reason of the great sweetness they felt in contemplation, they even gave up to forgetfulness the need of bodily refreshment.

All riches, dignities, honours, friends, and kinsfolk they renounced;[5] they desired to have nothing which appertained to the world; they scarce took things necessary for the sustenance of life; they grieved to serve their bodies even in necessity. Poor therefore were they in earthly things, but rich exceedingly in grace and virtues.[6] Outwardly they were destitute, but inwardly they were refreshed with grace and divine consolation.

To the world they were strangers, but near and familiar friends to God.[7] They seemed to themselves as nothing, and to this present world despicable; but they were precious and beloved in the eyes of God.[8] They stood firm in true humility, lived in simple obedience, walked in love and patience; and therefore they profited daily in the Spirit, and obtained great favour with God.

They were given for an example to all religious men; and they should more provoke us to profit well, than the number of the lukewarm to make us remiss.

2. O how great was the fervour of all religious persons in the beginning of their holy institution! How great was the devotion of their prayer! How great their ambition to excel others in virtue! What mighty discipline was then in force! How great reverence and obedience flourished in all things under the rule of a superior!

Their footsteps yet remaining, do testify that they were indeed holy and perfect men; who, fighting so valiantly, trod the world under their feet.

Now, he is accounted great who is not a transgressor, and who can with patience endure that which he hath undertaken. O the lukewarmness and negligence of our own condition! That we so quickly decline from the ancient fervour, and are come to be weary of life through sloth and lukewarmness.

Would to God the desire to grow in virtues did not wholly sleep in thee, who hast often seen the many examples of the devout!

→ CHAPTER NINETEEN ←

OF THE EXERCISES OF A GOOD RELIGIOUS PERSON

THE LIFE OF A GOOD RELIGIOUS PERSON OUGHT TO BE MIGHTY IN ALL virtues;[1] that he may inwardly be such, as outwardly he seemeth to men. And with reason there ought to be much more within, than is perceived without. For God beholdeth us;[2] whom we are bound most highly to reverence, wheresoever we are, and to walk in purity[3] like Angels in His sight.

Daily ought we to renew our purpose, and to stir up ourselves to fervour, as though we had for the first time today entered the religious life, and to say, "Help me, O Lord God! In this my good purpose, and in Thy holy service; and grant that I may now this day begin perfectly; for that which I have done hitherto is as nothing."

According to our purpose shall be the course of our spiritual profiting; and much diligence is necessary to him that will profit much.

And if he that firmly purposeth often faileth, what shall he do that seldom, or with little firmness, purposeth anything? It falleth out sundry ways that we leave off our purpose; yet the light omission of spiritual exercises seldom passeth without some loss to our souls. The purpose of just men dependeth not upon their own wisdom, but upon God's grace; on whom too they always rely for whatsoever they take in hand. For man proposeth, but God disposeth;[4] neither is the way of man in himself.

If an accustomed exercise be sometimes omitted, either for some act of piety, or profit to my brother, it may easily afterwards be recovered. But if out of a slothful mind, or out of carelessness, we lightly forsake the same, it is blameworthy enough, and will be felt to be hurtful.

Let us do the best we can, we shall still easily fail in many things.[5] Yet must we always purpose some certain course, and especially against those failings which do most of all hinder us.

2. We must diligently search into, and set in order both the outward and the inner man, because both of them are of importance to our progress in godliness.

If thou canst not continually recollect thyself, yet do it sometimes, at the least once a day, namely, in the morning or at eventide. In the morning fix thy good purpose; and at eventide examine thy ways, how thou hast behaved thyself this day in word, deed, and thought;[6] for in these perhaps thou hast oftentimes offended both God and thy neighbour.

Gird up thy loins like a man[7] against the vile assaults of the devil; bridle thy gluttony and thou shalt the better bridle all the desire of the flesh. Never be entirely idle; but either be reading, or writing, or praying, or meditating, or endeavouring something for the public good. Bodily exercises, nevertheless, must be used with discretion; neither are they to be practiced of all men alike.

Those exercises which are not common are not to be exposed to public view; for things private are practiced more safely at home. Nevertheless thou must beware that thou be not slack in those which are common, and more ready for those which concern thyself only. But having fully and faithfully accomplished all which thou art bound and enjoined to do, if thou hast any spare time, betake thee to thyself, as thy devotion shall desire.

All cannot use one kind of spiritual exercise, but one is more useful for this person, another for that. According to the seasonableness of times also, divers exercises are fitting: some have a better savour on festivals, others on working-days. In the time of temptation, we have need of some, and of others in time of peace and quietness. Some we like to have in mind when we are sad, and other some when we rejoice in the Lord.

About the time of the chief festivals, good exercises are to be renewed, and the prayers of the saints more fervently to be implored. From festival to festival we should make our purpose, as though we were then to depart out of this world, and to come to the eternal festival.

Therefore ought we carefully to prepare ourselves at holy times, and to live more devoutly, and to keep more exactly all our Rule, as though we were shortly at God's hands to receive the reward of our labours.

But if it be deferred, let us believe that we are not sufficiently prepared, and unworthy yet of so great *glory which shall be revealed in us*[8] in the time ordained; and let us endeavour to prepare ourselves better for our departure. *Blessed is that servant,* saith Luke the Evangelist, *whom his Lord when He cometh shall find watching: Verily I say unto you, He shall make him ruler over all His goods.*[9]

CHAPTER TWENTY

OF THE LOVE OF SOLITUDE AND SILENCE

SEEK A CONVENIENT TIME[1] TO RETIRE INTO THYSELF, AND MEDITATE often upon God's loving-kindnesses. Forsake curious questionings; but read diligently matters which rather yield contrition to thy heart, than occupation to thy head.

If thou wilt withdraw thyself from speaking vainly, and from gadding idly, as also from hearkening after novelties and rumours, thou shalt find time enough and suitable for meditation on good things.

The greatest Saints avoided, when they could, the society of men[2], and did rather choose to live to God, in secret.

A certain one hath said, "As oft as I have been among men, I returned home less a man than I was before."[3] And this we often find true, when we talk long together. It is easier altogether to hold one's peace, than not to speak more words than we ought. It is easier for a man to keep at home, than to keep himself well when he is abroad.

He therefore that intendeth to attain to the more inward and spiritual things of religion, must with Jesus depart from the multitude.[4]

2. No man doth safely appear abroad, but he who gladly hideth himself. No man doth safely speak, but he that willingly holdeth his peace.[5] No man doth safely rule, but he that is willingly in subjection. No man doth safely command, but he that hath learned well to obey. No man doth safely rejoice, unless he hath within him the witness of a good conscience.[6]

And yet always the security of the Saints was full of the fear of God. Neither were they the less anxious and humble in themselves, for that they shined outwardly with great virtues and grace. But the security of bad men ariseth from pride and presumption, and in the end it turneth to a man's own deceiving.

Never promise thyself security in this life, although thou seem to be a good monk, or a devout hermit. Oftentimes those who have been greater in the esteem of men have fallen into the heavier peril, by overmuch self-confidence. Wherefore to many it is more profitable not to be altogether free from temptations, but to be often assaulted, lest they should be too secure, and so perhaps be puffed up with pride; or else too freely yield to worldly comforts.

3. O how good a conscience would he keep, that did never seek after transitory joy, nor ever entangle himself with this world! O how great peace and quietness would he possess, that did cut off all vain anxiety, and think only upon divine things, and such as are profitable for his soul, and place all his hope in God!

No man is worthy of heavenly comfort, unless he have diligently exercised himself in holy contrition. If thou desirest to be truly contrite in heart, enter into thy secret chamber, and shut out the tumults of the world, as it is written, *In your chambers be ye contrite*.[7]

In thy chamber thou shall find what abroad thou shalt too often lose.[8] Thy chamber, if thou continuest therein, groweth sweet; and if thou keepest it little, it begetteth weariness. If in the beginning of thy religious life thou art content to remain in it, and keep to it well, it will afterwards be to thee a dear friend, and a most pleasant comfort. In silence and in stillness a devout soul profiteth, and learneth the hidden things of the Scriptures. There she findeth rivers of tears, wherein she may every night[9] wash and cleanse herself; that she may be so much the more familiar with her Creator, by how much the farther off she liveth from all worldly disquiet. Whoso therefore withdraweth himself from his acquaintance and friends, God will draw near unto him with His holy Angels.

4. It is better for a man to live hidden, and to take heed to himself, than to do signs and wonders while he neglecteth himself. It is

commendable in a religious person, seldom to go abroad, to shun being seen, to be unwilling even to look on men.

Why art thou desirous to see that which thou mayest not have? *The world passeth away, and the lust thereof*.[10] Our sensual desires draw us to rove abroad; but when the hour is past, what carriest thou home with thee but heaviness of conscience and distraction of heart? A merry going forth bringeth often a sad returning, and a merry evening maketh a sad morning.[11] So all carnal joy entereth gently, but in the end it biteth and stingeth to death.[12]

What canst thou see elsewhere, which thou seest not here?[13] Behold the Heaven and the earth and all the elements: for of these are all things created.

What canst thou see anywhere that can long continue under the sun? Thou thinkest perchance to satisfy thyself, but thou canst never attain it. Shouldst thou see all things present before thine eyes, what were it but an empty vision?[14]

Lift up thine eyes[15] to God in the highest, and pray him to pardon thy sins and negligences. Leave vain things to the vain; but be thou intent upon those things which God hath commanded thee. Shut thy door upon thee,[16] and call unto thee Jesus, thy Beloved. Stay with Him in thy closet; for thou shalt not find elsewhere so great peace. If thou hadst not gone abroad and hearkened to idle rumours, thou wouldest the better have remained in happy peace. But since thou delightest sometimes to hear novelties, it is but fit thou suffer disquietude of heart therefrom.

CHAPTER TWENTY-ONE

OF CONTRITION OF HEART

If thou wilt make any progress keep thyself in the fear of God,[1] and affect not too much liberty, but restrain all thy senses under discipline, and give not thyself over to foolish mirth. Give thyself to contrition of heart, and thou shalt find devotion. Contrition layeth open many good things, which distraction is wont quickly to destroy.

It is a wonder that any man can ever perfectly rejoice in this life, who considereth and weigheth his own state of exile, and the many perils of his soul. Through levity of heart, and small care for our failings, we become insensible of the sorrows of our souls; but oftentimes we vainly laugh, when we justly ought to weep. There is no true liberty nor right joy but in the fear of God accompanied with a good conscience.

Happy is he, who can cast off all distracting hindrances, and gather himself to the one single purpose of holy contrition. Happy is he, who can put away from him all that may defile his conscience or burden it.

2. Strive manfully; one custom is vanquished of another.

If thou canst let others alone in their works, they likewise shall gladly let thee alone in thine. Busy not thyself in matters of others; neither do thou entangle thyself with the affairs of thy betters. Have ever an eye to thyself first, and especially admonish thine own self before all thy beloved friends.

If thou hast not the favour of men, be not grieved at it;[2] but take this to heart, that thou dost not keep thyself so warily and circumspectly as it becometh the servant of God, and a devout religious man to behave. It is better oftentimes and safer that a man should not have many consolations in this life,[3] especially such as are according to the flesh. But that we have no divine consolations at all, or do very seldom feel them, the fault is ours; because we seek not after contrition of heart, nor do altogether forsake vain and outward comforts.

Know that thou art unworthy of divine consolation, and that thou art rather worthy of much tribulation. When a man is perfectly contrite, then is the whole world grievous and bitter unto him.[4]

3. A good man findeth always sufficient cause for mourning and weeping. For whether he consider himself or think of his neighbour, he knoweth that none liveth here without tribulation. And the more narrowly a man considereth himself, so much the more he sorroweth.

Matter of just sorrow and inward contrition are our faults and sins, in which we lie so enwrapt that rarely have we power to contemplate the things of Heaven.

Didst thou oftener think of thy death,[5] than of thy living long, there is no question but thou wouldst be more zealous to amend. If also thou didst consider deeply in thy heart the penalties that are to be in hell or in purgatory,[6] I believe thou wouldst willingly undergo labour and sorrow, and not be afraid of the greatest austerity. But because these things enter not to thy heart, and we still love those things only that delight us, therefore it is we remain cold and very sluggish.

It is often our want of spirit which maketh our miserable body so easily complain. Pray therefore unto the Lord with all humility, that He will give thee the spirit of contrition. And say with the Prophet, *Feed me, O Lord, with the bread of tears, and give me plenteousness of tears to drink*.[7]

➔ CHAPTER TWENTY-TWO ⬅

OF THE CONSIDERATION OF HUMAN MISERY

MISERABLE THOU ART, WHERESOEVER THOU BE, OR WHITHERSOEVER thou turn, unless thou turn thyself unto God.

Why art thou troubled when things succeed not as thou wouldest or desirest? Who is he that hath all things according to his mind?[1] Neither I nor thou, nor any man upon earth. There is none in this world, even though he be King or Pope, without some tribulation or perplexity. Who is he that hath the better lot? Assuredly he who is able to suffer something for God.

Many weak and unstable persons say, Behold! What a happy life doth that man lead,[2] how wealthy, how great he is, how powerful and exalted! But look to the riches of Heaven, and thou shalt see that all these temporal things are nothing, but are very uncertain, and rather burdensome than otherwise, because they are never possessed without anxiety and fear. Man's happiness consisteth not in having abundance of temporal goods,[3] but a moderate portion is sufficient for him.

Truly it is misery to live upon the earth.[4] The more spiritual a man desireth to be, the more bitter doth this present life become to him; because he perceiveth better and seeth more clearly the defects of human corruption. For to eat and to drink, to sleep, and to wake, to labour and to rest, and to be subject to the other necessities of nature, is truly a great misery and affliction to a religious man, who would gladly be set loose, and free from all sin. For the inner man is much weighed down with bodily necessities in this world. Therefore the

Prophet prayeth with great devotion to be enabled to be free from them, saying, *From my necessities deliver me, O Lord!*[5]

But woe unto them that know not their own misery; and a greater woe unto them that love this miserable and corruptible life![6] For some there be who so much doat upon it, that although by labour or by begging they can scarce get mere necessaries, yet if they might be able to live here always, they would care nothing at all for the Kingdom of God. O senseless and unbelieving in heart, who lie so deeply sunk in earth, that they can relish nothing but carnal things![7] But, miserable men, they shall in the end feel to their cost how vile and worthless that was which they were in love with.

Whereas the Saints of God and all the devout friends of Christ regarded not those things which pleased the flesh, nor those which flourished in this present time, but all their hope and endeavour panted after the good things which are eternal.[8] Their whole desire was carried upward to things durable and invisible, that the desire of things visible might not draw them to things below.

O my brother, lose not thy confidence of making progress towards the things of the Spirit; still thou hast time, the hour is not yet past.[9] Why wilt thou defer thy good purpose from day to day? Arise and in this very instant begin, and say, Now is the time to be doing, now is the time to be fighting, now is the fit time to be amending myself.

When thou art ill at ease and much troubled, then is the time to win most blessing. Thou must pass through fire and water[10] before thou come to the place of refreshing. Unless thou doest violence to thyself, thou shalt never get the victory over wickedness.

So long as we carry about us this frail body, we can never be without sin, or live without weariness and pain. We would gladly have rest from all misery, but seeing by sin we have lost our innocency, we have lost also the true felicity.[11] Therefore it becometh us to keep hold on patience, and to wait for the mercy of God, *till this iniquity be over-past*,[12] *and mortality be swallowed up of life!*[13]

2. O how great is human frailty, which is always prone to evil.[14] Today thou confessest thy sins, and tomorrow thou committest the very same thou hast confessed. Now, thou art purposing to take heed, and

after an hour thou so behavest thyself, as though thou hadst never any such purpose at all. Good cause have we therefore to humble ourselves,[15] and never to have any great conceit of ourselves: since we are so frail and so inconstant. Besides, that may quickly be lost by our own negligence, which, by the grace of God, with much labour we have scarce at length obtained.

What will become of us in the end, who so early wax lukewarm! Woe be unto us, if we will thus to give ourselves unto ease, as if already there were peace and safety, when as yet there appeareth no trace of true holiness in our conversation!

It would be very profitable for us like young beginners to be newly instructed again to good life,[16] if haply there might be some hope of future amendment, and greater spiritual profiting.

CHAPTER TWENTY-THREE

OF MEDITATION ON DEATH

VERY QUICKLY THERE WILL BE AN END OF THEE HERE;[1] LOOK WHAT will become of thee in another world. Today man is; and tomorrow he appeareth not. And when he is taken away from the eyes, quickly also he passeth out of mind.

O dulness and hardness of man's heart, which thinketh only upon the present, and doth not rather care for what is to come! Thou oughtest so to order thyself in every act and thought, as if today thou wert on the point to die.[2] If thou hadst a good conscience, thou wouldst not greatly fear death.[3] It were better to avoid sins, than to fly death.[4] If today thou art not prepared, how wilt thou be so tomorrow?[5] Tomorrow is a day uncertain, and how knowest thou if thou shalt have a tomorrow?

What availeth it to live long, when we amend ourselves so little! Alas! Length of days doth not always amend us, but often rather increaseth our fault! O that we had well spent but one day in this world! Many there are who count the years of their life in religion; and yet full slender oftentimes is the fruit of amendment. If to die is full of terrors, to live longer will perhaps be more perilous.

Blessed is he that always hath the hour of his death before his eyes,[6] and daily prepareth himself to die. If at anytime thou hast seen another man die, make account thou must also pass the same way.[7] When it is morning, think thou wilt not come to eventide. And when evening is come, dare not to promise thyself the morning. Always, therefore, be thou ready, and so live that death may never take thee unprepared.[8] Many die suddenly and when they look not for it; for *at an hour when we think not the Son of Man will come.*[9] When that last hour shall come, thou wilt begin to have a far different opinion of thy whole life that is past, and be exceeding sorry thou hast been so careless and remiss.

2. How wise and happy is he that now laboureth to be such an one in his life, as he wisheth to be found at his death! A perfect contempt of the world,[10] a fervent desire to go forward in virtue, the love of discipline, the toil of penance, the readiness of obedience, the denying of ourselves, and the bearing of any adversity whatsoever for the love of Christ, will give us great confidence we shall die happily.

Many good things canst thou do whilst thou art in health; but when thou art sick, I see not what thou art able to do. Few by sickness grow better; as also they who wander much on pilgrimage, seldom thereby become holy.

Put not thy confidence in friends and kindred, neither do thou put off thy welfare till hereafter; for men will sooner forget thee, than thou art aware of. Better it is to look to it betime, and do some good beforehand, than to hope in other men's help.[11] If thou art not careful for thyself now, who will be careful for thee hereafter?

Now time is very precious; *now are the days of salvation; now is the acceptable time*.[12] But alas! That thou shouldest not spend to more profit this time, wherein thou mightest purchase to live eternally hereafter. The time will come, when thou shalt desire one day or hour to amend in, and I know not that thou wilt obtain it. Ah, beloved, from how great danger wilt thou be able to free thyself, from how great fear deliver thyself, if only thou wilt be ever fearful and mindful of death!

Labour now to live so, that in the hour of death thou mayest rather rejoice than fear. Learn now to die to the world, that thou mayest then begin to live with Christ.[13] Learn now to contemn all things,[14] that thou mayest then freely go to Christ. Chastise thy body now by penance,[15] that thou mayest then have sure confidence.

3. Ah fool, why dost thou think to live long, when thou hast not one day that is safe![16] How many have been deceived and suddenly

snatched from the body! How often hast thou heard them saying, That man hath fallen by the sword; that man hath been drowned; that, by falling from a height hath broken his neck; that man died while eating; that hath come to his end while playing. One perished by fire, another by the steel, another of the plague, another at the hands of robbers; and thus death is the end of all, and man's life suddenly *passeth away like a shadow*.[17] Who shall remember thee when thou art dead? And who shall pray for thee?

Do, do now, my beloved, whatsoever thou art able to do; for thou knowest not when thou shalt die, neither knowest thou what shall befall thee after thy death. Whilst thou hast time, heap unto thyself everlasting riches.[18] Think on nothing but thy salvation; care for nothing but the things of God. Make now friends to thyself by honouring the Saints of God, and imitating their actions, that when thou failest in this life, *they may receive thee into everlasting habitations*.[19] Keep thyself as a *stranger and pilgrim upon the earth*[20] and as one to whom the affairs of this world do nothing appertain. Keep thy heart free, and lifted up to God, because thou hast here *no continuing city*.[21] Thither send thy daily prayers and sighs together with thy tears, that after death thy spirit may be found worthy to pass happily to the Lord. Amen.

CHAPTER TWENTY-FOUR

OF JUDGMENT, AND THE PUNISHMENTS OF SINNERS

IN ALL THINGS LOOK TO THE END; AND HOW THOU WILT STAND BEFORE that severe Judge[1] to whom nothing is hid, who is not appeased with gifts, nor admitteth excuses, but will judge according to right.

O wretched and foolish sinner, who sometimes art in terror at the countenance of an angry man, what answer wilt thou make to God who knoweth all thy wickedness![2] Why dost thou not provide for thyself[3] against the day of judgment, when no man can be excused or defended by another, but everyone shall be a sufficient burden for himself! Now is thy toil fruitful, thy weeping acceptable,[4] thy groaning audible, thy grief pacifieth God, and purgeth thy soul.

The patient man hath a great and wholesome purgatory,[5] who though he receive injuries, yet grieveth more for the malice of the other, than for his own wrong; who prayeth willingly for his adversaries,[6] and from his heart forgiveth their offences; who is not slack to ask forgiveness from others; who is sooner moved to compassion than to anger; who often doeth violence to himself, and laboureth to bring the flesh wholly into subjection to the spirit.

It is better to purge out our sins, and cut off our vices here, than to keep them to be purged away hereafter. Verily we deceive our own selves through the inordinate love we have for the flesh. What is it that that infernal fire shall feed upon, but thy sins? The more thou sparest thyself now and followest the flesh, so much the harder hereafter shall be thy punishment, and the greater fuel for burning thou storest up.

2. In what things a man hath sinned, in the same shall he be the more grievously punished. There shall the slothful be pricked forward with burning goads, and the gluttons be tormented with vast thirst and hunger. There shall the luxurious and lovers of pleasures be bathed in burning pitch and stinking brimstone; and the envious, like raging dogs, shall howl for very grief. There is no sin but shall have its proper torment. There the proud shall be filled with all confusion; the covetous shall be pinched with miserable penury.

There one hour of pain shall be more severe than a hundred years of the severest penance here! There is there no quiet, no comfort for the damned;[7] yet here we have some respite of our labours, and enjoy the comfort of our friends.

Be now anxious and sorrowful because of thy sins, that at the day of judgment thou mayest be secure with the blessed.

For then shall the righteous with great boldness stand against such as have straitened and oppressed them.[8] Then shall he stand for judgment, who doth now humbly submit himself to the judgments of men. Then shall the poor and humble have great confidence, but the proud man shall be compassed with fear on every side. Then will it be seen that he was wise in this world, who had learned for Christ to be a fool and despised.[9]

Then shall every affliction patiently suffered delight us, *when all iniquity shall shut her mouth.*[10] Then shall every devout man be glad, and every profane one shall mourn. Then the flesh which hath been beaten down shall more rejoice, than if it had been alway nourished in delicacies.[11] Then shall the poor attire shine gloriously, and the finely-wrought raiment shall grow dim. Then shall be more commended the poor cottage, than the gilded palace. Then will constant patience more avail us, than all the power of the world.

Then simple obedience shall be more highly extolled, than all worldly craftiness.[12] Then shall a good and clear conscience more rejoice a man, than learned philosophy. Then shall the contempt of riches weigh more than all the worldling's treasure. Then wilt thou be more comforted that thou hast prayed devoutly, than that thou hast fared daintily. Then wilt thou be more glad thou hast kept silence, than that thou hast talked much. Then will holy works avail more than many fair words. Then a strict life and severe penance will be more pleasing than all earthly delight.

Accustom thyself now to suffer a little, that thou mayest then be delivered from more grievous pains. Prove first here what thou canst endure hereafter. If now thou canst bear so little, how wilt thou then be able to endure eternal torments? If now a little suffering make thee so impatient, what will hell fire do hereafter? Behold, surely thou canst not have two paradises: to enjoy delights in this world, and after that to reign with Christ. Suppose thou hast to this day lived always in honours and delights, what would all this avail thee if it befell thee to die at this instant?[13]

All therefore is vanity,[14] but to love God and serve Him only. For he that loveth God with all his heart, is neither afraid of death, nor punishment, nor of judgment, nor of hell; for perfect love gives secure access to God.[15] But he that delighteth still to sin, what marvel is it if he fear both death and judgment? Yet it is good, although love be not yet of force to call thee back from sin, that at least the fear of hell should restrain thee. Nay, he that layeth aside the fear of God, can never continue long in good estate, but runneth quickly into the snares of the devil.

➔ CHAPTER TWENTY-FIVE ⟵

OF THE ZEALOUS AMENDMENT OF OUR WHOLE LIFE

Be watchful and diligent in the service of God;[1] and often bethink thyself wherefore thou camest hither, and why thou hast left the world. Was it not that thou mightest live to God, and become a spiritual man? Therefore be fervent to go forward,[2] for shortly thou shalt receive the reward of thy labours; there shall not be then any fear or sorrow in thy coasts.[3] Labour now but a little, and thou shalt find great rest, yea, perpetual joy.[4] If thou continuest faithful and fervent in doing good, no doubt but God will be faithful and liberal in rewarding thee[5] Thou oughtest to have a good hope[6] that thou wilt come to the palm of victory, but thou must not be secure, lest thou wax either slothful or proud.

2. When one[7] that was in anxiety of mind, often wavering between fear and hope, did once, being overcome with grief, prostrate himself in a Church before a certain altar in prayer, and pondered thus within himself, saying, "O if I knew that I should yet persevere!" he presently heard within him a divine answer, "If thou didst know this, what wouldest thou do? Do now what thou wouldest do then, and thou shalt be perfectly secure." And being herewith comforted and strengthened, he committed himself wholly to the divine will, and that anxious tossing ceased. And he willed not to search curiously, to know what things should befall him; but rather laboured to seek out what was the *acceptable and perfect will of God*[8] for the beginning and the accomplishing of every good work.

Hope in the Lord, and do good, saith the Prophet, *and dwell in the land, and thou shalt be fed in the riches thereof.*[9]

One thing there is that draweth many back from a spiritual progress and fervent amendment; dread of the difficulty, or rather the labour of the combat. However, they above others improve most in virtues, who strive like men to overcome those things which are most grievous and contrary unto them. For there a man improveth more and winneth fuller grace, where he more overcometh himself and mortifieth himself in spirit. Howbeit all men have not equally much to overcome and put to death. Yet he that is diligent and zealous, though he have more passions, shall be more mighty to go forward, than another that is of a more obedient temper but less fervent in the pursuit of virtues.

Two things especially help to great amendment, to wit, to withdraw ourselves violently from that to which nature is viciously inclined; and to labour earnestly for that good whereof a man is the more in need.

Be careful also the more to shun and conquer those things in thyself, which do commonly displease thee in others.

Gather some profit wheresoever thou be; so that if thou seest or hearest any good examples, kindle thyself to the imitation thereof. But if thou observest anything worthy of reproof, beware thou do not the same. And if at anytime thou hast done it, labour quickly to amend thyself. As thine eye observeth others,[10] so art thou by others noted again.

How sweet and pleasant a thing it is, to see brethren fervent and devout, obedient and well-disciplined![11] How sad and grievous a thing it is, to see them walk disorderly, not applying themselves to that for which they are called! How hurtful a thing it is, when they neglect the purpose of their calling and busy themselves in things not committed to their care!

3. Be mindful of the purpose thou hast embraced, and set always before thee the image of the Crucified. Good cause thou hast to be ashamed in looking upon the life of Jesus Christ, seeing thou hast not as yet endeavoured to conform thyself more unto Him, though thou hast been a long time in the way of God. A religious person that exerciseth himself seriously and devoutly in the most holy life and passion

of our Lord, shall there abundantly find whatsoever is profitable and necessary for him neither shall he need to seek any better thing, besides Jesus. O if Jesus crucified would come into our hearts,[12] how quickly and fully should we be taught!

A fervent religious person taketh and beareth well all that is commanded him. A careless and lukewarm religious person hath tribulation upon tribulation, and on all sides suffereth affliction, for he is void of inward consolation, and that which is outward he is forbidden to seek. A religious person that liveth not according to discipline, lieth open to grievous ruin. He that seeketh what is easier and more lax shall ever be in difficulties; for one thing or other will displease him.

How do so many other religious persons act who are confined with all strictness under the discipline of the cloister? They rarely go abroad, they live in abstraction from the world, they have the poorest fare, they wear coarse clothing; they labour much, they speak little, they watch long, they rise betimes, they continue long in prayers, they read frequently, and keep watch over themselves with all discipline. Observe the Carthusians, the Cistercians, and the monks and solitaries of various orders, how do they every night rise to sing Psalms to the Lord. And therefore it would be shameful that thou shouldst be slothful about so holy a work, when so great a multitude of religious persons have already commenced their hymns of praise unto God.

O that nothing else lay upon us to do, but with our mouth, and whole heart to praise our Lord God! O that thou mightest never have need to eat, nor drink, nor sleep; but mightest always praise God, and only employ thyself in spiritual exercises; then thou wouldest be much more happy than now, when for some or other necessity thou art in bondage to the flesh. Would God these necessities were not at all, but only the spiritual banquets of the soul, which, alas, seldom enough we taste.

When a man cometh to that estate, that he seeketh not his comfort from any creature, then first doth God begin to be altogether sweet to him. Then shall he be contented with whatsoever doth befall him in this world. Then shall he neither rejoice in great matters, nor be sorrowful for small; but entirely and confidently he committeth himself to God, who is unto him all in all;[13] to whom assuredly nothing doth perish nor die, but all things do live unto Him, and serve Him at a beck without delay.

Remember always thy end,[14] and how that time lost returneth not. Without care and diligence thou shalt never get virtue. If thou beginnest to wax lukewarm,[15] it will begin to be evil with thee. But if thou give thyself to fervour, thou shalt find much peace, and feel lighter toil through the assistance of God's grace, and the love of virtue. A man fervent and diligent is prepared for all things.

It is harder toil to resist vices and passions, than to sweat in bodily labours. He that avoideth not small faults, by little and little falleth into greater.[16] Thou wilt always rejoice in the evening, if thou spend the day profitably. Be watchful over thyself, stir up thyself, warn thyself, and whatsoever becometh of others, neglect not thyself. The more violence thou usest against thyself, the more shalt thou progress. Amen.

THE SECOND BOOK

ADMONITIONS PERTAINING TO INWARD THINGS

CHAPTER ONE

OF THE INWARD LIFE

THE KINGDOM OF GOD IS WITHIN YOU,[1] SAITH THE LORD. TURN THEE with thy whole heart[2] unto the Lord, and forsake this wretched world, and thy soul shall find rest. Learn to despise outward things, and to give thyself to things inward, and thou shalt perceive the Kingdom of God to come in thee. *For the Kingdom of God is peace and joy in the Holy Ghost*,[3] which is not given to the unholy. Christ will come unto thee, and show thee His consolation, if thou prepare for Him a worthy abode within thee. All His glory and beauty is from within,[4] and there He delighteth Himself. The inward man he often visiteth; and hath with him sweet discourse, pleasant solace, much peace, familiarity exceeding wonderful.

O faithful soul! Make ready thy heart for this Bridegroom, that He may vouchsafe to come unto thee and dwell within thee. For thus saith He, *If any love Me, he will keep My words, and We will come unto him, and will make our abode with him.*[5]

Give therefore a place unto Christ, and deny entrance to all others. When thou hast Christ, thou art rich, and hast enough. He Himself will be thy provider and faithful steward in all things, so that thou need not to trust in men. For men soon change, and quickly fail; but *Christ abideth forever*,[6] and standeth by us firmly unto the end. There is no great trust to be put in a frail and mortal man,[7] even though he be profitable and dear unto us: neither ought we to be much grieved if sometimes he cross and contradict us. They that today are with thee, tomorrow may be against thee; and often again do they turn round like the wind.

2. Put all thy trust in God,[8] let Him be thy fear, and thy love: He Himself shall answer for thee, and will do in all things what is best for thee. Thou hast not here *a continuing city*,[9] and wheresoever thou be, thou art a foreigner and pilgrim:[10] neither shalt thou ever have rest, unless thou be most inwardly united unto Christ. Why dost thou here gaze about, since this is not the place of thy rest? In Heaven ought to be thy dwelling-place,[11] and all earthly things are to be looked upon as it were by the way. All things are passing away,[12] and thou together with them. Beware thou cleave not unto them, lest thou be caught and perish. Let thy *meditation be on the Most High,*[13] and thy prayer for mercy directed unto Christ without ceasing.

If thou canst not contemplate high and heavenly things, rest thyself in the passion of Christ, and dwell willingly in His sacred wounds. For if thou fly devoutly unto the wounds and precious marks of the Lord Jesus, thou shalt feel great strengthening in tribulation: neither wilt thou much care for the slights of men, and wilt easily bear words of detraction. Christ was also in the world, despised of men, and in greatest necessity, forsaken by His acquaintance and friends, in the midst of slanders. Christ willed to suffer and be despised;[14] and dost thou dare complain of any man? Christ had adversaries and backbiters; and dost thou wish to have all men thy friends and benefactors? Whence shall thy patience attain her crown,[15] if no adversity befall thee? If thou art willing to suffer nought that is against thee, how wilt thou be the friend of Christ? Be strong with Christ, and for Christ, if thou desire to reign with Christ. If thou hadst but once perfectly entered into the secrets of the Lord Jesus, and tasted a little of His ardent love, then wouldest thou care nothing for thine own convenience, or inconvenience, but rather wouldest rejoice at slander offered thee; for the love of Jesus maketh a man despise himself.

A lover of Jesus and of the Truth, and a true inward Christian, and one free from unruly affections, can freely turn himself unto God, and lift himself above himself in spirit, and with profit remain at rest.

He to whom all things taste as they are, and not as they are said or esteemed to be, is truly wise,[16] and taught rather of God than men.[17] He that can live inwardly, and make small reckoning of things without, neither seeketh places, nor waiteth for times, for performing of religious exercises. A spiritual man quickly recollecteth himself, because he never poureth out himself wholly to outward things. He is not hindered by outward labour, or business which may be necessary for the time: but as things fall out, so he accommodateth himself to them. He that is well ordered and disposed within himself, careth not for the strange and perverse behaviour of men. So much is a man hindered and distracted, in proportion as he draweth outward things unto himself.

If it were well with thee, and thou wert well purified from sin, all things would fall out to thee for good,[18] and to thy advancement in holiness. For this cause many things displease, and often trouble thee; because thou art not yet perfectly dead unto thyself, nor separated from all earthly things. Nothing so defileth and entangleth the heart of man, as the impure love of creatures. If thou refuse to be comforted from without, thou wilt be able to contemplate the things of heaven, and often to rejoice within.

CHAPTER TWO

OF HUMBLE SUBMISSION

COUNT NOT OF GREAT IMPORTANCE WHO IS FOR THEE OR AGAINST thee;[1] but let this be thy aim and care, that God be with thee in everything thou doest. Have a good conscience, and God shall well defend thee.[2] For whom God willeth to help, no man's perverseness shall be able to hurt. If thou knowest how to be silent and suffer, without doubt thou shalt see the help of the Lord. Himself knoweth the time and manner of delivering thee, and therefore thou oughtest to resign thyself unto Him. It belongeth to God to help, and to deliver from all confusion.

It is often very profitable, to keep us more humble, that others know and rebuke our faults. When a man humbleth himself for his faults, then he easily pacifieth others, and lightly satisfieth those that are offended with him.

2. God protecteth the humble and delivereth him;[3] the humble He loveth and comforteth; unto the humble man He inclineth Himself; unto the humble He giveth great grace; and after his humiliation He raiseth him to glory. Unto the humble He revealeth His secrets,[4] and sweetly draweth and inviteth him unto Himself. The humble man, though he suffer confusion, is yet perfectly in peace; for that he resteth on God, and not on the world.

Do not think that thou hast made any progress, unless thou esteem thyself inferior to all.

CHAPTER THREE

OF A GOOD PEACEABLE MAN

KEEP THYSELF FIRST IN PEACE, AND THEN SHALT THOU BE ABLE TO pacify others. A peaceable man doth more good than he that is well learned. A passionate man turneth even good into evil, and easily believeth evil. A good peaceable man turneth all things to good. He that is well in peace, is not suspicious of any.[1] But he that is discontented and troubled, is tossed with divers suspicions: he is neither quiet himself, nor suffereth others to be quiet. He often speaketh that which he ought not to speak; and omitteth that which were more expedient for him to do. He considereth what others are bound to do,[2] and neglecteth that which he is bound to himself.

First, therefore, have a careful zeal over thyself,[3] and then thou mayest justly be zealous also towards thy neighbour. Thou knowest well how to excuse and colour thine own deeds, but thou art not willing to receive the excuses of others. It were more just that thou shouldest accuse thyself, and excuse thy brother. If thou wilt be borne withal, bear also with another.[4]

2. Behold, how far off thou art yet from true charity and humility, which knoweth not how to be angry with any or to be moved with indignation, but only against its own self. It is no great matter to associate with the good, and gentle; for this is naturally pleasing to all, and everyone willingly enjoyeth peace, and loveth those best that agree with him. But to be able to live peaceably with hard, and perverse, or

undisciplined persons, is a great grace, and an exceedingly commendable and manly deed.

3. Some there are that keep themselves in peace, and are in peace also with others. And there are some that neither are in peace themselves, nor leave others to be in peace: They are troublesome to others, but always more troublesome to themselves. And there are that keep themselves in peace, and study to bring others unto peace.

Nevertheless, our whole peace in this miserable life consisteth rather in humble sufferance, than in not feeling adversities. Whoso knoweth best how to suffer, will keep the greatest peace. That man is conqueror of himself, and lord of the world, the friend of Christ, and heir of heaven.

→ CHAPTER FOUR ←

OF A PURE MIND, AND SIMPLE INTENTION

BY TWO WINGS, A MAN IS LIFTED UP FROM THINGS EARTHLY, NAMELY, BY Simplicity and Purity. Simplicity ought to be in our intention; Purity in our affection. Simplicity tendeth toward God; Purity apprehendeth and tasteth Him.

2. No good action will hinder thee, if thou be inwardly free from inordinate affection. If thou intend and seek nothing else but the will of God and the good of thy neighbour, thou shalt thoroughly enjoy inward liberty.

If thy heart were right, then every creature would be unto thee a looking-glass of life, and a book of holy doctrine. There is no creature so small and mean, that it doth not set forth the goodness of God.[1] If thou wert inwardly good and pure,[2] then wouldest thou be able to see and understand all things well without hindrance. A pure heart penetrateth heaven and hell.

Such as everyone is inwardly, so he judgeth outwardly. If there is joy in the world, surely a man of pure heart possesseth it. And if there be anywhere tribulation and affliction, an evil conscience best knoweth it.

As iron put into the fire loseth its rust, and becometh altogether white and glowing, so he that wholly turneth himself unto God, putteth off all slothfulness, and is transformed into a new man. When a man beginneth to grow lukewarm, then he is afraid of a small labour, and willingly receiveth outward comfort. But when he once beginneth to overcome himself perfectly, and to walk manfully in the way of God; then he esteemeth less those things, which before he felt grievous unto him.

→ CHAPTER FIVE ←

OF THE CONSIDERATION OF ONE'S SELF

We cannot trust over much to ourselves,[1] because grace oftentimes is wanting to us, and understanding also.

Little light is there in us, and this we quickly lose by our negligence. Oftentimes too we perceive not our own inward blindness how great it is. Oftentimes we do evil, and excuse it worse.[2] We are sometimes moved with passion, and we think it zeal. We reprehend small things in others, and pass over our own greater matters.[3] Quickly enough we feel and weigh what we suffer at the hands of others; but we mind not how much others suffer from us. He that well and rightly considereth his own works, will find little cause to judge hardly of another.

2. The inward Christian preferreth the care of himself before all other cares.[4] And he that diligently attendeth unto himself, easily keepeth silence concerning others. Thou wilt never be thus inwardly devout, unless thou be silent concerning other men's matters, and look especially to thyself. If thou attend wholly unto thyself and God, thou wilt be but little moved with whatsoever thou seest abroad.[5]

Where art thou, when thou art not with thyself? And when thou hast run over all, what hast thou then profited, if thou hast neglected thyself? If thou desirest peace of mind and true unity of purpose, thou must still put all things behind thee, and look only upon thyself. Thou shalt then make great progress, if thou keep thyself at leisure from all temporal care. Thou shalt greatly fall back, if thou esteem anything temporal.

3. Let nothing be great unto thee, nothing high, nothing pleasing, nothing acceptable, except it be simply God, or cometh of God. Esteem all comfort vain,[6] which cometh to thee from any creature. A soul that loveth God, despiseth all things that are inferior unto God. God alone is everlasting, and of infinite greatness, filling all things; the soul's solace, and the true joy of the heart.

✧ CHAPTER SIX ✧

OF THE JOY OF A GOOD CONSCIENCE

THE GLORY OF A GOOD MAN, IS THE *TESTIMONY OF A GOOD CONSCIENCE.*[1]

Have a good conscience, and thou shalt ever have joy. A good conscience is able to bear very much, and is very joyful in adversities. An evil conscience is always fearful and unquiet.[2]

Sweetly shalt thou rest if thy heart do not blame thee. Never rejoice, but when thou hast done well. Sinners have never true joy, nor feel inward peace; because *there is no peace to the wicked, saith the Lord.*[3] And if they should say, *We are in peace, no evil shall fall upon us,*[4] *and who shall dare to hurt us?* Believe them not; for upon a sudden will arise the wrath of God, and their deeds shall be brought to nought, and their thoughts shall perish.

To glory in tribulation, is no hard thing for him that loveth; for so to glory is to glory in the Cross of the Lord.[5] Brief is the glory which is given and received from men.[6] The world's glory is ever accompanied by sorrow.

2. The glory of the good is in their consciences, and not in the tongues of men: The gladness of the just is of God,[7] and in God; and their joy is of the Truth. He that desireth true and everlasting glory, careth not for that which is temporal. And he that seeketh temporal glory, or despiseth it not from his soul, sheweth himself to love little the glory of heaven.

Great tranquillity of heart hath he that careth neither for the praises, nor the fault-finding of men. He will easily be content and pacified, whose conscience is pure. Thou art not the more holy, if thou art praised; nor the more worthless, if thou art found fault with. What thou art, that thou art; neither by words canst thou be made greater than what thou art in the sight of God.

If thou consider what thou art within thee, thou wilt not care what men talk of thee. Man looketh on the countenance, but God on the heart.[8] Man considereth the deeds, but God weigheth the intentions.

To be always doing well, and to esteem little of one's self, is the sign of an humble soul. To refuse to be comforted by any creature, is a sign of great purity, and inward confidence. He that seeketh no witness for himself from without, doth shew that he hath wholly committed himself unto God. *For not he that commendeth himself, the same is approved* (saith blessed Paul), *but whom God commendeth.*[9]

To walk inwardly with God, and not to be kept abroad by any affection, is the state of an inwardly Christian man.

➔ CHAPTER SEVEN ➔

OF THE LOVE OF JESUS ABOVE ALL THINGS

BLESSED IS HE THAT UNDERSTANDETH[1] WHAT IT IS TO LOVE JESUS, AND to despise himself for Jesus' sake. Thou oughtest to leave thy beloved, for thy Beloved;[2] for that Jesus will be loved alone above all things. The love of things created is deceitful and inconstant; the love of Jesus is faithful and persevering. He that cleaveth unto a creature, shall fall with that which is subject to fall; he that embraceth Jesus shall be made strong forever.

2. Love Him, and keep Him for thy friend, who, when all go away, will not forsake thee, nor suffer thee to perish in the end. Sometime or other thou must be separated from all, whether thou wilt or no. Keep close to Jesus both in life and in death, and commit thyself unto His faithfulness, who, when all fail, can alone help thee.

Thy Beloved is of that nature, that He will admit of no rival; but will have thy heart alone, and sit on His own throne as King. If thou couldest empty thyself perfectly from all creatures, Jesus would willingly dwell with thee.

3. Whatsoever thou reposest in men, out of Jesus, thou shalt find almost wholly lost. Trust not nor lean upon a reed shaken by the wind;[3] *for that all flesh is grass, and all the glory thereof shall wither away as the flower of grass.*[4]

Quickly shalt thou be deceived, if thou only look to the outward appearance of men. For if in others thou seekest thy comfort and profit, thou shalt too often feel loss. If thou seekest in all things Jesus, thou shalt surely find Jesus. But if thou seekest thyself, thou shalt also find thyself, but to thine own destruction. For man is more hurtful to himself if he seek not Jesus, than the whole world and all his adversaries.

→ CHAPTER EIGHT ←

OF FAMILIAR CONVERSE WITH JESUS

WHEN JESUS IS PRESENT, ALL IS GOOD AND NOTHING SEEMS DIFFICULT; but when Jesus is absent, all is hard.

When Jesus speaketh not inwardly to us, all other comfort is nothing worth; but if Jesus speak but one word, we feel great comfort. Did not Mary Magdalene rise immediately from the place where she wept, when Martha said to her, *The Master is come and calleth for thee*? [1] Happy hour! When Jesus calleth from tears to spiritual Joy.

How dry and hard art thou without Jesus! How foolish and vain, if thou desire anything out of Jesus! Is not this a greater loss, than if thou shouldest lose the whole world?[2] What can the world profit thee without Jesus? To be without Jesus, is a grievous hell; and to be with Jesus, a sweet paradise. If Jesus be with thee, no enemy shall be able to hurt thee.[3] He that findeth Jesus, findeth a good treasure,[4] yea, a Good above all good. And he that loseth Jesus loseth much indeed, yea, more than the whole world! Most poor is he who liveth without Jesus;[5] and he most rich who is well with Jesus.

2. It is great skill to know how to hold converse with Jesus; and to know how to keep Jesus, great wisdom. Be thou humble and peaceable, and Jesus will be with thee.[6] Be devout and quiet, and Jesus will stay with thee.

Thou mayest soon drive away Jesus, and lose His favour, if thou wilt turn aside to outward things. And if thou shouldest drive Him from thee, and lose Him, unto whom wilt thou flee, and whom wilt thou then seek for thy friend? Without a friend thou canst not live well; and if Jesus be not above all a friend to thee, thou shalt be indeed sad and desolate. Thou actest therefore like an idiot, if thou trust or rejoice in any other.[7] It is preferable to have all the world against us, rather than to have Jesus offended with us. Amongst all therefore that be dear unto us, let Jesus alone be specially beloved.

3. Love all for Jesus, but Jesus for Himself. Jesus Christ alone is singularly to be beloved: who alone is found good and faithful above all friends. For Him, and in Him, let as well friends as foes be dear unto thee; and all these are to be prayed for, that He would make them all to know and love Him.[8]

Never desire to be singularly commended or beloved, for that appertaineth only unto God, who hath none like unto Himself. Neither do thou desire that the heart of any should be set on thee, nor do thou set thy heart on the love of any; but let Jesus be in thee, and in every good man.

Be pure and free within, and not entangled with any creature. Thou oughtest to be unclothed and ever to carry thy heart pure towards God, if thou wouldest be free from the world and *see how sweet the Lord is*.[9] And truly, unless thou be prevented and drawn by His grace, thou shalt never attain to that happiness, to empty thyself of all, and take leave of all, that thou alone mayest with Him alone be made one. For when the grace of God cometh unto a man, then he is made able for all things. And when it goeth away, then shall he be poor and weak, and, as it were, left only for the scourge. In this case he ought not to be cast down, nor to despair; but at God's will to stand with even mind, and whatever come upon him to endure it for the glory of Jesus Christ; for after winter followeth summer, after night the day returneth, and after a tempest a great calm.[10]

CHAPTER NINE

OF THE WANT OF ALL COMFORT

It is no hard matter to despise human comfort, when we have divine. It is a great thing, yea, very great, to be able to want both human and divine comfort;[1] and, for God's honour, to be willing cheerfully to endure the heart's banishment; and to seek oneself in nothing, nor to regard one's own merit.

What great matter is it, if at the coming of grace thou be cheerful and devout? This hour is wished for of all men. Sweetly enough he rideth whom the grace of God carrieth. And what marvel if he feel not his burden, who is borne up by the Almighty, and led by the Sovereign Guide?

We are always willing to have something for our comfort; and with difficulty a man doth strip himself of self.

The holy martyr Laurence,[2] with his priest, overcame the world, because whatsoever seemed delightsome in the world he despised; and for the love of Christ he patiently suffered God's chief priest Sixtus, whom he most dearly loved, to be even taken away from him. By the love of the Creator, therefore, he overcame the love of man; and he rather chose what pleased God, than human comfort. So also do thou learn to leave even a near and dear friend, for the love of God. Nor do thou take it hard, when thou art deserted by a friend, as knowing that we all at last must be separated one from another.

A man must strive much and long within himself, before he can learn fully to master himself, and to draw his whole affection unto God. When a man standeth on himself, he easily slideth unto human comforts. But a true lover of Christ, and a diligent follower of virtues doth not fall back on comforts, nor seek such sensible sweetnesses; but rather seeketh hard exercises, and to bear severe labours for Christ.

2. When therefore spiritual comfort is given thee from God, receive it with thanksgiving; but understand that it is the gift of God, not thy deserving. Be not puffed up, be not too joyful nor vainly presumptuous; but rather be the more humble for that gift, more wary too and fearful in all thine actions; for that hour will pass away, and temptation will follow. When consolation is taken from thee, do not immediately despair; but with humility and patience wait for the heavenly visitation; for God is able to give thee back again more ample consolation.

This is nothing new nor strange unto them that have experience in the way of God; for the great Saints and ancient Prophets had oftentimes experience of such kind of vicissitudes. For which cause, one, while grace was present with him, said, *I said in my prosperity, I shall never be moved.*[3] But when this grace was absent, what he found in himself he goeth on to speak of, saying, *Thou didst turn Thy face from me, and I was troubled.* Yet in the midst of all this he doth not by any means despair, but more earnestly beseecheth the Lord, and saith, *Unto Thee, O Lord, will I cry, and unto my God will I complain.* At length he receiveth the fruit of his prayer, and testifieth that he was heard, saying, *The Lord hath heard me, and taken pity on me; the Lord is become my helper.* But wherein? *Thou hast turned,* saith he, *my sorrow into joy, and Thou hast compassed me about with gladness.* If great Saints were so dealt with, we that are weak and poor ought not to despair, if we be sometimes fervent and sometimes cold; for the Spirit cometh and goeth, according to the good pleasure of His own will.[4] For which cause blessed Job saith, *Thou visitest him early in the morning, and suddenly Thou provest him.*[5]

3. Whereupon then can I hope, or wherein ought I to trust, save in the great mercy of God alone, and in the hope alone of heavenly grace? For whether I have with me good men, or religious brethren and faithful friends; whether holy books or fair treatises, or sweet chanting and hymns, all these help but little, and have but little savour, when I am forsaken of grace, and left in mine own poverty. At such time there is

no better remedy than patience, and the denying of myself according to the will of God.[6]

I never found any so religious and devout, that he had not sometimes a withdrawing of grace, or felt not some decrease of zeal. There was never Saint so high caught up[7] and illuminated, who first or last was not tempted. For he is not worthy of the high contemplation of God, who hath not been exercised with some tribulation for God's sake. Temptation going before is wont to be a sign of ensuing comfort. For unto those that are proved by temptations, heavenly comfort is promised. *He that shall overcome,* saith He, *I will give him to eat of the Tree of life.*[8] But divine consolation is given, that a man may be bolder to bear adversities. There followeth also temptation, lest he should wax proud of any good. The devil sleepeth not,[9] neither is the flesh as yet dead; therefore cease not to prepare thyself to the battle; for on thy right hand and on thy left are enemies who never rest.

➛ CHAPTER TEN ➛

OF GRATITUDE FOR THE GRACE OF GOD

WHY SEEKEST THOU REST, SINCE THOU ART BORN TO LABOUR.[1] Dispose thyself to patience rather than to comfort, and to the bearing of the Cross, rather than to gladness.[2]

What secular person is there that would not willingly receive comfort and spiritual joy, if he could always have it? For spiritual comforts exceed all the delights of the world and pleasures of the flesh. For all worldly delights are either vain or unclean; but spiritual delights are only pleasant and honest, sprung from virtues, and infused by God into pure minds.

But these divine comforts can no man always enjoy according to his desire; for the time of temptation ceaseth not.

But false freedom of mind and great confidence of ourselves is very contrary to the heavenly visitation.

God doth well for us in giving the grace of comfort; but man doth evil in not returning all again unto God with thanksgiving. And therefore the gifts of grace cannot flow in us, because we are unthankful to the Giver, and return them not wholly to the Head-fountain.[3] For grace ever attendeth him that duly giveth thanks; and from the proud shall be taken that which is wont to be given to the humble.

I desire not that consolation which taketh from me contrition; nor do I aim at that contemplation which leadeth to haughtiness of mind. For not all that is high, is holy; nor all that is sweet, good; nor every desire, pure; nor is everything that is dear unto us, pleasing to God. Willingly do I accept of that grace, whereby I may ever be found more humble, and more full of fear, and may become more ready to renounce myself.

2. He that is taught by the gift of grace, and schooled by the rod of its withdrawing, will not dare to attribute any good to himself, but will rather acknowledge himself poor and naked. Give unto God that which is God's,[4] and ascribe unto thyself that which is thine own; that is, give thanks to God for His grace; and feel that to thyself alone the fault, and the fit punishment of the fault, are due.

Set thyself always in the lowest place,[5] and the highest shall be given thee; for the highest cannot stand without the lowest. The chiefest Saints before God, are the least before themselves; and the more glorious they are, so much within themselves the humbler. Those that are full of truth and heavenly glory, are not greedy of vain-glory. Those that are firmly settled and grounded in God, can no wise be puffed up. And they that ascribe all unto God, what good soever they have received, seek not glory one of another, but wish for that glory which is from God alone; and desire above all things that God may be praised in them, and in all His Saints; and after this very thing they are ever striving.

Be therefore thankful for the least gift, so shalt thou be meet to receive greater. Let the least be unto thee even as the greatest, yea the most contemptible gift as of especial value. If thou consider the worth of the Giver, no gift will seem little, or of too mean esteem. For that cannot be little which is given by the Most High God. Yea, if He should give punishment and stripes, it ought to be matter of thankfulness; because He doth it always for our welfare, whatsoever He permitteth to happen unto us.

He that desireth to keep the grace of God, let him be thankful for grace given, and patient for the taking away thereof: let him pray that it may return; let him be cautious and humble, lest he lose it.

CHAPTER ELEVEN

HOW FEW ARE THE LOVERS OF THE CROSS OF JESUS

JESUS HATH NOW MANY LOVERS OF HIS HEAVENLY KINGDOM, BUT FEW bearers of His Cross. Many He hath that are desirous of consolation, but few of tribulation. Many He findeth that share His table, but few His fasting. All desire to rejoice with Him, few are willing to endure anything for Him. Many follow Jesus unto the breaking of bread; but few to the drinking of the Cup of His Passion.[1] Many reverence His miracles, few follow the shame of His Cross. Many love Jesus so long as no adversities befall them. Many praise and bless Him, so long as they receive any consolations from Him. But if Jesus hide Himself, and leave them but a little while, they fall either into complaining, or into too much dejection of mind.

But they who love Jesus for the sake of Jesus, and not for some special comfort of their own, bless Him in all tribulation and anguish of heart, as well as in the highest comfort. Yea, although He should never be willing to give them comfort, Himself notwithstanding they would ever praise, and wish to be always giving thanks. O how powerful is the pure love of Jesus, which is mixed with no self-interest, or self-love!

Are not all those to be called hirelings, who are ever seeking consolations? Do they not shew themselves to be rather lovers of themselves than of Christ, who are always thinking of their own advantage and profit?[2]

2. Where shall one be found who is willing to serve God for nought?[3] Rarely is anyone found so spiritual as to be stript of all things. For who

shall find a man that is indeed poor in spirit, and stript of every created thing? *From afar, yea, from the ends of the earth, is his price.*[4]

If a man should give all his substance, yet is it nothing.[5] And if he should practice great penance, still it is little. And if he should attain to all knowledge, still he is afar off. And if he should have great virtue, and very fervent devotion, yet there is much wanting to him; especially, one thing, which is for him most chiefly necessary. What is that? That, forsaking all, he forsake himself, and go forth wholly from himself,[6] and retain nothing of self-love. And when he hath done all that he knoweth ought to be done, let him think that he hath done nothing. Let him not weigh that much, which might be much esteemed; but let him pronounce himself to be in truth an unprofitable servant, as the Truth saith, *When you shall have done all things that are commanded you, say, we are unprofitable servants.*[7]

Then may he be truly poor and naked in spirit, and say with the Prophet *I am alone and poor.*[8] Yet no man richer than he, no man more powerful, no man more free: for he is able to leave himself and all things, and to set himself in the lowest place.

→ CHAPTER TWELVE ←

OF THE KING'S HIGH WAY OF THE HOLY CROSS

UNTO MANY THIS SEEMETH AN HARD SAYING, *DENY THYSELF, TAKE UP thy cross, and follow Jesus.*[1] But much harder will it be to hear that last word, *Depart from Me, ye cursed, into everlasting fire.*[2] For they who now willingly hear and follow the word of the Cross, shall not then fear[3] to hear the sentence of everlasting damnation. This sign of the Cross shall be in the heaven, when the Lord shall come to judgment.[4] Then all the servants of the Cross, who in their life-time conformed themselves unto Christ crucified, shall draw near unto Christ the Judge with great confidence. Why therefore fearest thou to take up the Cross which leadeth thee to a kingdom?

In the Cross is salvation, in the Cross is life, in the Cross is protection against our enemies, in the Cross is infusion of heavenly sweetness, in the Cross is strength of mind, in the Cross joy of spirit, in the Cross the height of virtue, in the Cross the perfection of holiness. There is no salvation of the soul, nor hope of everlasting life, but in the Cross. Take up therefore thy Cross and follow Jesus,[5] and thou shalt go into life everlasting. He went before, bearing His Cross,[6] and died for thee on the Cross; that thou also mayest bear thy Cross and desire to die on the Cross. For if thou be dead with Him, thou shalt also in like manner live with Him.[7] And if thou share His punishment, thou shalt also share His glory.[8]

Behold! In the Cross all doth consist, and in our dying thereon all lieth; for there is no other way unto life, and unto true inward peace, but the way of the holy Cross, and of daily mortification. Walk where thou wilt, seek whatsoever thou wilt, thou shalt not find a higher way above, nor a safer way below, than the way of the holy Cross.

Dispose and order all things according to thy will and judgment, and thou shalt not find but that thou must always suffer somewhat, either willingly or against thy will, and so thou shalt ever find the Cross. For either thou shalt feel pain in thy body, or in thy soul thou shalt suffer tribulation of spirit. Sometimes thou shalt be forsaken of God, sometimes thou shalt be troubled by thy neighbour; and, what is more, oftentimes thou shalt be wearisome to thine own self. Neither canst thou be delivered or eased by any remedy or comfort; but so long as it pleaseth God thou oughtest to bear it. For God will have thee learn to suffer tribulation without comfort; and that thou subject thyself wholly to Him, and by tribulation become more humble. No man so feeleth from his heart the passion of Christ, as he to whom it hath befallen to suffer the like.

The Cross therefore is always ready, and everywhere waiteth for thee. Thou canst not escape it whithersoever thou runnest; for wheresoever thou goest thou carriest thyself with thee, and ever shalt find thyself. Turn thee above, turn thee below, turn thee without, turn thee within, and in all these places thou shalt find the Cross; and everywhere of necessity thou must hold fast patience, if thou wilt have inward peace, and win an everlasting crown.

2. If thou bear the Cross cheerfully, it will bear thee, and lead thee to the desired end, to wit, where there shall be an end of suffering; though here this shall not be. If thou bear it unwillingly, thou makest for thyself a load, and burdenest thyself the more, and yet notwithstanding thou must bear it. If thou cast away one cross, without doubt thou shalt find another, and perhaps a heavier one.

Thinkest thou to escape that which no mortal man could ever avoid? Which of the Saints in the world was without cross and tribulation? For not even our Lord Jesus Christ was ever one hour without the anguish of His Passion, so long as He lived. *Christ,* saith He, *must needs suffer, and rise again from the dead, and so enter into His glory.*[9] And how dost thou seek any other way than this royal way, which is the way of the holy Cross? The whole life of Christ was a Cross and Martyrdom;

and dost thou seek rest and joy for thyself? Thou art deceived, thou art deceived, if thou seek any other thing than to suffer tribulations; for the whole of this mortal life is full of miseries,[10] and signed on every side with crosses. And the higher a person hath advanced in the Spirit, so much the heavier crosses he oftentimes findeth; because the grief of his banishment increaseth with his love.

3. Nevertheless, this man, though so many ways afflicted, is not without refreshing comfort, for that he perceiveth very much fruit to grow unto him by the enduring of his own cross. For whilst he willingly putteth himself under it, all the burden of tribulation is turned into the confidence of Divine comfort. And the more the flesh is wasted by affliction, so much the more is the spirit made strong by inward grace.[11] And sometimes he is so strengthened by the desire of tribulation and adversity, for the love of conformity to the Cross of Christ, that he would not wish to be without pain and tribulation;[12] because he believeth that he shall be unto God so much the more acceptable, the more and the heavier things he can suffer for Him.

This is not the power of man, but it is the grace of Christ, which can and doth so much in frail flesh; so that what naturally it always abhorreth and fleeth from, this by fervour of spirit it doth encounter and love. It is not according unto man to bear the Cross, to love the Cross, to chastise the body, and bring it into subjection, to flee honours, willingly to suffer reproaches, to despise himself and wish to be despised, to endure all adversities and losses, and to desire no prosperity in this world. If thou look to thyself, nothing of this kind shalt thou be able of thyself to accomplish.[13] But if thou trust in the Lord, fortitude shall be given thee from heaven, and the world and the flesh shall be made subject to thy sway. Neither yet shalt thou fear thy enemy the devil, if thou be armed with faith, and signed with the Cross of Christ.

Set thyself therefore, like a good and faithful servant of Christ, to bear manfully the Cross of thy Lord, who out of love for thee was crucified. Prepare thyself to bear many adversities and divers troubles in this miserable life; for so it will be with thee, wheresoever thou art, and so surely thou shalt find it, wheresoever thou hide thyself. So it must be; nor is there any remedy or means to escape from tribulation and pain of evils, but only to endure thyself. Drink of the Lord's cup[14] with all thine heart, if thou desire to be His friend, and to have part with Him. As for comforts, leave them to God; let Him do therein as shall best please Him. But do thou set thyself to suffer tribulations, and account them the greatest comforts; *for the sufferings of this present time,* although thou alone couldest suffer them all, *are not worthy to be compared with the future glory* which is to be won.[15]

4. When thou shalt come to this estate, that tribulation[16] shall seem sweet, and thou shalt relish it for Christ's sake; then think it to be well with thee, for thou hast found Paradise upon earth. As long as it is grievous to thee to suffer, and thou desirest to flee it, so long shalt thou be ill at ease, and the desire of escaping tribulation will follow thee everywhere. If thou dost set thyself to that thou oughtest, namely, to suffering, and to death, it will quickly be better with thee, and thou shalt find peace.

Although thou shouldest have been caught up even unto the third heaven with Paul,[17] thou art not for this secured that thou shalt suffer no adversity. *I will shew him,* saith Jesus, *how great things he must suffer for My name.*[18] To suffer, therefore, remaineth for thee, if it please thee to love Jesus, and to serve Him perpetually. O that thou wert worthy to suffer something for the Name of Jesus![19] How great glory would remain for thee; what joy would arise to all God's Saints; how great edification also to thy neighbour! For all men recommend patience; few, however, are they who are willing to suffer. With great reason oughtest thou cheerfully to suffer some little for Christ; since many suffer more grievous things for the world.

5. Know for certain, that thou oughtest to lead a dying life.[20] And the more any man dieth to himself, so much the more doth he begin to live unto God. No man is fit to comprehend things heavenly, unless he submit himself to the bearing of adversities for Christ's sake. Nothing is more acceptable to God, nothing more wholesome to thee in this world, than to suffer cheerfully for Christ. And if it were for thee to choose, thou oughtest rather to suffer adversities for Christ, than to be refreshed with many consolations; because thou wouldest thus be more

like unto Christ, and more conformable to all the Saints. For our worthiness, and the progress of our spiritual estate, standeth not in many sweetnesses and comforts; but rather in thoroughly enduring great afflictions and tribulations.

Indeed, if there had been any better thing, and more profitable to a man's salvation, than suffering, surely Christ would have shewn it by word and example. For both the disciples that followed Him, and all who desire to follow Him, he plainly exhorteth to the bearing of the Cross, and saith, *If any will come after Me, let him deny himself, and take up his Cross, and follow Me.*[21] So that when we have read to the end and searched through all, let this be the final conclusion, *That through many tribulations we must enter into the Kingdom of God.*[22]

THE THIRD BOOK

OF INTERNAL CONSOLATION

CHAPTER ONE

OF CHRIST'S SPEAKING INWARDLY TO THE FAITHFUL SOUL

I will hearken what the Lord God speaketh in me.[1] Blessed is the soul which heareth the Lord speaking within her,[2] and from His mouth receiveth the word of consolation. Blessed are the ears that catch the pulses of the Divine whisper,[3] and give no heed to the whisperings of this world. Blessed indeed are those ears which listen not after the voice which is sounding without, but for the Truth teaching inwardly. Blessed are the eyes that are shut to outward things, but intent on things inward. Blessed are they that enter far into things within, and endeavour to prepare themselves more and more, by daily exercises, for the receiving of heavenly secrets. Blessed are they who are glad to have time to spare for God, and who shake off all worldly hindrances.

2. Consider these things, O my soul, and shut up the door of thy sensual desires, that thou mayest hear what the Lord thy God speaketh in thee.[4]

Thus saith thy Beloved, *I am thy salvation,*[5] thy Peace, and thy Life: keep thyself with Me, and thou shalt find peace. Let go all transitory things, and seek the things eternal. What are all transitory objects but seductive things? And what can all creatures avail thee, if thou be forsaken by the Creator?

Renounce therefore all things, and labour to please thy Creator, and to be faithful unto Him, that so thou mayest be able to attain unto true blessedness.

→ CHAPTER TWO ←

THAT THE TRUTH SPEAKETH INWARDLY WITHOUT NOISE OF WORDS

SPEAK, O LORD, FOR THY SERVANT HEARETH.[1] *I AM THY SERVANT, GRANT me understanding, that I may know Thy testimonies.*[2] *Incline my heart to the words of Thy mouth:* let Thy speech *distil as the dew.*[3]

The children of Israel in times past said unto Moses, *Speak thou unto us, and we will hear: Let not the Lord speak unto us, lest haply we die.*[4] Not so, Lord, not so, I beseech Thee: but rather with the prophet Samuel, I humbly and earnestly entreat, *Speak, Lord, for Thy servant heareth.*

2. Let not Moses speak unto me, nor any of the prophets, but rather do Thou speak, O Lord God, the Inspirer and Enlightener of all the prophets; for Thou alone without them canst perfectly instruct me, but they without Thee will profit nothing.

They may indeed sound forth words, but they cannot give the Spirit. Beautiful is their speech, but if Thou be silent, they kindle not the heart. They give the letter, but Thou openest the sense; they bring forth mysteries, but Thou unlockest the meaning of things that are sealed. They declare commandments, but Thou helpest us to fulfill them. They point out the way, but Thou givest strength to walk in it. They work only from without, but thou instructest and enlightenest hearts. They water outwardly, but Thou givest the increase.[5] They cry aloud in words, but Thou to the hearing impartest understanding.

Let not Moses therefore speak unto me, but Thou, O Lord my God, the Everlasting Truth; lest haply I die, and prove unfruitful, if I be only warned outwardly, and not set on fire within, lest it turn to my condemnation, the word heard and not fulfilled, known and not loved, believed and not kept. Speak therefore, Lord, for Thy servant heareth; for *Thou hast the words of eternal life.*[6] Speak Thou unto me, to the comfort, however imperfect, of my soul, and to the amendment of my whole life, and to Thy praise and glory and honour everlasting.

CHAPTER THREE

THAT THE WORDS OF GOD ARE TO BE HEARD WITH HUMILITY, AND THAT MANY WEIGH THEM NOT

MY SON, HEAR MY WORDS, WORDS OF GREATEST SWEETNESS, SURPASSING all the knowledge of the philosophers and wise men of this world. *My words are Spirit and Life*,[1] and not to be weighed by the understanding of man. They are not to be drawn forth for vain self-pleasing, but to be heard in silence, and to be received with all humility and great affection.

And I said, *Blessed is the man whom Thou shalt instruct, O Lord, and shalt teach out of Thy law, that Thou mayest give him rest from the evil days*,[2] and that he be not desolate upon earth.

2. I, saith the Lord, have taught the Prophets from the beginning,[3] and cease not, even to this day, to speak to all; but many are deaf, and hardened to My voice. Most men do more willingly listen to the world than to God; they sooner follow the desire of their own flesh, than God's good pleasure.

The world promiseth things temporal and mean, and is served with great eagerness: I promise things most high and eternal, and the hearts of mortals grow dull. Who is there that in all things serveth and obeyeth Me with so great care as the world and its lords are served withal? *Be ashamed, O Sidon, saith the sea.*[4] And if thou ask the cause, hear wherefore. For a small income, a long journey is run; for everlasting life, many scarce once lift a foot from the ground. A pitiful reward is sought after; for a single piece of money sometimes there is shameful strife at law; for a vain matter and a slight promise men fear not to toil day and night. But, ah shame! For a good that changeth not, for a reward that cannot be reckoned, for the highest honour, and glory without end, they grudge even the least fatigue. Be ashamed, therefore, thou slothful and complaining servant, that they are found more ready to destruction than thou to life. They rejoice more in vanity than thou dost in the truth.

Sometimes, indeed, they are disappointed of their hope; but My promise deceiveth none,[5] nor sendeth him away empty that trusteth in Me. What I have promised, I will give; what I have said, I will fulfill; if only any man remain faithful in My love even to the end. I am the Rewarder of all good men,[6] and the strong Approver of all who are devoted to Me.

Write thou My words in thy heart, and meditate diligently on them; for in time of temptation they will be very needful. What thou understandest not when thou readest, thou shalt know in the day of visitation. In two several ways, I am wont to visit Mine elect, namely with temptation and with consolation. And I daily read two lessons to them, one in reproving their vices, another in exhorting them to the increase of virtues.

He that hath My words and despiseth them, *hath One that shall judge him in the last day*.[7]

3. *A Prayer to implore the grace of Devotion.*

O Lord my God! Thou art all my good things. And who am I, that I should dare speak to Thee?[8] I am Thy poorest, meanest servant, and a vile worm, much more poor and contemptible than I know or dare express.

Yet do Thou remember me, O Lord, because I am nothing, I have nothing, and I can do nothing. Thou alone art Good, Just, and Holy; Thou canst do all things, Thou suppliest all things, Thou fillest all things, only the sinner Thou leavest empty. *Remember Thy tender mercies*,[9] and fill my heart with Thy grace, Thou who willest not that Thy works should be void. How can I bear up myself in this miserable life, unless Thou strengthen me with Thy mercy and grace?

Turn not Thy face away from me;[10] delay not Thy visitation; withdraw not thy consolation, lest my soul become as a thirsty land unto Thee.[11] Teach me, O Lord, to do Thy will;[12] teach me to live worthily and humbly in Thy sight; for Thou art my Wisdom, Who dost truly know me, and didst know me before the world was made, and before I was born in the world.

→ CHAPTER FOUR ←

THAT WE OUGHT TO LIVE IN TRUTH AND HUMILITY BEFORE GOD

MY SON, WALK THOU BEFORE ME IN TRUTH, AND IN THE SIMPLICITY OF thine heart seek Me evermore.[1] He that walketh before Me in truth shall be defended from evil attacks, and the Truth shall set him[2] free from seducers, and from the slanders of unjust men. *If the Truth shall have made thee free, thou shalt be free indeed*,[3] and shalt not care for the vain words of men.

O Lord, it is true. According as Thou sayest, so, I beseech thee, let it be with me; let Thy Truth teach me, itself guard me, and preserve me to an end of safety. Let it set me free from all evil affection and inordinate love; and I shall walk with Thee in great liberty of heart.

2. I will teach thee (saith the Truth) those things which are right and pleasing in My sight.

Reflect on thy sins with great displeasure and grief; and never esteem thyself to be anything, because of good works.

In truth thou art a sinner; thou art subject to and entangled with many passions. Of thyself thou always tendest to nothing; speedily art thou cast down, speedily overcome, speedily confused, speedily dissolved. Thou hast nothing whereof thou canst glory,[4] but many things for which thou oughtest to account thyself vile; for thou art much weaker than thou art able to comprehend.

Let nothing therefore seem much unto thee of all the things thou doest. Let nothing seem great, nothing precious and wonderful, nothing worthy of estimation, nothing high, nothing truly commendable and to be desired, but that alone which is eternal. Let the eternal Truth be above all things pleasing to thee. Let thy own extreme unworthiness be always displeasing to thee. Fear nothing so much, blame nothing, flee nothing, so much as thy vices and sins; which ought to be more unpleasing to thee than any losses whatsoever of things earthly.

Some walk not sincerely in My sight,[5] but led by a certain curiosity and arrogance wish to know My secrets, and to understand the deep things of God, neglecting themselves and their own salvation. These oftentimes, when I resist them, for their pride and curiosity do fall into great temptations and sins. Fear the judgments of God; dread the wrath of the Almighty. Do not, however, discuss the works of the Most High, but search diligently thine own iniquities, in how great things thou hast offended, and how many good things thou hast neglected.

Some carry their devotion only in books, some in pictures, some in outward signs and figures. Some have Me often in their mouth; but little there is in their heart.[6]

Others there are who, being illuminated in their understandings, and purged in their affection, do always pant after things eternal, are unwilling to hear of earthly things, and do serve the necessities of nature with grief; and these perceive what the Spirit of Truth speaketh in them,[7] for He teacheth them to despise earthly, and to love heavenly things; to neglect the world, and to desire Heaven all the day and night.[8]

✧ CHAPTER FIVE ✧

OF THE WONDERFUL EFFECT OF DIVINE LOVE

I BLESS THEE, O HEAVENLY FATHER, FATHER OF MY LORD JESUS Christ, for that Thou hast vouchsafed to remember me that am poor. *O Father of mercies and God of all comfort,*[1] thanks be unto Thee, who sometimes with Thy comfort refreshest me, unworthy as I am of all comfort. I will always bless and glorify Thee, with Thy only-begotten Son, and the Holy Ghost, the Comforter, forever and ever. Ah, Lord God, Thou Holy Lover of me, when Thou comest into my heart, all that is within me shall rejoice. Thou art my Glory and the exultation of my heart; Thou art my Hope and *Refuge in the day of my trouble.*[2]

But because I am as yet weak in love, and imperfect in virtue, I have need to be strengthened and comforted by Thee; visit me therefore often, and instruct me with all holy discipline. Set me free from evil passions, and heal my heart of all inordinate affections; that being inwardly healed and throughly cleansed, I may be made ready to love, strong to suffer, steady to persevere.

2. Love is a great thing, yea, altogether a great good; by itself it maketh light everything that is heavy, and it beareth evenly all that is uneven. For it carrieth a burden which is no burden,[3] and maketh everything that is bitter, sweet and tasteful. The noble love of Jesus driveth a man to do great things, and stirreth him up to be always longing for what is more perfect. Love willeth to be on high, and not to be kept back by anything low and mean. Love willeth to be free, and estranged from all worldly affection, that so its inward sight may not be hindered; that

it may not be entangled by any temporal prosperity, or by any adversity subdued.

Nothing is sweeter than Love, nothing stronger, nothing higher, nothing wider, nothing more pleasant, nothing fuller nor better in Heaven and earth; because Love is born of God,[4] and cannot rest but in God, above all created things. A lover flieth, runneth, and rejoiceth; he is free, and is not holden. He giveth all for all, and hath all in all; because he resteth in One Highest above all things, from whom all that is good floweth and proceedeth. He respecteth not the gifts, but turneth himself above all goods unto the Giver.

Love oftentimes knoweth no measure, but is fervent beyond all measure. Love feeleth no burden, thinketh nothing of labours, attempteth what is above its strength, pleadeth no excuse of impossibility; for it thinketh all things possible for itself and all things lawful. It is therefore strong for all things, and it completeth many things, and bringeth them to effect, where he who doth not love, fainteth and lieth down. Love is watchful, and sleeping slumbereth not.[5] Though wearied, it is not tired; though pressed, it is not straitened; though alarmed, it is not confounded; but as a lively flame and burning torch, it forceth its way upwards, and securely passeth through all. If any man love, he knoweth what is the cry of this voice. For it is a loud cry in the ears of God, that ardent affection of the soul, when it saith, "My God, my Love, Thou art all mine, and I am all Thine."

Enlarge thou me in Love, that with the inward palate of my heart I may learn to taste how sweet it is to love, and in Love to be dissolved and to bathe myself. Let me be holden by Love, mounting above myself, through excessive fervour and wonder. Let me sing the song of Love, let me follow Thee, my Beloved, on high; let my soul spend itself in Thy praise, rejoicing through Love. Let me love Thee more than myself, nor love myself but for Thee; and in Thee all that truly love Thee, as the law of Love commandeth, shining out from Thyself.

Love is swift, sincere, kindly-affectioned, pleasant and delightsome; brave, patient, faithful, prudent, long-suffering, manly, and never seeking itself.[6] For where a person seeketh himself, there he falleth from Love.[7]

Love is circumspect, humble, and upright; not yielding to softness, or to lightness, nor attending to vain things; it is sober, chaste, firm, quiet, and guarded in all the senses.

Love is subject and obedient to its superiors, to itself mean and despised, unto God devout and thankful, trusting and hoping always in Him, even then when God is not sweet unto it: for without sorrow none liveth in love. He that is not prepared to suffer all things, and to stand to the will of his Beloved, is not worthy to be called a lover.[8] A lover ought to embrace willingly all that is hard and bitter, for the sake of his Beloved; nor for things that fall out against one to turn away from Him.

→ CHAPTER SIX ←

OF THE PROVING OF A TRUE LOVER

MY SON, THOU ART NOT YET A VALIANT AND WISE LOVER.

Wherefore, O Lord?

Because for a slight opposition thou failest from thy undertakings, and too eagerly seekest consolation. A valiant lover standeth firm in temptations, and giveth no credit to the crafty persuasions of the Enemy. As I please him in prosperity, so in adversity I displease him not.[1] A wise lover regardeth not so much the gift of Him who loveth, as the love of Him who giveth. He esteemeth affection rather than value, and setteth all gifts below the Beloved. A noble-minded lover resteth not in the gift, but in Me above every gift.

All is not therefore lost, if sometimes thou hast less feeling for Me or My saints than thou wouldest. That good and sweet affection which thou sometimes feelest, is the effect of grace present, and a sort of foretaste of thy native land of heaven: but hereon thou must not lean too much, for it cometh and goeth. But to strive against evil motions of the mind which befall thee, and to reject[2] with scorn a suggestion of the devil, is a notable sign of virtue, and shall have great reward.

Let not strange fancies therefore trouble thee, on whatsoever matter they may be, which are forced into thy mind. Bravely keep thy purpose, and an upright intention towards God. Neither is it an illusion that sometimes thou art suddenly rapt into ecstasy, and presently returnest again unto the wonted follies of thy heart. For these thou dost rather unwillingly suffer, than commit: and so long as they displease thee, and thou strivest against them, it is matter of reward, and no loss.

Know that the ancient Enemy doth strive by all means to hinder thy desire to good, and to keep thee void of all religious exercises; particularly from reverence towards the saints, from the devout remembrance of My Passion, from the profitable calling to mind of sins, from the guard of thine own heart, and from the firm purpose of advancing in virtue. Many evil thoughts he forceth on thee, that so he may cause in thee a wearisomeness and horror, to call thee back from prayer and holy reading. Humble confession is displeasing unto him; and if he could, he would cause thee to cease from Holy Communion.

Believe him not, nor regard him, although he should often set for thee snares of deceit. Charge him with it when he suggesteth evil and unclean thoughts; say unto him, "Away thou unclean Spirit![3] Blush, thou miserable wretch! Most unclean art thou that bringest such things unto mine ears. Begone from me, thou wicked Seducer! Thou shalt have no part in me: but Jesus shall be with me as a strong Warrior, and thou shalt stand confounded. I had rather die, and undergo any torment, than consent unto thee. Hold thy peace and be dumb; I will hear thee no more, though thou shouldest work me many troubles. *The Lord is my Light and my Salvation, whom shall I fear?*[4] *If whole armies should stand together against me, my heart shall not fear. The Lord is my Helper and my Redeemer.*"[5]

2. Fight like a good soldier:[6] and if thou sometimes fall through frailty, take again strength greater than the former, trusting in My more abundant Grace; and take great heed against vain pleasing of thyself, and pride. Through this are many led into error, and sometimes fall into blindness almost incurable. Let this fall of the proud, presuming foolishly of themselves, serve thee for a warning, and keep thee ever humble.

CHAPTER SEVEN

OF CONCEALING GRACE UNDER THE GUARD OF HUMILITY

MY SON, IT IS MORE PROFITABLE FOR THEE AND MORE SAFE, TO CONCEAL the grace of devotion; not to lift thyself on high, nor to speak much thereof, or to dwell much thereon; but rather to despise thy very self, and to fear this grace, as given to one unworthy of it.

This disposition must not be too earnestly cleaved unto, for it may be quickly changed to the contrary. Think when thou art in grace, how miserable and needy thou art wont to be without grace.

Nor is it in this only that thy progress in spiritual life consisteth, when thou hast the grace of comfort; but rather when with humility, self-denial, and patience, thou endurest the withdrawing thereof; provided thou do not then become listless in the zeal of prayer, nor suffer the rest of thy accustomed duties to be at all neglected. But do thou cheerfully perform what lieth in thee, according to the best of thy power and understanding; and do not, because of the dryness or anxiety of mind which thou feelest, wholly neglect thyself. For there are many who when things do not well succeed with them, presently become impatient or slothful. For the way of man is not always in his power,[1] but it belongeth unto God to give, and to comfort, when He will, and how much He will, and whom He will; as it shall please Him, and no more.

2. Some unadvised persons, to gain the grace of devotion, have overthrown themselves; because they attempted more than they were able to perform, not weighing the measure of their own littleness, but

rather following the desire of their heart, than the judgment of their reason. And because they presumed on greater matters than was pleasing to God, they therefore quickly lost His grace. They who had set their nests[2] in Heaven were made helpless and vile outcasts; to the end that being humbled and made poor, they might learn not to fly with their own wings, but to trust under My feathers.[3]

They that are yet but novices and inexperienced in the way of the Lord, unless they govern themselves by the counsel of discreet persons, may easily be deceived and broken to pieces. And if they will rather follow their own feelings than trust to others who are more experienced, their end will be dangerous, at least if they are unwilling to be drawn back from their own fond conceit. It is seldom the case that they who are self-wise endure humbly to be governed by others. Better it is to have a small portion of good sense with humility,[4] and a slender understanding, than great treasures of many sciences with vain self-pleasing. Better it is for thee to have little, than much of that which may make thee proud.

3. He acteth not very discreetly, who wholly giveth himself over to joy, forgetting his former poverty, and that chastened fear of the Lord, which is afraid of losing the grace which hath been offered. Nor again is he very valiantly wise who in time of adversity or any heaviness, beareth himself with too much despondency, and reflecteth and thinketh of Me less confidingly than he ought. He who in time of peace is willing to be over secure,[5] shall be often found in time of war too much dejected and full of fears. If thou hadst the wit always to continue humble and moderate within thyself, and also well to restrain and govern thy spirit, thou wouldest not so quickly fall into danger and offence.

It is good counsel, that when a spirit of fervour is kindled within thee, thou shouldest consider how it will be, when that light shall leave thee. And when this doth happen, then remember that the light may return again; which as a warning to thyself and for Mine own glory, I have withdrawn for a time.[6] Such a trial is oftentimes more profitable, than if thou shouldest always have things prosper according to thy will. For a man's deserts are not to be reckoned by this, whether he have many visions and consolations, or be skilled in the Scriptures, or be set in a higher station than others; but whether he be grounded in true humility, and full of divine charity; if he be always purely and sincerely seeking God's honour; if he think nothing of and unfeignedly despise himself,[7] and even rejoice more to be despised and put low by others, than to be honoured by them.

CHAPTER EIGHT

OF A MEAN CONCEIT OF OURSELVES IN THE SIGHT OF GOD

I WILL SPEAK UNTO MY LORD, THOUGH I AM BUT DUST AND ASHES.[1]

If I esteem myself to be anything more, behold, Thou standest against me, and my iniquities bear true witness, and I cannot contradict it. But if I abase myself, and reduce myself to nothing, and shrink from all self-esteem, and grind myself to (what I am) dust, Thy grace will be favourable to me, and Thy light near unto my heart; and all self-esteem, how little soever, shall be swallowed up in the valley of my nothingness, and perish forever.

There Thou shewest Thyself unto me, what I am, what I have been, and whither I am come; for I am nothing, and I knew it not. If I be left to myself, behold! I am nothing, and altogether weakness; but if Thou for an instant look upon me, I am forthwith made strong, and am filled with new joy. And a great marvel it is, that I am so suddenly lilted up, and so graciously embraced by Thee, who of mine own weight am always sinking to the depths.

This is the work of thy love, freely preventing me, and relieving me in so many necessities, guarding me also from pressing dangers, and snatching me (as I may truly say) from evils out of number. For indeed by loving myself amiss, I lost myself;[2] and by seeking Thee alone, and purely loving Thee, I have found both myself and Thee; and by that love have more deeply reduced myself to nothing. Because Thou, O sweetest Lord, dealest with me above all desert, and above all that I dare hope for or ask.

2. Blessed be Thou, my God: for although I be unworthy of any benefits, yet Thy noble bounty and infinite goodness never ceaseth to do good even to the ungrateful,[3] and to those who are turned away far from Thee.

Turn Thou us unto Thee, that we may be thankful, humble, and devout; for Thou art our salvation, our courage, and our strength.

CHAPTER NINE

THAT ALL THINGS ARE TO BE REFERRED UNTO GOD, AS THEIR LAST END

MY SON, I OUGHT TO BE THY SUPREME AND ULTIMATE END, IF THOU truly desire to be blessed. With this intention thy affections will be purified, which are too often perversely twisted towards self and towards creatures. For if in anything thou seekest thyself, immediately within thyself thou faintest and driest up.

Refer all things therefore unto Me in the first place, for I am He who hath given all. Thus think of everything as flowing from the Highest Good;[1] and therefore unto Me as their Spring must all be brought back.

2. From Me, the small and the great, the poor and the rich, draw, as from a living fountain, the water of life;[2] and they that willingly and freely serve Me, shall receive *grace for grace*.[3] But he who desireth to glory in things out of Me,[4] or to take pleasure in some private good, shall not be grounded in true joy, nor be enlarged in his heart, but shall many ways be encumbered and straitened.

Nothing therefore oughtest thou to ascribe to thyself of good, neither do thou attribute virtue unto any man; but give all unto God, without whom man hath nothing.

I have given all;[5] I will to have all again; and with great strictness do I require a return of thanks. This is the Truth whereby vain-glory is put to flight. And if heavenly grace enter in, and true charity, there will be no envy nor narrowness of heart, neither will self-love have place.

For divine charity overcometh all things, and enlargeth all the powers of the soul.

If thou rightly judge, thou wilt rejoice in Me alone, in Me alone thou wilt hope; for *none is good save God alone,*[6] who is above all things to be praised, and in all to be blessed.

CHAPTER TEN

THAT TO DESPISE THE WORLD AND SERVE GOD, IS SWEET

NOW I WILL SPEAK AGAIN, O LORD, AND WILL NOT BE SILENT; I WILL speak in the ears of my God, my Lord, and my King, who is on high.

O how great is the multitude of Thy sweetness, O Lord, which Thou hast laid up for them that fear Thee.[1] But what art Thou to those who love Thee? What to those who serve Thee with their whole heart? Truly unspeakable is the sweetness of contemplating Thee, which Thou bestowest on them that love Thee. In this especially Thou hast shewed me the sweetness of Thy charity: that when I was not, Thou madest me; when I went far astray from Thee, Thou broughtest me back again, that I might serve Thee, and hast commanded me to love Thee.[2]

O Fountain of love unceasing, what shall I say concerning Thee? How can I forget Thee, who hast vouchsafed to remember me, even after I had wasted away and perished? Thou hast shewed mercy to Thy servant beyond all hope; and hast exhibited favour and loving-kindness beyond all desert.

What return shall I make to Thee for this grace?[3] For it is not granted to all to forsake all, to renounce the world, and to undertake the life of solitude. Is it any great thing that I should serve Thee,[4] whom the whole creation is bound to serve? It ought not to seem much to me, to serve Thee; but rather this doth appear much to me, and wonderful, that Thou vouchsafest to receive into Thy service one so poor and unworthy, and to make him one of Thy beloved servants. Behold! All things are Thine which I have, and whereby I serve Thee.[5] And yet contrariwise, Thou rather servest me than I Thee. Behold!

Heaven and earth, which Thou hast created for the service of man, are ready at hand, and do daily perform whatever Thou hast commanded. And this is too little; nay, even angels hast Thou appointed to minister to man.[6] But that which excelleth all this is, that Thou Thyself hast vouchsafed to serve man, and hast promised that Thou wouldest give Thyself unto him.

What shall I give Thee for all these thousands of benefits? I would I could serve Thee all the days of my life. I would I were able, at least for one day, to do Thee some worthy service. Truly Thou art worthy of all service, of all honour, and everlasting praise. Truly Thou art my Lord, and I Thy poor servant, who am bound to serve Thee with all my might, neither ought I ever to be disdainful of Thy praises. And this I wish to do, this I desire; and whatsoever is wanting unto me, do Thou vouchsafe to supply.

2. It is a great honour, and a great glory, to serve Thee, and despise all things for Thee. For they shall have great grace, who shall have willingly subjected themselves to Thy most holy service. They shall find the sweetest consolation of the Holy Ghost,[7] who for Thy love have renounced all carnal delight. They shall attain great freedom of mind, who for Thy Name's sake enter into the narrow way,[8] and have left off all worldly care.

O sweet and delightful service of God,[9] by which a man is made truly free and holy! O sacred state of religious servitude, which maketh a man equal to the Angels, pleasing to God, terrible to devils, and worthy to be commended of all the faithful! O service worthy to be embraced and ever desired, in which the Greatest Good is offered; and joy is won, which shall endlessly remain!

CHAPTER ELEVEN

THAT THE LONGINGS OF OUR HEARTS ARE TO BE EXAMINED AND RULED

MY SON, IT IS NEEDFUL FOR THEE STILL TO LEARN MANY THINGS MORE, which thou hast not even yet well learned.

What are these, O Lord?

That thou set thy longing[1] wholly according to My good pleasure; and that thou be not a lover of thyself, but an earnest follower of My will.

Various longings oftentimes inflame thee, and drive thee forwards with vehemence; but consider whether thou be moved for My honour, or rather for thine own advantage. If I Myself be the cause, thou wilt be well content with whatsoever I shall ordain; but if there lurk in thee any self-seeking,[2] behold, this it is that hindereth thee and weigheth thee down. Beware therefore thou lean not too much upon preconceived desire, without asking my counsel, lest perhaps afterwards it repent thee, or thou be displeased with that which at first pleased thee, and for which thou wast earnestly zealous, thinking it the best. For not every affection which seemeth good is immediately to be followed; nor again is every contrary affection at the first to be avoided.

2. It is sometimes expedient to use a curb, even in good endeavours and longings, lest through importunity thou incur distraction of mind; lest by thy want of self-government thou beget a scandal unto others; or again, being thwarted by others, thou become suddenly confounded, and fall. Sometimes however thou must use violence,[3] and resist manfully thy sensual appetite, nor regard what the flesh

would, or would not;[4] but rather for this taking pains, that even perforce it may be made subject to the Spirit.[5] And so long ought it to be chastised and to be forced to remain under servitude, until it be prepared for all things and learn to be content with a little, and to be pleased with simple things, nor to murmur against aught that suiteth it not.

→ CHAPTER TWELVE ←

OF THE GROWTH OF PATIENCE IN THE SOUL, AND OF THE STRUGGLE AGAINST CONCUPISCENCE

O LORD MY GOD, PATIENCE IS VERY NECESSARY FOR ME,[1] AS I PLAINLY see, for many things in this life do happen contrary unto us. For whatever plans I shall devise for my own peace, my life cannot be without war and pain.[2]

It is so, My son. But My will is, that thou seek not that peace which is void of temptations, or which feeleth nothing contrary; but rather think that thou hast then found peace, when thou art exercised with sundry tribulations,[3] and tried in many crosses.

If thou say, that thou art not able to suffer many things, how wilt thou endure hereafter the fire of purgatory? Of two evils the less is alway to be chosen. That thou mayest therefore avoid the future everlasting punishment, endeavour to endure present evils with an even mind for God's sake.

Dost thou think that the men of this world suffer nothing, or but a little? Not so shalt thou find it even if thou ask of those who enjoy the greatest delights. But thou wilt say, they have many delights, and follow their own wills, and therefore they do not much weigh their own afflictions. Be it so, that they do have whatsoever they will; but how long dost thou think it will last? Behold, *even as the smoke they shall vanish that prosper in the world*,[4] and there shall be no memory of their past joys! Yea, even while they are yet alive, they do not rest in them without bitterness, and weariness, and fear. For from the self-same thing in which they imagine their delight to be, oftentimes they receive the penalty of sorrow. Justly are they dealt with, that because inordinately they seek and follow after delights, they enjoy them not without shame and bitterness. O how brief, how false, how inordinate and filthy, are all those pleasures. Yet so drunken and blind are men that they understand it not; but like dumb beasts, for the poor enjoyment of this corruptible life, they incur the death of the soul.

2. Thou therefore, My son, *go not after thy lusts, but from thine own will refrain thyself.*[5] *Delight in the Lord, and He shall give thee the requests of thine heart.*[6] For if thou desire true delight, and to be of the more plentifully comforted; behold, in the contempt of all worldly things, and in the cutting off all base delights, shall be thy blessing, and abundant consolation shall be rendered to thee. And the more thou withdrawest thyself from all solace of creatures, so much the sweeter and more powerful consolations shalt thou find in Me.

But at the first, thou shalt not without some sadness, and the toil of conflict, attain unto these. In thy way shall stand inbred habit, but by better habit shall it be entirely overcome. The flesh will murmur against thee; but with fervency of spirit shalt it be bridled. The Old Serpent shall sting and irritate thee, but by prayer he shall be put to flight; moreover also, by useful labour shall his great approach be barred against him.

→ CHAPTER THIRTEEN ←

OF THE OBEDIENCE OF ONE IN HUMBLE SUBJECTION, AFTER THE EXAMPLE OF JESUS CHRIST

My son, he that endeavoureth to withdraw himself from obedience, withdraweth himself from grace; and he who seeketh for himself private benefits,[1] loseth those which are common.

He that doth not cheerfully and freely submit himself to his superior, it is a sign that his flesh is not as yet perfectly obedient unto him, but oftentimes kicketh and murmureth against him. Learn thou therefore quickly to submit thyself to thy superior, if thou desire to keep thine own flesh under the yoke. For more speedily is the outward enemy overcome, if the inward man be not laid waste. There is no worse nor more troublesome enemy to the soul than thou art unto thyself, if thou be not well in harmony with the Spirit. It is altogether necessary that thou take up a true contempt for thyself, if thou desire to prevail against flesh and blood. Because as yet thou lovest thyself too inordinately, therefore thou art afraid to resign thyself wholly to the will of others.

2. And yet, what great matter is it, if thou, who art but dust and nothing, subject thyself to a man for God's sake, when I, the Almighty and the Most Highest, who created all things of nothing, humbly subjected Myself to man for thy sake? I became of all men the most humble and the most abject,[2] that thou mightest overcome thy pride with My humility. O dust! Learn to be obedient. Learn to humble thyself, thou earth and clay, and to bow thyself down under the feet of all men. Learn to break thine own wishes, and to yield thyself to all subjection. Be fiercely

hot against thyself, and suffer no swelling of pride to dwell in thee: but shew thyself so humble and so very small, that all may be able to walk over thee, and to tread thee down as the mire of the streets.[3]

What hast thou, O vain man, to complain of? What canst thou answer, foul sinner, to them that upbraid thee, thou who hast so often offended God, and so many times deserved hell? But Mine eye spared thee, because thy soul was precious in My sight; that thou mightest know My love, and ever be thankful for My benefits; also that thou mightest continually give thyself to true subjection and humility, and endure patiently the contempt which belongeth to thee.

CHAPTER FOURTEEN

OF THE DUTY OF CONSIDERING THE SECRET JUDGMENTS OF GOD, THAT SO WE BE NOT LIFTED UP FOR ANYTHING GOOD IN US

THOU THUNDEREST FORTH THY JUDGMENTS OVER ME, O LORD. THOU shakest all my bones with fear and trembling, and my soul is very sore afraid. I stand astonished; and I consider that *the Heavens are not pure in Thy sight.*[1] If in Angels Thou didst find wickedness,[2] and didst not spare even them, what shall become of me? Stars tell from Heaven,[3] and what can I presume who am dust? They whose works seem commendable have fallen into the depths, and those who did eat the bread of Angels,[4] I have seen delighting themselves with the husks of swine.[5]

No sanctity is there therefore, if Thou, O Lord, withdraw Thine hand. No wisdom availeth, if Thou cease to guide. No courage helpeth, if Thou leave off to preserve. No chastity is secure, if Thou do not protect it. No custody of our own availeth, if Thy sacred watchfulness be not present. For, left to ourselves, we sink and perish; but being visited of Thee, we are raised up and live. Unstable truly are we, but through Thee we are strengthened; we wax lukewarm, but by Thee we are inflamed.

2. O how humbly and meanly ought I to think of myself! How ought I to esteem it as nothing, if I should seem to have ought of good! With what profound humility ought I to submit myself to Thy unfathomable judgments, O Lord; where I find myself to be nothing else than

Nothing, and still Nothing! O weight unmeasurable! O sea that cannot be passed over, where I discover nothing of myself save only and wholly Nothing!

Where then is the lurking place of glory? Where the confidence conceived of virtue? Swallowed up is all vain-glorying in the deep of Thy judgments over me. What is all flesh in Thy sight? Shall the clay glory against him that formeth it?[6] How can he be lilted up with vain words whose heart is truly subject to God?[7] Not all the world shall lift up him whom the Truth hath subjected unto itself: neither shall he, who hath firmly settled his whole hope in God, be moved with the tongues of any who praise him. For even they themselves who speak, behold they all are nothing, for they will pass away with the sound of their words; but *the Truth of the Lord remaineth forever.*[8]

→ CHAPTER FIFTEEN ←

IN EVERYTHING WHICH WE DESIRE, HOW WE OUGHT TO STAND AFFECTED, AND WHAT WE OUGHT TO SAY

My son, say thou thus in everything; "Lord, if this be pleasing unto Thee, so let it be.[1] Lord, if it be to Thy honour, in Thy Name let this be done. Lord, if Thou seest it expedient for me, and approvest it to be useful, then grant unto me that I may use this to Thine honour. But if Thou knowest it will be hurtful unto me, and no profit to the health of my soul, take away any such desire from me."

For not every desire proceedeth from the Holy Spirit, even though it seem unto a man right and good. It is difficult to judge truly whether a good Spirit or the contrary drive thee to desire this or that; or whether by thine own spirit thou be moved thereunto. Many have been deceived in the end, who at the first seemed to be led on by a good Spirit.

Therefore whatever occurreth to the mind as desirable, must always be desired and prayed for in the fear of God and with humility of heart; and chiefly thou must commit the whole matter to Me with special resignation of thyself, and thou must say, "O Lord, Thou knowest what is the better way, let this or that be done, as Thou shalt please. Give what Thou wilt, and how much Thou wilt, and when Thou wilt. Deal with me as Thou knowest, and as best pleaseth Thee, and is most for Thy honour. Set me where Thou wilt, and deal with me in all things just as Thou wilt. I am in Thy hand: turn me round, and turn me back again, even as a wheel. Behold, I am Thy servant, prepared for all things; for I desire not to live unto myself, but unto Thee; and O that I could do it worthily and perfectly!"

2. *A prayer that the will of God may be fulfilled.*

O most merciful Jesus, grant to me Thy Grace, that it maybe with me, and labour with me,[2] and persevere with me even to the end.

Grant me always to desire and to will that which is to Thee most acceptable and most dear. Let Thy will be mine, and let my will ever follow Thine, and agree perfectly with it. Let my will and nill be all one with Thine, and let me not be able to will or not to will anything else, but what Thou willest or willest not.

Grant that I may die to all things that are in the world, and for Thy sake love to be contemned, and not known in this generation. Grant to me above all things that can be desired, to rest in Thee, and in Thee to have my heart at peace. Thou art the true peace of the heart, Thou its only rest; out of Thee all things are hard and restless. *In this peace, in this self-same thing,* that is, in Thee, the one Chiefest Eternal Good, *I will sleep and rest.*[3] Amen.

✧ CHAPTER SIXTEEN ✧

THAT TRUE COMFORT IS TO BE SOUGHT IN GOD ALONE

WHATSOEVER I CAN DESIRE OR IMAGINE FOR MY COMFORT, I LOOK FOR it not here but hereafter. For if I might alone have all the comforts of the world, and were able to enjoy all the delights thereof,[1] it is certain that they could not long endure.

Wherefore, O my soul, thou canst not be fully comforted,[2] nor have perfect refreshment, except in God, the Comforter of the poor, and Patron of the humble. Wait a little while, O my soul, wait for the divine promise, and thou shalt have abundance of all good things in Heaven.

If thou desire inordinately the things that are present, thou shalt lose those which are heavenly and eternal. Let temporal things be used, but things eternal desired.

Thou canst not be satisfied with any temporal good, because thou wast not created to enjoy these. Although thou shouldest possess all created good, yet couldest thou not be happy thereby nor blessed; but in God, who created all things, consisteth thy whole blessedness and felicity;[3] not such as is seen and commended by the foolish lovers of the world, but such as the good and faithful servants of Christ wait for, and of which the spiritual and pure in heart, whose conversation is in Heaven,[4] sometimes have a foretaste.

Vain and brief is all human comfort. Blessed and true is the comfort which is received inwardly from the Truth.

2. A devout man beareth everywhere about with him his own Comforter Jesus, and saith unto Him, "Be Thou present with me, O Lord Jesu, in

every time and place. Let this be my consolation, to be cheerfully willing to do without all human comfort. And if Thy consolation be wanting, let Thy will, and just trial of me be unto me as the greatest comfort; *for Thou wilt not always be angry, neither wilt Thou threaten forever.*"[5]

✧ CHAPTER SEVENTEEN ✧

THAT ALL OUR ANXIETIES ARE TO BE PLACED ON GOD

My son, suffer Me to do with thee what I please; I know what is expedient for thee. Thou thinkest as man; thou judgest in many things as human feelings persuade thee.

O Lord, what Thou sayest is true. Greater is Thy anxiety for me,[1] than all the care that I can take for myself. For he standeth but very totteringly, who casteth not all his anxiety upon Thee.[2]

O Lord, if only my will may remain right and firm towards Thee, do with me whatsoever it shall please Thee. For it cannot be anything but good, whatsoever Thou shalt do with me. If Thou willest me to be in darkness, be Thou blessed; and if Thou willest me to be in light, be Thou again blessed. If Thou vouchsafe to comfort me, be Thou blessed; and if Thou willest me to be afflicted, be Thou ever equally blessed.

2. My son, such as this ought to be thy state, if thou desire to walk with Me. Thou oughtest to be as ready to suffer as to rejoice. Thou oughtest as cheerfully to be destitute and poor, as full and rich.

O Lord, cheerfully will I suffer for Thy sake,[3] whatever Thou shalt will to come upon me. From Thy hand I am willing to receive indifferently good and evil, sweet and bitter, joy and sorrow, and for all that befalleth me, to give Thee thanks.

Keep me safe from all sin, and I shall fear neither death[4] nor hell. So as Thou cast me not from Thee forever, nor *blot me out of the book of life*,[5] whatever tribulation may come upon me shall not hurt me.

CHAPTER EIGHTEEN

THAT TEMPORAL MISERIES MUST BE BORNE PATIENTLY, AFTER THE EXAMPLE OF CHRIST

MY SON, I CAME DOWN FROM HEAVEN,[1] FOR I THY SALVATION; I took upon Me thy miseries,[2] not necessity but charity drawing Me thereto; that thou thyself mightest learn patience, and bear temporal miseries without grudging. For from the hour of My birth,[3] even until My death on the cross, I was not without suffering of grief. I suffered great want of things temporal; I often heard many complaints against Me; I endured calmly disgraces and revilings; for benefits I received ingratitude; for miracles, blasphemies; for teaching, reproofs.

2. O Lord, for that Thou wert patient in Thy life-time, herein especially fulfilling the commandment of Thy Father,[4] worthy it is that I, a most miserable sinner, according to Thy will should bear myself patiently, and for my welfare endure the burden of this corruptible life as long as Thou Thyself shalt will. For although this present life be burdensome to our feelings, yet notwithstanding it is now by Thy grace made very gainful; and by Thy example and the footsteps of Thy Saints, more bright and bearable to the weak. It is, moreover, much more full of consolation than it was formerly in the old Law, when the gate of Heaven remained shut; and the way also to Heaven seemed darker, when so few took care to seek after the kingdom of Heaven.[5] Moreover also they who then were just and meet to be saved, could not enter into the heavenly kingdom, before Thy Passion, and the due satisfaction of Thy holy Death.

O how great thanks am I bound to render unto Thee, that Thou hast vouchsafed to shew unto me and to all faithful people the good and the right way to Thine eternal kingdom! For Thy life is our way, and by holy patience we walk toward Thee who art our Crown. If Thou hadst not gone before us and taught us, who would care to follow? Alas, how many would remain behind and afar off, if they did not gaze upon Thy glorious example! Behold, even yet we are lukewarm, though we have heard of so many of Thy miracles and teachings; what would become of us, if we had not so great light[6] whereby to follow Thee!

→ CHAPTER NINETEEN ←

OF THE ENDURANCE OF INJURIES, AND WHO IS APPROVED TO BE TRULY PATIENT

What is it thou sayest, My son? Cease to complain, when thou considerest My Passion, and the sufferings of other holy ones. Thou hast *not yet made resistance unto blood.*[1] It is but little which thou sufferest, in comparison of those who suffered things so many, who were so strongly tempted, so heavily afflicted, so many ways tried and exercised.[2] Thou oughtest therefore to call to mind the more heavy sufferings of others, that so thou mayest the easier bear thy own very small troubles. And if they seem unto thee not very small, then beware lest thy impatience be the cause thereof. However, whether they be small or whether they be great, endeavour patiently to undergo them all. The better thou disposest thyself to suffer, so much the more wisely thou doest, and so much the greater reward shalt thou receive; thou shalt also more easily endure, if both in mind and by habit thou art diligently prepared thereunto.

Do not say,

"I cannot endure to suffer these things at the hands of this man, nor ought I to endure things of this sort; for he hath done me grievous harm, and reproacheth me with things which I never thought of; but of another I will willingly suffer, and will look upon them as things which I ought to suffer." Foolish is such a thought; it considereth not the virtue of patience, nor by whom it will be crowned; but rather, weigheth the persons, and the injuries offered to itself. He is not truly patient, who willeth to suffer only so much as he think good, and from whom he please. But the truly patient man mindeth not by whom he is exercised, whether by his superior, by one of his equals, or by an inferior; whether by a good and holy man, or by one that is perverse and unworthy. But indifferently from every creature, how much soever, or how often soever anything adverse befall him, he taketh all thankfully as from the hand of God, and esteemeth it a great gain: for with God it is impossible that anything, how small soever, if only it be suffered for God's sake, should pass without its reward.

Be thou therefore prepared for the fight, if thou wilt have the victory. Without a combat thou canst not come to the crown of patience.[3] If thou willest not to suffer, thou refusest to be crowned. But if thou desirest to be crowned, strive manfully, endure patiently. Without labour there is no arriving at rest, nor without fighting can the victory be reached.

2. O Lord, let that become possible to me by grace, which by nature seemeth to me impossible. Thou knowest that I am able to suffer but little, and that I am quickly cast down, when a slight adversity ariseth. For Thy Name's sake, let every exercise of tribulation be made loveable and desirable to me; for to suffer and to be disquieted for Thy sake is very wholesome for my soul.

CHAPTER TWENTY

OF THE ACKNOWLEDGING OF OUR OWN INFIRMITY; AND OF THE MISERIES OF THIS LIFE

I WILL CONFESS AGAINST MYSELF MINE OWN UNRIGHTEOUSNESS;[1] I WILL confess my weakness unto Thee, O Lord. Oftentimes a small matter it is that casteth down and maketh me sad. I resolve that I will act with courage, but when even a small temptation cometh, I am at once in a great strait. It is sometimes a very trifle, whence a heavy temptation ariseth. And whilst I am thinking myself tolerably safe, and when I feel it not, I sometimes find myself almost entirely overcome by a slight breath.

Behold therefore, O Lord, my low estate,[2] and my frailty which is every way known unto Thee. Have mercy on me, and deliver me out of the mire, that I stick not fast therein,[3] that I remain not utterly cast down forever. This is that which oftentimes striketh me backwards, and confoundeth me in Thy sight, that I am so subject to fall, and weak in resisting my passions. And although I do not altogether consent, yet their continued assaulting is troublesome and grievous unto me; and it is exceeding weary to live thus daily in conflict. From hence my weakness becometh known unto me, in that hateful phantoms do always much more easily rush in than depart.

Most mighty God of Israel, Thou zealous Lover of faithful souls! O that Thou wouldst consider the labour and sorrow of Thy servant, and stand by him in all things, to whatsoever he reacheth forward! Strengthen me with heavenly courage, lest the old man, the miserable flesh, not as yet fully subject to the Spirit, prevail and get the upper hand; against which, it will be needful for me to fight, so long as I breathe in this most miserable life.

2. Alas, what a kind of life is this, where tribulation and miseries are never wanting; where all is full of snares and enemies! For when one tribulation or temptation retreateth, another cometh on; yea, and while the first conflict yet lasteth on, many others come unexpected one after another.

And how can a life be loved that hath so many embitterments, and is subject to so many calamities and miseries? How too can it be called life, that begetteth so many deaths and plagues? And yet it is loved, and many seek to delight themselves therein. The world is oftentimes blamed for being deceitful and vain, and yet it is not easily abandoned, because the desires of the flesh bear so great a sway. But some things draw us to love the world, others to contemn it. *The lust of the flesh, the lust of the eyes, and the pride of life,*[4] do draw us to the love of the world; but the pains and miseries that justly follow them bring forth a hatred of the world and a weariness thereof. But alas, vicious pleasure overcometh the mind that is addicted to the world; and to be under thorns[5] it esteemeth a delight, because it hath neither seen nor tasted the sweetness of God, and the inward pleasantness of virtue.

But they who perfectly contemn the world, and study to live to God under holy discipline, these are not ignorant of the divine sweetness promised to those who truly renounce the world; they also very clearly see how grievously the world erreth, and is in many ways deceived.

→ CHAPTER TWENTY-ONE ←

THAT WE ARE TO REST IN GOD ABOVE ALL THINGS WHICH ARE GOOD, AND ABOVE ALL HIS OWN GIFTS

ABOVE ALL THINGS, AND IN ALL THINGS, O MY SOUL, THOU SHALT REST in the Lord always, for He Himself is the everlasting Rest of the Saints.

Grant me, O most sweet and loving Jesus, to rest in Thee above every creature,[1] above all health and beauty, above all glory and honour, above all power and dignity, above all knowledge and subtilty, above all riches and arts, above all joy and gladness, above all fame and praise, above all sweetness and comfort, above all hope and promise, above all desert and desire; above all gifts and favours that Thou canst give and pour upon us, above all mirth and exultation that the mind can receive and feel; finally, above Angels and Archangels, and above all the host of Heaven, above all things visible and invisible, and above all that Thou my God art not.

Because Thou, O Lord my God, art above all things the best; Thou alone art most high, Thou alone most powerful, Thou alone most sufficient and most full, Thou alone most sweet and most full of consolation; Thou alone art most lovely and loving, Thou alone most noble and glorious above all things; in Whom all good things together both perfectly are, and ever have been, and shall be. And therefore it is too small, and unsatisfying, whatsoever Thou bestowest on me besides Thyself, or revealest unto me of Thyself, or promisest, whilst Thou art not seen, nor fully obtained. For surely my heart cannot truly rest, nor be entirely contented, unless it rest in Thee,[2] and surmount all gifts and every creature.

O Thou most beloved Bridegroom of my soul, Jesu Christ, Thou most pure Lover, Thou Lord of all creation: who will give me the wings of true liberty, that I might flee away and rest in Thee![3] O when shall it be fully granted me, to consider in quietness of mind and see how sweet Thou art, O Lord my God! When shall I fully gather up myself into Thee, that by reason of my love to Thee I may not feel myself, but Thee alone, above all thought and measure, in a manner not all men know. But now I oftentimes groan, and bear my unhappiness with grief. Because many evils occur in this vale of miseries, which do often trouble, sadden, and over-cloud me; often hinder and distract me, allure and entangle me, so that I can have no free access unto Thee, nor enjoy the sweet welcomings which are ever ready with the blessed spirits.

Let my sighs move Thee and my manifold desolation here on earth, O Jesu, Thou Brightness of the eternal glory,[4] Thou Comfort of the pilgrim soul. With Thee is my tongue without voice, and my very silence speaketh unto Thee. How long doth my Lord delay to come? Let Him come unto me His poor despised servant, and make me glad. Let Him put forth His hand, and deliver me in my misery from all anguish. Come, O come; for without Thee no day nor hour shall be glad; for Thou art my gladness, and without Thee my table is empty. In misery am I, and in a manner imprisoned and loaded with fetters, until Thou refresh me with the light of Thy presence, and grant me liberty, and shew a friendly countenance toward me. Let others seek what else they please instead of Thee; but for me, nothing else meanwhile pleaseth nor shall please me, but Thou only, my God, my hope, my everlasting salvation. I will not hold my peace, nor cease to pray, until Thy grace return again, and Thou speak inwardly unto me.

2. Behold, here I am. Behold, I come unto thee, because thou hast called upon Me. Thy tears and the desire of thy soul, thy humiliation and thy contrition of heart, have inclined and brought Me unto thee.

3. And I said, Lord, I have called Thee, and have desired to enjoy Thee, being ready to spurn all things for Thy sake. For Thou didst first stir me up that I might seek Thee. Blessed be Thou therefore, O Lord, that hast shewed this goodness to Thy servant, according to the

multitude of Thy mercies. What hath Thy servant more to say before Thee? Save that he greatly humble himself in Thy sight, ever mindful of his own iniquity and vileness. For there is none like unto Thee[5] in all the wonderful things of Heaven and earth. Thy works are very good, Thy judgments true, and by Thy providence the universe is ruled. Praise therefore and glory be unto Thee, O Wisdom of the Father; let my mouth, my soul, and all created things together, praise and bless Thee.

CHAPTER TWENTY-TWO

OF THE REMEMBRANCE OF GOD'S MANIFOLD BENEFITS

OPEN, O LORD, MY HEART IN THY LAW, AND I TEACH ME TO WALK IN Thy commandments.[1] Grant me to understand Thy will, and with great reference and diligent consideration to remember Thy benefits, as well in general as in particular, that henceforward I may be able worthily to give Thee thanks. But I know, and confess, that I am not able, even in the least point, to give Thee due thanks and praises. I am less than any of the benefits bestowed upon me:[2] and when I consider Thine excellency, before its greatness my spirit fainteth.

2. All that we have in soul and in body, and whatsoever we possess outwardly or inwardly, by nature or beyond nature, are Thy benefits, and do proclaim Thee bountiful, merciful, and good, from whom we have received all good things.

Although one have received more, another less, all notwithstanding are Thine, and without Thee even the least blessing cannot be had.

He that hath received greater cannot glory of his own desert, nor extol himself above others, nor insult over the lesser; for he is the greatest and the best, who ascribeth least unto himself, and who in rendering thanks is the most humble and the most devout. And he that esteemeth himself viler than all men, and judgeth himself most unworthy, is fittest to receive the greater blessings.

But he that hath received fewer, ought not to be out of heart, nor to take it grievously, nor envy him that is richer; but rather he should turn his mind to Thee, and exceedingly praise Thy goodness, for that Thou bestowest Thy gifts so bountifully, so freely, and so willingly, without respect of persons.

All things proceed from Thee, and therefore in all Thou art to be praised.

3. Thou knowest what is fit to be given to everyone; and why this man should have less, and that more, this is not for us to judge, but for Thee with whom are exactly marked every man's deserts.

Wherefore, O Lord God, I even esteem it a great mercy, not to have much of that which outwardly and in the opinion of men seemeth worthy of glory and applause. For so it cometh, that he who considereth the poverty and unworthiness of his own person, is so far from conceiving grief or sadness, or from being cast down thereat, that he rather taketh great comfort, and is glad; because Thou, O God, hast chosen the poor and humble and the despised of this world for Thyself,[3] for Thy familiar friends and household. Witnesses are Thy Apostles themselves, whom Thou hast *made princes over all the earth.*[4] And yet they lived in the world without complaint,[5] so humble and simple, without all malice and deceit, that they even rejoiced to suffer reproaches for Thy Name;[6] and what the world abhorreth, themselves embraced with great affection.

Nothing therefore ought so to rejoice him that loveth Thee and knoweth Thy benefits, as Thy will toward him, and the good pleasure of Thine eternal appointment. And herewith he ought to be so contented and comforted, that he would as willingly be the least, as another would wish to be the greatest; and he would be as peaceable and contented in the last place as in the first; as willing to be a despised cast-away, of no name or great report, as to be preferred in honour before others, and to be greater in the world than they. For Thy will and the love of Thy honour ought to surpass all things, and to comfort him more, and please him better, than all the benefits which he either hath received or can receive.

CHAPTER TWENTY-THREE

OF FOUR THINGS THAT BRING MUCH INWARD PEACE

My son, now will I teach thee the way of peace and true liberty.

Do, O Lord, as Thou sayest, for this is well-pleasing to me to hear.

Be desirous, My son, to do the will of another rather than thine own.[1] Choose always to have less rather than more.[2] Seek always the lower place, and to be inferior to everyone.[3] Wish always, and pray, that the will of God be wholly done in thee.[4] Behold, such a man entereth within the borders of peace and rest.

O Lord, this short discourse of Thine containeth within itself much perfection.[5] It is little to be spoken, but full of meaning, and abundant in fruit. For if it could faithfully be kept by me, trouble ought not so easily to arise in me. For as often as I feel myself unquiet and weighed down, I find that I have gone back from this doctrine. But Thou who canst do all things, and ever lovest the profiting of my soul, add unto me greater grace, that I may be able to fulfill Thy words, and to complete my salvation.

2. *A prayer against evil thoughts.*

O Lord my God, be not Thou far from me; my God, have regard to help me:[6] for there have risen up against me sundry thoughts, and great fears, afflicting my soul. How shall I pass through unhurt? How shall I break them to pieces?

I, saith He, *will go before thee, and will humble the great ones of the earth*; I will open the doors of the prison, and reveal unto thee hidden secrets.[7]

Do, O Lord, as Thou sayest, and let all evil thoughts fly from before Thy face. This is my hope, my one only consolation, to flee unto Thee from my inmost heart, and to wait patiently for Thy consolation.

3. *A prayer for mental illumination.*

O good Jesus, enlighten Thou me with the clear shining of an inward light, and remove away all darkness from the habitation of my heart. Repress Thou my many wandering thoughts, and break in pieces those temptations which violently assault me. Fight Thou strongly for me, and vanquish the evil beasts, I mean the alluring desires of the flesh; that so *there may be peace in Thy power*,[8] and that Thine abundant praise may resound in Thy holy court, that is, in a pure conscience. Command the winds and tempests; say unto the sea, Be still;[9] say to the north wind, Blow not; and there shall be a great calm.

Send out Thy light and Thy truth,[10] that they may shine upon the earth; for I am earth *without form and void*,[11] until Thou enlighten me. Pour forth Thy grace from above, shower upon my heart the dew of Heaven, supply fresh streams of devotion to water the face of the earth, that it may bring forth fruit good and excellent. Lift Thou up my mind which is pressed down by a load of sins, and draw up my whole desire to things heavenly; that having tasted the sweetness of supernal happiness, it may be irksome to me to think of earthly things.

Do Thou pluck me away, and deliver me from all unenduring comfort of creatures; for no created thing can give full rest and comfort to my desires. Join Thou me to Thyself with an inseparable band of love; for Thou even alone dost satisfy him that loveth Thee; and without Thee all things are vain and frivolous.

CHAPTER TWENTY-FOUR

OF AVOIDING CURIOUS ENQUIRY INTO THE LIFE OF ANOTHER

My son, be not curious, nor trouble thyself with idle anxieties.[1] What is this or that to thee? *Follow thou Me.*[2] For what is it to thee, whether that man be such or such, or whether this man do or speak this or that? Thou shalt not need to answer for others, but shalt give account for thyself.[3] Why therefore dost thou entangle thyself? Behold, I know all men, and do see all things that are done under the sun; also I understand how it is with everyone, what he thinketh, what he willeth, and to what end his intention aimeth. Unto Me therefore all things are to be committed; but do thou keep thyself in perfect peace, and let go the unquiet, to be as unquiet as he will. Whatsoever he shall have done or said, shall come upon him, for Me he cannot deceive.

2. Be not careful for "the shadow of a great name,"[4] nor for the familiar friendship of many, nor for the private affection of men. For these things beget distractions, and great darkness in the heart. Willingly would I speak My word, and reveal My hidden things unto thee, if thou wouldest diligently observe My coming, and open unto Me the door of thine heart. Be thou circumspect, and watchful in prayer, and in all things humble thyself.

CHAPTER TWENTY-FIVE

WHEREIN FIRM PEACE OF HEART AND TRUE SPIRITUAL PROGRESS CONSISTETH

MY SON, I HAVE SPOKEN; *PEACE I LEAVE WITH YOU, MY PEACE I GIVE UNTO you: not as the world giveth, give I unto you.*[1] Peace is what all desire, but all do not care for the things that make for true peace. My peace is with the humble and gentle of heart; in much patience shall thy peace be. If thou wilt hear Me and follow My voice, thou shalt be able to enjoy much peace.

What then shall I do?

In every matter look to thyself, what thou doest and what thou sayest; and direct thy whole intention unto this, that thou mayest please Me alone, and neither desire or seek anything besides Me. But of the words or deeds of others judge nothing rashly; neither do thou entangle thyself with things not committed unto thee; and it shall be that thou art little or seldom disturbed. But never to feel any disturbance at all, nor to suffer any trouble of heart or body, belongeth not to the present time, but to the state of eternal Rest.

2. Think not therefore that thou hast found true peace, if thou feel no heaviness; nor that then all is well, if thou art vexed with no adversary; nor that this is to be perfect, if all things happen according to thy desire. Neither do thou then esteem at all highly of thyself, or account thyself to be specially beloved, if thou be in a state of great devotion and sweetness; for it is not by these things that a true lover of virtue is known, nor in these things consisteth the progress and perfection of a man.

Wherein then, O Lord?

In giving thyself over with all thy heart to the divine Will, not seeking thine own things, either in great or in small, either in time or in eternity. So shalt thou keep one even countenance, in thanksgiving, amidst prosperity and adversity, weighing all things with an equal balance. Be thou so brave, and so long-suffering in hope, that when inward comfort is withdrawn, thou mayest prepare thy heart to suffer even greater things; and do not justify thyself, as though thou oughtest not to suffer these afflictions or any so great, but justify Me in whatsoever I appoint, and praise My Holy Name. Then thou art walking in the true and right way of peace, and thou shalt have undoubted hope to see My face again with great delight. For if thou attain to the full contempt of thyself, know that thou shalt then enjoy abundance of peace, as great as thy state of sojourning is able to possess.

⇢ CHAPTER TWENTY-SIX ⇠

OF THE EXCELLENCY OF A FREE MIND, WHICH IS RATHER WON BY HUMBLE PRAYER THAN BY READING

O Lord, this is the business of a perfect man, never to relax his mind from attentive thought of heavenly things, and amidst many cares to pass by, as it were, without care; not as one destitute of all feeling, but by a certain privilege of a free mind, cleaving to no creature with inordinate affection.

2. I beseech Thee, most gracious God, preserve me from the cares of this life, that I be not too much entangled therein; from the many necessities of the body, that I be not ensnared by pleasure; from whatsoever is an obstacle to the soul, that I be not broken with troubles and overthrown. I do not say from those things which worldly vanity with its whole affection compasseth, but from those miseries, which as punishments by the common curse of mortality,[1] do weigh down and hinder the soul of Thy servant, that it cannot enter into the freedom of the Spirit, so often as it would.

3. O my God, Thou sweetness ineffable, turn for me into bitterness all carnal comfort, which draweth me away from the love of things eternal, and in evil manner allureth me to itself by the view of some present delightsome good. Let me not be overcome, O my God, let me not be overcome by flesh and blood;[2] let not the world and the brief glory thereof deceive me; let not the devil and his cunning give me a fall. Give me strength to resist, patience to endure, and constancy to

persevere. Give me instead of all the comforts of the world, the most sweet unction of Thy Spirit, and in place of carnal love, pour in the love of Thy Name.

Behold, meat, drink, raiment, and all the other necessaries for the maintenance of the body, are burdensome unto a fervent spirit. Grant me to use such refreshments moderately, and not to be entangled with an over-great desire of them. To cast away all things is not lawful, because nature is to be sustained; but to require superfluities, and those things that give the more delight, the holy Law forbiddeth; for then the flesh would wax wanton against the Spirit. Herein, I beseech Thee, let Thy hand govern me and teach me, that there may be no excess.

CHAPTER TWENTY-SEVEN

THAT IT IS PRIVATE LOVE WHICH MOST HINDERETH FROM THE CHIEFEST GOOD

MY SON, THOU OUGHTEST TO GIVE ALL FOR ALL, AND TO BE NOTHING of thyself. Know that the love of thyself doth thee more hurt than anything in the world. According to the love and affection which thou bearest towards anything, so doth it more or less cleave to thee. If thy love be pure,[1] simple, and well-ordered, thou shalt be free from the bondage of things.

Do not covet that which it is not lawful to have. Do not have that which may entangle thee, and deprive thee of inward liberty. Strange it is that thou committest not thyself wholly unto Me, from the bottom of thy heart, with all things thou canst have or desire. Why art thou consumed with vain grief?[2] Why weary thyself with superfluous cares? Stand to My good pleasure, and thou shalt suffer no loss.

If thou seek this or that, and wouldest be in such or such a place, the better to enjoy thine own profit and pleasure, thou shalt never be at quiet, nor free from anxiety; for in every instance somewhat will be found wanting, and in every place there will be someone to cross thee.

Man's welfare then lieth not in obtaining or multiplying any external thing, but rather in despising it, and utterly rooting it out from the heart. And this thou must understand not only of income of money and riches, but of seeking after honour also, and the desire of vain praise, all which pass away with this world.

The place giveth little defense if the spirit of fervour be wanting, neither shall that peace long continue, which is sought abroad;[3] if the state of thy heart be destitute of a true foundation, that is, unless thou stand stedfast in Me, thou mayest change but not better thyself. For when occasion ariseth and is laid hold of, thou shalt find what thou didst flee from, and more also.

2. *A prayer for a clean heart, and Heavenly Wisdom.*

Confirm me, O God, by the grace of Thy Holy Spirit.[4] Grant me might to be strengthened in the inner man,[5] and to empty my heart of all useless anxiety and distress;[6] not to be drawn away with sundry desires of anything whatever, whether mean or precious, but to look on all things as passing away, and on myself also no less as about to pass away with them. For nothing is abiding under the sun, where *all things are vanity and vexation of spirit*.[7] O how wise is he that so considereth them!

Grant me, O Lord, heavenly wisdom,[8] that I may learn above all things to seek and to find Thee, above all things to relish and to love Thee, and to think of all other things as being, what indeed they are, at the disposal of Thy wisdom. Grant me prudently to avoid him that flattereth me, and to endure patiently him that opposeth me. Because this is great wisdom, not to be moved with every wind of words,[9] nor to give ear to an ill-flattering siren; for thus we shall go on securely in the way which we have begun.

CHAPTER TWENTY-EIGHT

AGAINST THE TONGUES OF SLANDERERS

MY SON, TAKE IT NOT GRIEVOUSLY IF SOME THINK ILL OF THEE,[1] AND speak that which thou wouldest not willingly hear. Thou oughtest to judge the worst of thyself, and to think no man weaker than thyself.

If thou dost walk inwardly, thou wilt not much weigh fleeting words. It is no small prudence to keep silence in an evil time,[2] and inwardly to turn thyself to Me, and not to be troubled by the judgment of men.

2. Let not thy peace be in the tongues of men; for whether they interpret well or ill of thee thou art not therefore another man.

Where are true peace and glory? Are they not in Me?[3] And he that neither coveteth to please men, nor feareth to displease them, shall enjoy much peace. From inordinate love and vain fear ariseth all disquietness of heart and distraction of the thoughts.

→ CHAPTER TWENTY-NINE ←

HOW WE OUGHT TO CALL UPON GOD, AND TO BLESS HIM, WHEN TRIBULATION IS UPON US

Blessed be Thy Name, O Lord, forever;[1] who hast willed that this temptation and tribulation should come upon me. I cannot escape it, but must needs flee to Thee, that Thou mayest help me, and turn it to my good.

2. Lord, I am now in tribulation, and my heart is ill at ease, for I am much troubled with the present suffering. And now, O Beloved Father, *what shall I say*? I am caught amidst straits; *save me from this hour. Yet for this cause came I unto this hour,*[2] that Thou mayest be glorified, when I shall have been greatly humbled, and by Thee delivered. *Let it please Thee, Lord, to deliver me*;[3] for, poor wretch that I am, what can I do, and whither shall I go without Thee? Grant me patience, O Lord, even now in this moment. Help me, my God, and then I will not fear, how grievously soever I be afflicted.

And now amidst these things what shall I say? Lord, *Thy will be done*;[4] I have well deserved to be afflicted and weighed down. Assuredly I ought to bear it; and O that I may bear it with patience, until the tempest pass over, and better come! Howbeit Thy Almighty hand hath power to take even this temptation from me, and to assuage the violence thereof, that I sink not utterly under it; as oftentimes heretofore Thou hast dealt with me, O my God, my Mercy! And the more difficult it is to me, so much the more easy to Thee is *this change of the right hand of the most Highest*.[5]

CHAPTER THIRTY

OF SEEKING THE DIVINE AID, AND CONFIDENCE OF RECOVERING GRACE

MY SON, I AM THE LORD, *THAT GIVETH STRENGTH IN THE DAY OF tribulation.*[1] Come thou unto Me, whenever it shall not be well with thee.[2]

This it is which most of all hindereth heavenly consolation, that thou art too slow in turning thyself unto prayer. For before thou dost earnestly ask of Me, thou seekest in the meanwhile many comforts, and refreshes! Thyself in outward things. And hence it cometh to pass that all doth little profit thee, until thou well consider that it is I who rescue them that hope in Me; and that out of Me, there is neither powerful help, nor profitable counsel, nor lasting remedy.

But do thou, having now recovered breath after the tempest, gather strength again in the light of My tender mercies; for I am at hand, saith the Lord, to repair all, not only entirely, but also abundantly and with increase. Is there anything hard to Me? Or shall I be like one that saith and doeth not?[3] Where is thy faith? Stand firmly and with perseverance; be long-suffering, and a man of courage; comfort will come to thee in due time. Wait for Me, yea, wait; I will come and heal thee.[4]

2. It is a temptation that vexeth thee, and a vain fear that affrighteth thee. What else doth anxiety about future accidents bring thee, but sorrow upon sorrow? *Sufficient for the day is the evil thereof.*[5] It is a vain thing and unprofitable, to be either disturbed or pleased about future things, which perhaps will never come to pass. But it belongeth

to man's nature to be deluded with such imaginations; and it is a sign of a mind as yet weak, to be so easily drawn away at the suggestions of the Enemy. For himself careth not whether it be by things true or false that he delude and deceive thee; nor whether he overthrow thee with the love of present, or the fear of future things. *Let not therefore thy heart be troubled, neither let it be afraid.*[6] Trust in Me, and have confidence in My mercy.[7] When thou thinkest thyself far off from Me, oftentimes I am the nearer. When thou countest almost all to be lost, then oftentimes the greater gain of reward is close at hand. All is not lost, when anything falleth out contrary. Thou oughtest not to judge according to present feeling; nor so to take any heaviness, or give thyself over to it, from whencesoever it cometh, as though all hope of rising therefrom were quite taken away. Think not thyself wholly left, although for a time I have sent thee some tribulation, or even have withdrawn thy desired comfort; for this is the passage to the Kingdom of Heaven.

And without doubt it is more expedient for thee and the rest of My servants, that ye be exercised with adversities, than that ye should have all things according to your desires. I know the secret thoughts, and that it is very expedient for thy welfare that thou be left sometimes without taste of spiritual sweetness, lest thou shouldest be puffed up with thy prosperous estate, and shouldest will to please thyself in that which thou art not. That which I have given, I can take away; and I can restore it again when I please. When I give it, it is Mine; when I withdraw it, I have not taken anything that is thine; for Mine is *every good gift and every perfect gift.*[8] If I send upon thee affliction, or any cross whatever, repine not, nor let thy heart fail thee; I can quickly succour thee, and turn all thy burden into joy. Howbeit I am righteous, and greatly to be praised when I deal thus with thee.

If thou art wise, and considerest what the truth is, thou never oughtest for adversities to be so cast down and made sad, but rather to rejoice and give thanks. Yea, thou wilt account this thine especial joy, that I afflict thee with sorrows, and do not spare thee. *As the Father hath loved Me, I also love you,*[9] I said unto My beloved disciples; whom certainly I sent not out to temporal joys, but to great conflicts; not to honours, but to contempts; not to idleness, but to labours; not to rest, but to bring forth much *fruit with patience.*[10] Remember thou these words, My son!

➔ CHAPTER THIRTY-ONE ⬅

OF THE DISREGARD OF EVERY CREATURE, THAT SO THE CREATOR MAY BE FOUND

O Lord, I stand much in need of yet greater grace, if I ought to reach that place, where no man nor any creature shall be a hindrance unto me.

For as long as anything holdeth me back, I cannot freely fly to Thee. He was longing to fly freely who said, *Who shall give me wings like a dove, and I will fly away and be at rest*![1] What is more at rest than the single eye?[2] And what is more free than he that desireth nothing upon earth? A man ought therefore to mount over every creature, and perfectly to forsake himself and stand in a trance, and see that Thou, the Creator of all things, hast nothing amongst creatures like unto Thyself. Unless too a man be disentangled from all creatures, he cannot freely attend unto divine things. For that is the reason why there are few contemplative men to be found, because few have the knowledge to withdraw themselves fully from things about to perish and from creatures.

To obtain this there is need of much grace, which may elevate the soul, and carry it away above itself.

And unless a man be elevated in spirit, and freed from all creatures, and wholly united unto God, whatsoever he knoweth, and whatsoever he hath, is of no great weight. For a long while shall he be small, and lie grovelling below, who esteemeth anything great, but the One only Infinite Eternal Good. And whatsoever is not God, is nothing, and ought to be accounted as nothing.

There is great difference between the wisdom of an illuminated and devout man, and the knowledge of a learned and studious clerk. Far more noble is that learning which floweth from above, from the divine out-pouring, than that which is painfully acquired by the wit of man.

3. Many are found that desire contemplation, but they have no mind to practice the things that are required thereunto. It is a great hindrance, that men rest in signs and sensible things, and take little care about the perfect mortification of themselves.

I know not what it is, or by what spirit we are led, or what we pretend, we that seem to be called spiritual, that we take so much pains, and are so full of anxiety about transitory and mean things, while we but seldom, and hardly at all with full recollection of mind, think of our own inward concerns. Alas, presently after a slight recollection we burst forth abroad, and weigh not our works with strict examination. We mind not where our affections lie, nor bewail the impurity that is in all our actions. For *all flesh had corrupted his way*, and therefore did the great deluge ensue.[3] Since then our inward affection is much corrupted, our actions thence proceeding, which are the proof of the lack of inward strength, must needs be corrupted also. From a pure heart proceedeth the fruit of a good life.[4]

We ask how much a man hath done; but from what degree of virtue he acteth, is not so carefully weighed. We enquire whether he hath been courageous, rich, handsome, skilful, a good writer, a good singer, or a good labourer; but how poor he is in spirit, how patient and meek, how devout and spiritual, of this most men hold their peace. Nature respecteth the outward things of a man, Grace turneth itself to the inward. The one is often disappointed; the other hopeth in God, and so is not deceived.

CHAPTER THIRTY-TWO

OF SELF-DENIAL, AND RENOUNCING EVERY EVIL APPETITE

MY SON, THOU CANST NOT POSSESS PERFECT LIBERTY UNLESS THOU wholly renounce thyself.[1]

Bound in fetters are all they who seek their own interest, and are lovers of themselves; covetous, inquisitive, wandering in a circle, seeking ever soft and delicate things, not the things of Jesus Christ, but oftentimes devising and framing that which will not stand. For it shall perish altogether, whatsoever is not born of God.

Keep this short and perfect word: Let go all and thou shalt find all; leave desire and thou shalt find rest. Weigh this thoroughly in thy mind, and when thou hast fulfilled it, thou shalt understand all things.

2. O Lord, this is not the work of one day, nor children's sport; nay, in this short word is included all the perfection of religious persons.

3. My son, thou oughtest not to turn away, nor at once be cast down, when thou hearest the way of the perfect; but shouldest rather be stirred up to higher things, and at least in desire to sigh after them.

I would it were so with thee, and thou wert arrived at this, to be no longer a lover of thyself, but didst stand merely at My beck, and at his whom I have appointed a father over thee; then shouldest thou exceedingly please Me, and all thy life would pass away in joy and peace. Thou hast yet many things to part with, which unless thou wholly resign unto Me, thou shalt not attain to that which thou dost ask.

4. *I counsel thee to buy of Me gold tried in the fire, that thou mayest become rich;*[2] that is, the heavenly Wisdom, which treadeth under foot all that is mean and low. Put aside earthly wisdom, and all seeking to please the world and thyself.

I said that thou must buy mean things instead of things which, among men, are precious and exalted. For true heavenly Wisdom doth seem very mean, and small, and almost given up to forgetfulness, because she hath no high thoughts of herself, nor seeketh to be magnified upon earth. Many indeed praise her with their mouth, but in their life they are far from her; yet is she the *pearl of great price,*[3] which is hidden from many.

CHAPTER THIRTY-THREE

OF INCONSTANCY OF HEART, AND OF HAVING OUR FINAL INTENTION DIRECTED UNTO GOD

MY SON, TRUST NOT TO THY FEELING, WHICH NOW IS; QUICKLY SHALL it be changed into another. As long as thou livest, thou art subject to mutability,[1] even against thy will; so that thou art found one while merry, another while sad; one while quiet, another while troubled; now devout, then undevout; now diligent, then listless; now grave, and then light.

2. But he that is wise and well instructed in the Spirit standeth above these changeful things; not heeding what he feeleth in himself or which way the wind of instability bloweth; but so that the whole intention of his mind maketh progress to the due and desired end. For thus he will be able to continue throughout one and the self-same and unshaken; in the midst of so many various issues the single eye of his intention being directed unceasingly towards Me.

And the purer the eye of the intention is,[2] with so much the more constancy doth a man pass through divers storms.

But in many the eye of a pure intention waxeth dim, for their regard is quickly drawn aside to some pleasurable object which meeteth them. For it is rare to find one who is wholly free from all blemish of self-seeking. So the Jews of old came to Bethany to Martha and Mary, *not for Jesus' sake only, but that they might see Lazarus.*[3]

The eye of our intention therefore is to be purged, that it may be single and right;[4] and is to be directed towards Me, beyond all the various objects which may come between.

CHAPTER THIRTY-FOUR

THAT GOD IS SWEET ABOVE ALL THINGS, AND IN ALL THINGS, TO HIM THAT LOVETH HIM

BEHOLD, MY GOD, AND MY ALL! WHAT CAN I DESIRE MORE, AND WHAT happier thing can I long for? O sweet and delicious word? But to him only who loveth the Word, not the world, nor the things that are in the world.

My God, and my all! To him that understandeth, enough hath been said; and to repeat it often, is delightful to him that loveth. Forasmuch as when Thou art present, all things are delightful, but when Thou art absent, all things are a loathing. Thou makest a quiet heart, and great peace, and festal joy. Thou makest us to think well of all circumstances, and in all to praise Thee; neither can anything please long without Thee; but if it must needs be pleasant and of a good savour, Thy grace must be present, and it must be seasoned with the seasoning of Thy Wisdom. What will not be of good savour unto him to whom Thou savourest well? And him to whom Thou savourest not, what shall have power to please?

But the wise men of the world, and they also who relish the things of the flesh, are found wanting in Thy Wisdom;[1] for in the world is found the utmost vanity, and in the flesh is found death. But they that follow Thee by the contempt of worldly things, and mortification of the flesh, are known to be truly wise; for they are brought over from vanity to truth, from the flesh to the spirit. To these God savoureth well; and what good soever is found in creatures, they wholly refer unto the praise of their Maker. Different, however, yea, very different is the savour of the Creator and of the creature, of Eternity and of time, of Light uncreated and of light received.

2. O everlasting Light, surpassing all created luminaries, *flash forth Thy lightning*[2] from above, piercing all the most inward parts of my heart. Make clean, make glad, make bright and make alive my spirit, with all the powers thereof, that I may cleave unto Thee in ecstasies of joy. O when will that blessed and desired hour come, that Thou mayest satisfy me with Thy Presence, and be unto me all in all! So long as this is not granted me I shall not have full joy.

Still, alas? The old man doth live in me,[3] he is not wholly crucified, is not perfectly dead. Still lusteth he mightily against the Spirit, and stirreth up inward wars, nor suffereth the kingdom of the soul to be in peace.

But thou that rulest the power of the sea, and stillest the lifting up of its waves,[4] arise and help me! *Scatter the nations that desire war;*[5] crush Thou them in Thy might. Display Thy wonderful works, I beseech Thee, and let Thy right hand be glorified; for there is no other hope or refuge for me, save in Thee, O Lord my God.[6]

⇾ CHAPTER THIRTY-FIVE ⇽

THAT THERE IS NO SECURITY FROM TEMPTATION IN THIS LIFE

MY SON, THOU ART NEVER SECURE IN THIS LIFE, BUT AS LONG AS THOU livest,[1] thou needest always spiritual armour. Thou dwellest among enemies, and art fought against on the right hand and on the left.[2]

If therefore thou defend not thyself on every side with the shield of patience, thou wilt not be long without a wound. Moreover, if thou set not thy heart fixedly on Me, with a sincere wish to suffer all things for Me, thou wilt not be able to bear the heat of this combat, nor to attain to the palm of the blessed. Thou oughtest therefore manfully to go through all, and to use a strong hand against whatsoever withstandeth thee.

For to him that overcometh is manna given,[3] and for the indolent there remaineth much misery.

2. If thou seek rest in this life, how wilt thou then attain to the everlasting rest? Dispose not thyself for much rest, but for great patience. Seek true peace, not in earth, but in Heaven; not in men, nor in any other creature, but in God alone.

For the love of God thou oughtest cheerfully to undergo all things, that is to say, labours and pains; temptations, vexations, anxieties, necessities, infirmities, injuries, slanders, reproofs, humiliations; confusions, corrections, and despisings. These help to virtue; these are the trial of a novice in Christ; these frame the heavenly crown. I will give an everlasting reward for a short labour, and infinite glory for transitory confusion.

3. Thinkest thou that thou shalt always have spiritual consolations at thine own will? My saints had not such always, but they had many afflictions, and sundry temptations, and great forsakings. Nevertheless in all these they bore themselves up patiently, and trusted rather in God than in themselves; knowing that the *sufferings of this time are not worthy to be compared with winning the future glory.*[4] Wilt thou have that at once, which many after many tears and great labours have hardly obtained?

Wait for the Lord, behave thyself manfully, and be of good courage;[5] do not distrust, do not leave thy place, but steadily expose both body and soul for the glory of God. I will reward thee most plenteously; I will be with thee in every tribulation.[6]

CHAPTER THIRTY-SIX

AGAINST THE VAIN JUDGMENTS OF MEN

MY SON, CAST THY HEART FIRMLY ON THE LORD, AND FEAR NOT THE judgment of men, when conscience proveth thee holy and guiltless.

It is a good and happy thing to suffer in such a way; nor will this be grievous to a heart which is humble, and which trusteth rather in God than in itself. Many men say many things, and therefore little confidence is to be placed in them. Moreover also, to satisfy all is not possible.

Although Paul endeavoured to please all in the Lord, and was made *all things to all men*,[1] yet he held it a very small thing that he should be judged of man's judgment.[2] He did abundantly for the edification and salvation of others as much as lay in his power to do;[3] yet could he not hinder but that he was by others sometimes judged, sometimes despised. Therefore he committed all to God, who knew all; and against the face of men who spake unjust things, or thought vanities and lies, and boasted themselves as they listed, he defended himself, with humility and patience. Sometimes however he made answer, lest for the weak his silence should beget scandal.[4]

2. *Who art thou that thou shouldest fear a mortal man?*[5] Today he is, and tomorrow he is not seen.[6] Fear God, and thou shalt not shrink from the terrors of men. What power hath any man over thee by words or injuries? He hurteth himself rather than thee, nor shall he be able to avoid the judgment of God,[7] whosoever he be. Do thou have God before thine eyes, and contend not with peevish words. And though

for the present thou seem to be worsted, and to suffer shame, which thou deservedst not, do not therefore repine, neither do thou lessen thy crown by impatience.[8] But rather lift thou up thine eyes unto Me in Heaven, who am able to deliver thee from all shame and wrong, and to render to every man according to his works.[9]

⇒ CHAPTER THIRTY-SEVEN ⇐

OF PURE AND ENTIRE RESIGNATION OF OURSELVES, FOR THE OBTAINING FREEDOM OF HEART

My son, forsake thyself, and thou shalt find Me.[1] Stand without choosing, and without any self-seeking; and thou shalt always be a gainer. For even greater grace shall be added to thee, the moment thou dost resign thyself, provided thou dost not turn back to take thyself again.

2. Lord, how often shall I resign myself? And wherein shall I forsake myself?

Always, and at every hour; as well in small things as in great. I except nothing, but in all things I will thee to be found naked. Otherwise, how canst thou be Mine, and I thine, unless thou be stript of all self-will both within and without? The sooner thou doest this, the better it will be with thee; and the more fully and sincerely thou doest it, so much the more shalt thou please Me, and so much the greater shall be thy gain.

Some there are who resign themselves, but with certain exceptions; for they put not their full trust in God, and therefore they study how to provide for themselves. Some also at first do offer all, but afterwards being assailed with temptation, they return again to their own ways, and therefore make no progress in the path of virtue. These shall not attain to the true liberty of a pure heart, nor to the favour of sweet familiarity with Me, unless they first make an entire resignation and a daily sacrifice of themselves. Without this, no union that beareth fruit standeth firm nor shall stand.

3. I have very often said unto thee, and now again I say the same: Forsake thyself,[2] resign thyself, and thou shalt enjoy great inward peace. Give all for all; ask for nothing, require back nothing; abide purely and unhesitatingly in Me, and thou shalt possess Me; thou shalt be free in heart, and darkness shall not tread thee down.[3] Let this be thine endeavour, this thy prayer, this thy desire; that thou mayest be stript of all selfishness, and naked follow the naked Jesus; mayest die to thyself, and live eternally to Me. Then shall fail all vain imaginations, evil perturbations, and superfluous cares. Then also immoderate fear shall depart, and inordinate love shall die.

✧ CHAPTER THIRTY-EIGHT ✧

OF GOOD GOVERNMENT IN THINGS EXTERNAL, AND OF HAVING RECOURSE TO GOD IN DANGERS

MY SON, TOWARDS THIS THOU OUGHTEST WITH ALL DILIGENCE TO endeavour, that in every place, and in every external action or occupation, thou mayest be inwardly free, and thoroughly master of thyself; and that all things be under thee, and not thou under them; that thou be lord and master of thine own actions, not a slave or a hireling. Rather thou shouldest be as a freed man and a true Hebrew, passing over into the lot and freedom of the sons of God; who stand upon things present, and contemplate things eternal; who look on transitory things with the left eye, and with the right on the things of Heaven; whom temporal things draw not to cleave unto them; rather they draw temporal things to serve them well, in such ways as they are ordained by God, and appointed by the great Work-master, who hath left nothing in His creation without due order.

2. If too in every event thou stand not in outward seeming, nor with a carnal eye survey things seen or heard, but presently in every affair dost enter with Moses into the Tabernacle[1] to ask counsel of the Lord, thou shalt sometimes hear the Divine Oracle, and shalt return instructed concerning many things, both present and to come. For Moses always had recourse to the Tabernacle for the dissolving of doubts and questions, and fled to the help of prayer, for support under dangers and the iniquity of men. So oughtest thou in like

manner to take refuge within the closet of thine heart,[2] very earnestly craving the divine favour.

For we read, that for this cause Joshua and the children of Israel were deceived by the Gibeonites, because *they asked not* beforehand *at the mouth of the Lord*,[3] but trusting too easily to sweet words, by feigned piety were deluded.

✧ CHAPTER THIRTY-NINE ✧

THAT A MAN SHOULD NOT BE FRETFUL IN MATTERS OF BUSINESS

My son, commit always to Me thy cause, I will dispose well of it in due time. Wait for My ordering of it, and thou shalt find thy good therefrom.

O Lord, most cheerfully do I commit all unto Thee, for my thinking can little avail. Would that I did not so much dwell on future events, but gave myself up without reluctance to Thy good pleasure.

2. My son, oftentimes a man vehemently struggleth for somewhat he desireth, but when he hath attained unto it, he beginneth to be of another mind; for the affections remain not firmly around the same thing, but rather drive us from one thing to another. It is no very small thing for a man to forsake himself even in things thatare very small.

The true profiting of a man is the denying of himself; and a man that hath denied himself is exceeding free and secure. But the old Enemy,[1] who always setteth himself against all that are good, ceaseth at no time from tempting, but day and night plotteth grievous lyings-in-wait to cast the unwary, if he can, headlong into the snare of deceit. *Watch ye, and pray,* saith the Lord, *that ye enter not into temptation.*[2]

CHAPTER FORTY

THAT MAN HATH NO GOOD OF HIMSELF, NOR OF ANYTHING CAN HE GLORY

Lord, what is man, that Thou art mindful of him, or the son of man, that Thou visitest him?[1] What hath man deserved, that Thou shouldest grant him Thy favour? O Lord, what cause can I have to complain, if Thou forsake me? Or if Thou do not that which I desire, what can I justly say against it? Surely this I may truly think and say; Lord, I am nothing, I can do nothing, I have nothing that is good of myself, but in all things I am falling away, and am ever tending to nothing. And unless Thou help me, and inwardly inform me, I become altogether lukewarm and ready to fall to pieces.

But Thou, Lord, art Thyself always the same, and endurest forever;[2] always good, just, and holy; doing all things well, justly, and holily, and ordering them in wisdom. Whereas I that am more ready to go backward than forward, do not ever continue in one estate, for *seven times are passed over me*.[3] Nevertheless it soon becometh better, when it so pleaseth Thee, and when Thou dost stretch forth Thy helping hand; for Thou canst help me alone without human aid, and so greatly strengthen me, that my countenance shall be no more changed to sadness, but that in Thee alone shall my heart be turned and be at rest.

Wherefore, if I knew well how to cast off all human consolation, either for the attainment of devotion, or because of mine own necessities, which enforce me to seek after Thee, (for no mortal man can comfort me,) then might I well hope in Thy grace, and rejoice in the gift of new consolation.

2. Thanks be unto Thee, from whom all cometh, whensoever it goeth well with me.

But I am before Thee, vanity and nothing, a man unstable and weak. Whereof then can I glory? Or for what do I desire to be respected? Is it for being nothing? This too is most vain. Empty glory is in truth an evil pest, the greatest of vanities; because it draweth from true glory, and robbeth of heavenly grace. For whilst a man pleaseth himself, he displeaseth Thee; whilst he gapeth after the praise of men, he is deprived of true virtues.

But true glory and holy exultation is to glory in Thee,[4] and not in himself; to rejoice in Thy Name, not in his own virtue, nor to take delight in any creature except it be for Thy sake.

Praised be Thy Name, not mine; magnified be Thy work, not mine: blessed be Thy Holy Name, but to me let no part of men's praises be given.[5] Thou art my glory, Thou art the joy of my heart. In Thee will I glory and rejoice all the day, but *as for myself, I will glory in nothing, but in mine infirmities*.[6]

Let the Jews seek the glory that cometh of another,[7] I will ask for that which cometh from God alone. Truly all human glory, all temporal honour, all worldly exaltation, compared to Thy eternal glory, is vanity and folly. O my God, my Truth, and my Mercy, O Blessed Trinity, to Thee alone be praise, honour, power and glory, throughout all ages, world without end.

→ CHAPTER FORTY-ONE ←

OF THE CONTEMPT OF ALL TEMPORAL HONOUR

MY SON, MAKE IT NO MATTER OF THINE, IF THOU SEE OTHERS HONOURED and exalted, but thyself contemned and debased. Lift up thy heart into Heaven to Me, and the contempt of men on earth shall not grieve thee.

2. Lord, we are in blindness, and are quickly misled by vanity.

If I look rightly into myself, never hath harm been done me by any creature; and therefore I cannot justly complain before Thee. But because I have often and grievously sinned against Thee, every creature doth justly take arms against me. Unto me, therefore, shame and contempt are justly due, but unto Thee praise, honour, and glory.

And unless I prepare myself with cheerful willingness to be despised and forsaken of every creature, and to be esteemed entirely nothing, I cannot obtain inward peace and stability, nor be spiritually enlightened, nor be fully united unto Thee.

→ CHAPTER FORTY-TWO ←

THAT OUR PEACE IS NOT TO BE SET ON MEN

My son, if thou rest thy peace on any person, because of thine own feelings and because thou livest with him, thou shalt be unstable and entangled. But if thou have recourse unto the ever-living and abiding Truth, the desertion or death of a friend will not grieve thee. In Me ought thy love for thy friend to be grounded; and for My sake is he to be beloved, whosoever seemeth good to thee, and is very dear unto thee in this life. Without Me friendship hath no strength, nor shall endure; neither is that love true and pure, which is not knit by Me.

2. Thou oughtest to be so dead to such affections towards beloved men, that (so far as thou art concerned) thou wouldest choose to be without all human sympathy. So much the nearer man draweth unto God, the farther he retireth from all earthly comfort. So much the higher also he ascendeth unto God, the lower he descendeth in himself and the meaner he is in his own sight. But he that attributeth any good unto himself, hindereth God's grace from coming unto him; because the Grace of the Holy Spirit ever seeketh an humble heart.[1] If thou couldest but perfectly bring thyself to nothing, and empty thyself of all created love, then ought I with great grace to overflow into thee. When thou lookest to the creatures, the countenance of the Creator is withdrawn from thee. Learn in all things to overcome thyself, for the sake of thy Creator; then shalt thou have power to attain unto divine knowledge. How little soever anything be, if it is inordinately loved and regarded, it keepeth thee back from the Highest, and corrupteth the soul.

CHAPTER FORTY-THREE

AGAINST VAIN AND WORLDLY KNOWLEDGE

My son, let not the fair and subtle sayings of men move thee. *For the Kingdom of God is not in word, but in power.*[1] Give heed to My words, which kindle the heart, and enlighten the mind; they produce contrition, and they supply manifold consolation.

Never read thou a word for this, that thou mayest appear more learned or more wise. Be studious for the mortification of thy sins; for this will profit thee more than the knowledge of many hard questions. When thou shalt have read and learnt many things, thou must needs ever return to one Beginning.

I am *He that teacheth man knowledge*;[2] and I bestow on little children a clearer understanding than can be taught by man. He to whom I speak, shall quickly be wise, and shall profit much in the Spirit. Woe be to them that enquire many curious things of men, and take small care about the way of serving Me! The time will come, when the Master of masters, Christ the Lord of Angels, shall appear, to hear the lessons of all, that is, to examine the consciences of everyone. And then will He *search Jerusalem with candles*, and the hidden things of darkness shall be laid open,[3] and the arguings of men's tongues shall be silent.

2. I am He who in one instant do lift up the humble mind to comprehend more reasonings of eternal Truth, than if one had studied ten years in the schools.

I teach without noise of words, without confusion of opinions, without the pride of honour, without the scuffling of arguments.

I am He who instruct men to despise earthly things, to loathe things present, to seek things eternal, to relish things eternal; to flee honours, to endure offences, to place all hope in Me, out of Me to desire nothing, and above all things ardently to love Me. For a certain one,[4] by loving Me from his heart, learned things divine, and was wont to speak marvellous things. He profited more by forsaking all things, than by studying subtleties.

Nevertheless, to some men I speak common things, to others things special; to some I shew Myself sweetly in signs and figures, whilst to some I reveal mysteries in much light. The voice of books is one, but it informeth not all alike; for inwardly I am the teacher, the Truth, the searcher of the heart, the discerner of thoughts, the promoter of actions, distributing to every man as I shall judge meet.

→ CHAPTER FORTY-FOUR ←

OF NOT FETCHING TROUBLE TO OURSELVES FROM OUTWARD THINGS

My son, in many things it is thy duty to be ignorant, and to esteem thyself as one dead upon the earth, and to whom the whole world is crucified.[1] Many things too there are which it is thy duty to pass by with a deaf ear, and be rather mindful of those which belong unto thy peace. It is more profitable to turn away one's eyes from things that displease, and to leave to each person his own opinion, than to wait upon contentious discourses. If thou stand well with God, and thou regard His judgment, thou shalt very easily endure to be as one defeated.

2. O Lord, to what a pass are we come! Behold, we bewail a temporal loss; for a pitiful gain we toil and run; while spiritual harm passeth away into forgetfulness, and hardly at last do we return to a sense of it. That which little or nothing profiteth, is minded, and that which is especially needful, is negligently passed over; because the whole man doth slide away to things external, and unless he speedily come to himself, he willingly lieth sunk in outward things.

→ CHAPTER FORTY-FIVE ←

THAT CREDIT IS NOT TO BE GIVEN TO ALL, AND THAT MAN IS PRONE TO OFFEND IN WORDS

Grant me help, O Lord, out of tribulation, for vain is the salvation of man![1] How often have I not met with faithfulness there, where I thought I possessed it! How often too have I found it there, where beforehand I least expected it! Vain therefore is hope in men; but the salvation of the righteous is in Thee, O God! Blessed be Thou, O Lord my God, in all things that befall us.

Weak are we and unstable; quickly are we deceived and altogether changed. Who is the man that is able in all things so warily and circumspectly to keep himself, as never to come into any deception or perplexity? But he that trusteth in Thee, O Lord, and seeketh Thee with a single heart, doth not so easily slip.[2] And if he fall into any tribulation, be he never so much entangled, yet shall he quickly through Thee be drawn out, or by Thee be comforted; for Thou wilt not forsake him that hopeth in Thee even to the end.

Rare is a faithful friend, that continueth in all his friend's distresses. Thou, O Lord, Thou alone art most faithful at all times, and beside Thee there is none other like unto Thee.

2. O how wise was that holy soul which said, *My mind is firmly settled, and is grounded in Christ.*[3] If thus it were with me, the fear of man would not so easily vex me, nor darts of words move me.

Who is sufficient to foresee, who to guard against, all future evils? If even things that are foreseen oftentimes hurt us, how can unforeseen evils otherwise than grievously smite us? But wretch as I am, why have I not foreseen better for myself? Why too have I so easily given credit to others? But we are men, nothing else are we but frail men, even though by many we are reputed and called Angels.

Whom shall I trust, O Lord? Whom but Thee? Thou art the Truth, who deceivest not nor canst be deceived. And on the other side, *every man is a liar*,[4] weak, unconstant, and subject to fall, especially in words; and therefore we must scarce ever immediately give credit to that which on the face of it seemeth to sound right.

How wisely hast thou warned us to beware of men; and, that *a man's foes are they of his own household*;[5] and not to believe, if one should say, *Lo here, or Lo there*.[6]

I have been taught by my own hurt, and I would it may make me more cautious, and not more unwise. "Be wary," saith one, "be wary, keep to thyself what I say to thee"; and whilst I keep silence, and think it is secret, he cannot himself keep that which he desired me to keep, but presently betrayeth both me and himself, and is gone.

From such tales and heedless persons protect me, O Lord, that I neither fall into their hands, nor ever commit such things myself. Give the word of truth and steadfastness to my mouth, and remove far from me a crafty tongue. What I am not willing to suffer, I ought by all means to beware of doing.

3. O how good it is and tending to peace, to be silent about other men, and not to believe indifferently all that is said, nor too easily to tell it further;[7] to lay one's self open to few; and ever to be seeking after Thee as the searcher of the heart:[8] and not to be carried about with every wind of words, but to desire that all things both within and without, be accomplished according to the pleasure of thy will!

How safe is it, for the keeping of heavenly grace, to avoid estimation of men, and not to seek those things which seem to cause admiration abroad; but to pursue with all diligence the things which bring amendment of life and godly zeal! How many hath virtue harmed, by being known and over-hastily commended! How truly profitable hath grace been when preserved in silence, in this frail life, which we are told is all temptation and warfare.

→ CHAPTER FORTY-SIX ←

OF PUTTING OUR TRUST IN GOD WHEN THE ARROWS OF WORDS ASSAIL US

My son, stand steadily, and put thy trust in Me;[1] for what are words, but words? They fly through the air, but a stone they cannot hurt. If thou art guilty, think that thou wouldest gladly amend thyself; if thou art conscious of no fault, consider that thou wouldest gladly endure this for God's sake.[2] Little enough it is, that sometimes thou shouldest endure even words, since thou hast not yet the courage to bear hard stripes.

And why do such small matters go to thy heart, but because thou art yet carnal,[3] and regardest men more than thou oughtest? For it is because thou art afraid of being despised, that thou art unwilling to be reproved for thy faults, and seekest the over-shadowing of excuses. But look better into thyself, and thou shalt acknowledge that the world is yet alive in thee, and a vain desire to please men. For when thou shrinkest from being abased and confounded for thy failings, it is evident surely that thou art neither truly humble, nor truly dead to the world, nor is the world crucified to thee.

But hear My word, and thou shalt not care for ten thousand words of men. Behold, if all should be spoken against thee that could be most maliciously invented, what would it hurt thee, if thou wouldst suffer it to pass entirely away, and make no more reckoning of it than of a mote? Could it pluck so much as one hair from thy head?[4]

But he that hath no heart within him, nor hath God before his eyes, is easily moved with a word of dispraise. Whereas he that trusteth in Me, and hath no wish to stand by his own judgment, shall be free from the fear of men. For I am the judge[5] and the discerner of all secrets; I well understand how the matter passed; I know him that offereth the injury, and him that suffereth it. From Me proceeded that word; by My permission this hath happened; *that the thoughts of many hearts may be revealed.*[6] I shall judge the guilty, and the innocent; but by a secret judgment I have thought fit beforehand to prove them both. The testimony of men oftentimes deceiveth; My judgment is true; it shall stand, and shall not be overthrown; it commonly lieth hid, and is manifest but to few in every matter; yet it never erreth, nor can err, although to the eyes of the foolish it may seem not right.

To me therefore men ought to run in every judgment, and not to lean on their own opinion. For the just man will not be disturbed,[7] whatsoever befalleth him from God. Even if an unjust charge be brought against him, he will not much care. Nor again will he vainly exult, if through others he be justly vindicated. For he considereth that *I am He that searcheth the hearts and reins,*[8] Who judge not according to the outward face, and human appearance. For oftentimes that in My sight is found worthy of blame, which in the judgment of men is thought worthy of praise.

2. O Lord God, *the just Judge, strong and patient*,[9] Thou who knowest the frailty and wickedness of men, be Thou my strength, and all my confidence, for mine own conscience sufficeth me not. Thou knowest what I know not; and therefore under all blame I ought to humble myself, and to bear it meekly. Of Thy mercy then forgive me whenever I have acted otherwise, and grant me once more the grace of more thorough endurance. Because better to me is Thine overflowing pity for the obtaining of pardon, than my own fancied righteousness to warn off the secret misgivings of conscience. Although I know nothing against myself, yet I cannot hereby justify myself;[10] for without Thy mercy, *in Thy sight shall no man living be justified.*[11]

CHAPTER FORTY-SEVEN

THAT ALL GRIEVOUS THINGS ARE TO BE ENDURED FOR THE SAKE OF ETERNAL LIFE

MY SON, BE NOT WEARIED OUT BY THE LABOURS WHICH THOU HAST undertaken for My sake, nor let tribulations cast thee down ever at all; but let My promise strengthen and comfort thee under every circumstance. I am well able to reward thee, above all measure and degree.

Thou shalt not long toil here, nor always be oppressed with griefs. Wait a little while, and thou shalt see a speedy end of thine evils. There will come an hour when all labour and tumult shall cease. Poor and brief is all that which passeth away with time.

Do in earnest what thou doest; labour faithfully in My vineyard;[1] I will be thy recompence. Write, read, chant, mourn, keep silence, pray, endure crosses manfully; life everlasting is worth all these battles, and greater than these. Peace shall come in one day which is known unto the Lord, and there shall be *not day nor night*[2] (that is, of this present time), but unceasing light, infinite brightness, stedfast peace, and secure rest. Then thou shalt not say, *Who shall deliver me from the body of this death?*[3] Nor cry, *Woe is me, that my sojourning is prolonged!*[4] For death shall be cast down headlong, and there shall be salvation which can never fail, no more anxiety, blessed joy, companionship sweet and noble.

2. O if thou hadst seen the everlasting crowns of the Saints in heaven,[5] and with how great glory they now rejoice, who once were esteemed by this world as contemptible, and in a manner unworthy of life itself;

truly thou wouldest forthwith humble thyself even to the earth, and wouldest rather seek to be under all, than to have command so much as over one. Neither wouldest thou long for this life's pleasant days, but rather wouldest rejoice to suffer affliction for God, and esteem it thy greatest gain to be reputed as nothing amongst men. O if these things had a sweet savour unto thee, and pierced to the bottom of thy heart, how couldest thou dare so much as once to complain! Are not all painful labours to be endured for the sake of life eternal? It is no small matter, to lose or to gain the Kingdom of God.

Lift up thy face therefore unto Heaven; behold, I and all My saints with Me, who in this world had great conflict, do now rejoice, now are comforted, now secure, now at rest, and shall remain with Me everlastingly in the Kingdom of My Father.

CHAPTER FORTY-EIGHT

OF THE DAY OF ETERNITY, AND THIS LIFE'S STRAITNESSES

O MOST BLESSED MANSION OF THE CITY WHICH IS ABOVE![1] O MOST clear day of eternity, which night obscureth not, but the highest Truth ever enlighteneth! O day ever joyful, ever secure, and never changing to the opposite. O that that day had shone upon us, and that all these temporal things were at an end! To the Saints indeed it shineth glorious with perpetual brightness; but only afar on, and *as through a glass*,[2] to those who are pilgrims on the earth. The Citizens of Heaven do know how full of gladness is that day, but "the banished sons of Eve"[3] bewail the bitterness and tediousness of this.

The days of this life are few and evil,[4] full of sorrows and straitnesses. Here a man is defiled with many sins, ensnared with many passions, held fast by many fears, racked with many cares, distracted with many curiosities, entangled with many vanities, compassed about with many errors, worn away with many labours, burdened with temptations, enervated by pleasures, tormented with want.

O when shall be the end of these evils? When shall I be delivered from the miserable bondage of my sins?[5] When shall I be mindful, O Lord, of Thee alone?[6] When to the full shall I rejoice in Thee? When shall I be without all hindrance in true liberty, without all heaviness of mind and body? When shall I have solid peace, peace secure and undisturbed, peace within and peace without, peace every way assured? O good Jesu, when shall I stand to behold Thee? When shall I contemplate the glory of Thy Kingdom? When wilt Thou be unto me all in all? O when shall I be with Thee in Thy Kingdom, which Thou hast prepared for Thy beloved ones from all eternity?

I am left, a poor and banished man, in the land of mine enemies, where there are daily wars and very great calamities.

2. Comfort my banishment, assuage my sorrow; for my whole desire sigheth after Thee. For all is a burden to me, whatsoever this world offereth for consolation. I long to enjoy Thee most inwardly, but I cannot attain unto it. I desire to cling fast to things heavenly, but temporal things and unmortified passions weigh me down. With the mind I wish to be above all things, but with the flesh I am enforced against my will to be beneath them. Thus, unhappy man that I am,[7] I fight against myself, and am become grievous to mine own self, whilst my spirit seeketh to be above, and my flesh to be below. O what do I inwardly suffer, whilst in my mind I dwell on things heavenly, and presently whilst I pray, a multitude of fleshly things hasten upon me.

O my God, be not Thou far from me, nor turn away in wrath from Thy servant.[8] *Flash forth Thy lightning, and scatter them; shoot out Thine arrows,*[9] and let all the imaginations of the Enemy be confounded. Gather in, and call home my senses unto Thee; make me to forget all worldly things; grant me to cast away speedily and to scorn all sinful phantoms. Succour me, O Thou eternal Truth, that no vanity may move me. Come to me, Thou heavenly sweetness, and let all impurity flee from before Thy face.

Pardon me also, and in mercy deal gently with me, as often as in prayer I think on aught beside Thee.

For truly I confess, that I am wont to be exceeding distracted. For oftentimes I am not where I am bodily standing or sitting; but rather there I am, whither my thoughts do carry me. Where my thoughts are, there am I; and commonly there are my thoughts, where my affection is. That readily hasteneth to me, which naturally bringeth delight, or by custom is pleasing. And for this cause, Thou that art Truth itself hast plainly said, *For where thy treasure is, there thy heart is also.*[10] If I love Heaven, I willingly muse on heavenly things. If I love the world, I rejoice with the felicity of the world, and grieve for the adversity thereof. If I love the flesh, I constantly imagine those things that belong to the flesh. If I love the Spirit, I delight to think on things spiritual. For whatsoever things I love, of these do I willingly speak and hear, and carry home with me the forms thereof.

But blessed is the man,[11] who for Thy sake, O Lord, granteth leave to depart unto all creatures, who doth violence to his nature, and through fervour of the Spirit crucifieth the lusts of the flesh; that so with a serene conscience he may offer a pure prayer unto Thee, and all earthly things both outwardly and inwardly being excluded, he may be meet to be admitted into the angelical choirs.

→ CHAPTER FORTY-NINE ←

OF THE DESIRE OF ETERNAL LIFE, AND HOW GREAT REWARDS ARE PROMISED TO THOSE THAT STRUGGLE

MY SON, WHEN THOU PERCEIVEST THE DESIRE OF ETERNAL BLISS TO BE poured on thee from above, and longest to depart out of the tabernacle of the body, that thou mayest be able to contemplate My brightness, without shadow of turning; open thy heart wide, and receive this holy inspiration with thy whole desire. Give fullest thanks to the Heavenly Goodness, which treateth thee with such condescension, visiteth thee mercifully, stirreth thee up fervently, sustaineth thee powerfully, lest through thine own weight thou sink down to earthly things. For thou dost not obtain this by thy own thought or endeavour, but by the mere condescension of heavenly grace and divine regard; to the end that thou mayest make further progress in all virtues, and in greater humility, and prepare thyself for future conflicts, and mayest earnestly strive to cleave unto Me with the whole affection of thy heart, and to serve Me with a fervent will.

2. My son, oftentimes the fire burneth, but the flame ascendeth not up without smoke. So likewise the desires of some men burn towards heavenly things, and yet they are not free from temptation of carnal affection. And therefore they act not altogether purely for the honour of God, in that they make such earnest requests to Him.

Such also oftentimes is thy desire, which thou hast pretended to be so earnest. For that is not pure and perfect, which is tinctured with self-seeking. Ask not for that which is delightful and profitable to thee, but for that which is acceptable to Me, and tendeth to My honour; for if thou judgest aright, thou oughtest to prefer and follow My appointment, rather than thine own desire, or anything that is desired.

I know thy desire, and have heard thy many groanings. Already thou willest to be in the glorious liberty of the sons of God;[1] already dost thou delight in the everlasting habitation, and the heavenly country which is full of joy: but that hour is not yet come; still there remaineth another time, and that a time of war,[2] a time of labour and of trial. Thou desirest to be filled with the Chiefest Good, but thou canst not attain it at once. *I am*;[3] wait thou for Me (saith the Lord) *until the Kingdom of God shall come.*[4]

Thou art still to be tried upon earth, and to be exercised in many things. Comfort shall be sometimes given thee, but the abundant fulness thereof is not granted. *Take courage therefore, and be strong*,[5] as well in doing as in suffering things contrary to nature.

It is thy duty to put on the new man,[6] and to be changed into another person.[7] It is thy duty oftentimes to do what thou wouldst not; and what thou wouldst do, it is thy duty to leave. That which pleaseth others, shall go well forward; that which pleaseth thee, shall not speed. That which others say, shall be heard; what thou sayest, shall be accounted nothing. Others shall ask and shall receive; thou shalt ask but shalt not obtain. Others shall be great in the mouth of men, but about thee there shall be silence. To others this or that shall be committed, but thou shalt be accounted useful for nought. At this nature will sometimes be troubled, and it is a great thing if thou bear it with silence. In these and many like instances, the faithful servant of the Lord is wont to be tried, how far he can deny and in all things break himself.

There is scarcely anything wherein thou hast such need to die to thyself, as in seeing and suffering those things that are adverse to thy will; especially when that is commanded to be done, which seemeth unto thee inconvenient, or useless. And because thou being set under authority darest not resist the higher power, therefore it seemeth hard to thee to walk at another's nod, and to give up all thine own opinion.

But consider, My son, the fruit of these labours, the end coming swiftly, and the reward exceeding great; and thou wilt not from these things have heaviness, but the strongest comfort of thy patience. For instead of that little of thy will, which now thou so readily forsakest, thou shalt always have thy will in Heaven. There surely thou shalt find all that thou mayest wish, all that thou shalt be able to desire. There thou shalt have within thy reach all good, without fear of losing it. There shall thy will be ever one with Me; it shall not covet any outward or private thing. There none shall withstand thee, no man shall complain of thee, no man hinder thee, nothing come in thy way; but all things thou canst desire shall be there together present, and refresh thy whole affection, and fill it up to the brim. There I will give thee glory for the reproach which here thou sufferedst, *the garment of praise for heaviness*,[8] for the lowest place a kingly throne forever. There shall the fruit of obedience appear, the labour of penance shall rejoice, and humble subjection shall be gloriously crowned.

At present then bend thyself humbly under the hands of all, and care not who said this or commanded it. But to this take especial care, that whether thy superior, or thy inferior, or thine equal, require anything of thee, or hint at anything, thou take it all in good part, and with a sincere will endeavour to fulfill it. Let one seek this, another that; let this man glory in this, the other in that, and be praised a thousand thousand times; but do thou rejoice neither in this, nor in that, but in thine own contempt, and in the good pleasure and honour of Me alone. This is what thou art to wish, that whether it be by life or by death God may be always glorified in thee.[9]

CHAPTER FIFTY

HOW A DESOLATE MAN OUGHT TO OFFER HIMSELF INTO THE HANDS OF GOD

O LORD GOD, HOLY FATHER, BE THOU BLESSED BOTH NOW AND FOR evermore, because as thou wilt, so is it done, and what Thou doest is good. Let Thy servant rejoice in Thee, not in himself nor in anything else; for Thou alone art the true gladness, Thou art my hope and my crown, Thou art my joy and my honour, O Lord. What hath Thy servant, but what he hath received from Thee,[1] even without any merit of his? Thine are all things, which Thou hast given, and which Thou hast made.

I am poor, and in my labours, from my youth;[2] and my soul is sorrowful sometimes even unto tears; sometimes also my spirit is of itself disquieted, by reason of impending sufferings. I long after the joy of peace; the peace of Thy sons I earnestly crave, who are fed by Thee in the light of Thy consolation. If Thou give peace, if Thou pour into me holy joy, the soul of Thy servant shall be full of melody, and devout in Thy praise. But if Thou withdraw Thyself (as very often Thou art wont), he will not be able to run the way of Thy commandments;[3] but rather he will bow his knees, and smite his breast, because it is not now with him as it was in times past, when Thy candle shined upon his head,[4] and under the shadow of Thy wings[5] he was protected from the temptations which assaulted him.

2. O righteous Father, and ever to be praised, the hour is come that Thy servant is to be proved. O beloved Father, meet and right it is that in this hour Thy servant should suffer something for Thy sake. O

Father, evermore to be honoured, the hour is come, which from all eternity Thou didst foreknow should come; that for a short time Thy servant should outwardly be oppressed, but inwardly should ever live with Thee. Let him be for a little while held cheap, and humbled, and fail in the sight of men; be wasted with sufferings and languors; that he may rise again with Thee in the morning dawn of the new Light, and be glorified in Heaven.

Holy Father, Thou hast so appointed it, and so hast willed; and that is fulfilled which Thyself hast commanded. For this is a favour to Thy friend, for Thy love to suffer and be afflicted in the world: how often soever, and by whom soever Thou permittest it to befall him. Without thy counsel and providence, and *without cause, nothing is done in the earth*.[6] It is good for me, Lord, that Thou hast humbled me,[7] that I may learn Thy righteous judgments, and may cast away all haughtines' of heart, and all presumptuousness. It is profitable for me, that *shame hath covered my face*,[8] that I may seek to Thee for consolation rather than to men. I have learned also hereby to dread Thy unsearchable judgment, who afflictest the just with the wicked, though not without equity and justice.

I give Thee thanks, for that Thou hast not spared my sins, but hast worn me down with bitter stripes, inflicting sorrows and sending afflictions upon me within and without. There is none else under Heaven who can comfort me, but Thou only, O Lord my God, the Heavenly Physician of souls, who strikest and healest, who *bringest down to hell and bringest back again*.[9] Thy discipline is over me, and Thy very rod itself shall instruct me.

Behold, O beloved Father, I am in Thy hands, under the rod of Thy correction I bow myself. Smite my back and my neck, that so I may bend my crookedness to Thy will. Make me a dutiful and humble disciple, as Thou art wont to be kind, that I may walk at Thy every nod. Unto Thee I commend myself and all that is mine, to be corrected: better it is to be punished here, than hereafter.

Thou knowest all things generally, and in particular, and there is nothing hidden from Thee in man's conscience. Before things are done, Thou knowest that they will come to pass; and Thou hast no need that any should teach or admonish Thee of what is going on here on the earth. Thou knowest what is expedient for my profiting, and how greatly tribulation serveth to scour oft the rust of sins. Do with me according to Thy desired good pleasure, and disdain me not for my sinful life, known to none so well and clearly as to Thee alone.

Grant me, O Lord, to know that which is worth knowing, to love that which is worth loving, to praise that which pleaseth Thee most, to esteem that which to Thee seemeth precious, to abhor that which in Thy sight is unclean.

Suffer me not to judge according to the sight of the outward eyes, nor to give sentence according to the hearing of the ears of ignorant men;[10] but with a true judgment to discern between things visible and spiritual, and above all to be ever searching after the good pleasure of Thy will. The minds of men are often deceived in their judgments; the lovers of the world too are deceived in loving only things visible. What is a man ever the better, for being by man esteemed great? The deceitful in extolling the deceitful playeth him false, the vain man the vain, the blind man the blind, the weak man the weak; and in truth doth rather put him to shame, while he vainly praiseth him. "*For what everyone is in Thy sight, so much is he, and no more*,"[11] saith humble S. Francis.

CHAPTER FIFTY-ONE

THAT A MAN OUGHT TO TAKE HIS STAND IN WORKS OF HUMILITY, WHEN HE FAILETH FROM THE HIGHEST WORKS

MY SON, THOU ART NOT ABLE ALWAYS TO STAND IN THE MORE FERVENT desire of virtue, nor to persist in the higher stage of contemplation; but thou must needs sometimes by reason of original corruption descend to inferior things, and bear the burden of this corruptible life, though against thy will, and with wearisomeness. As long as thou carriest a mortal body, thou shalt feel weariness and heaviness of heart. Thou oughtest therefore in the flesh oftentimes to bewail the burden of the flesh; for that thou canst not employ thyself unceasingly in spiritual studies and divine contemplation.

2. Then it is expedient for thee to flee to humble and outward works, and to refresh thyself with good actions; to expect with a firm confidence My coming and heavenly visitation; to bear patiently thy banishment and the dryness of thy mind, till again by Me thou art visited, and set free from all anxieties. For I will cause thee to forget thy painful toils, and thoroughly to enjoy inward quietness. I will spread open before thee the pleasant fields of the Scriptures, that with an enlarged heart thou mayest begin to run the way of My commandments.[1] And thou shalt say, *The sufferings of this present time are not worthy to be compared with the future glory, that shall be revealed in us.*[2]

CHAPTER FIFTY-TWO

THAT A MAN OUGHT NOT TO ACCOUNT HIMSELF AS WORTHY OF COMFORT, BUT RATHER AS DESERVING OF STRIPES

O Lord, I am not worthy of Thy consolation, nor of any spiritual visitation; and therefore Thou dealest justly with me, when Thou leavest me poor and desolate. For though I could shed a sea of tears, still I should not be worthy of Thy consolation. I am not then worthy of anything but to be scourged and punished; because grievously and often I have offended Thee, and in many things have greatly sinned. Wherefore, when the true reason is weighed, I am not worthy even of the least consolation.

But Thou, O gracious and merciful God, who willest not that Thy works should perish, *to shew the riches of Thy goodness upon the vessels of mercy,*[1] vouchsafest even beyond all his desert to comfort Thy servant above the manner of men. For Thy consolations are not like to the communings of men.

What have I done, O Lord, that Thou shouldest bestow any heavenly comfort upon me? I remember that I have done nought of good, but that I have been always prone to sin, and slow to amendment. This is true, and I cannot deny it. If I should say otherwise, Thou wouldest stand against me,[2] and there would be none to defend me. What have I deserved for my sins, but hell and everlasting fire? I confess in very truth that I am worthy of all scorn and contempt, nor is it fit that I should be remembered amongst Thy devout servants. And although I be unwilling to hear this, yet, notwithstanding, I will for the truth's sake lay open my sins, even against myself, that so the more readily I may be accounted worthy to obtain Thy mercy. What shall I say, in that I am guilty, and full of all confusion? My mouth can utter nothing but this word only, "I have sinned, O Lord! I have sinned:[3] have mercy on me, pardon me." Suffer me a little, *that I may bewail my grief, before I go into the land of darkness, a land covered with the shadow of death.*[4]

2. What dost Thou so much require of a guilty and miserable sinner, as that he be contrite, and that he humble himself for his offences? Of true contrition and humbling of the heart, is born hope of forgiveness; the troubled conscience is reconciled; the grace which was lost, is recovered; man is preserved from the wrath to come; and God and the penitent soul meet together with a holy kiss. Humble contrition for sins is an acceptable sacrifice unto Thee, O Lord,[5] giving forth a savour far sweeter in Thy sight than the perfume of frankincense. This is also the pleasant ointment,[6] which Thou wouldest should be poured upon Thy sacred feet; for a *contrite and humbled heart* Thou never hast despised.[7] Here is the place of refuge from the face of the Enemy's anger; here is amended and washed away whatever defilement hath been anywhere else contracted.

→ CHAPTER FIFTY-THREE ←

THAT THE GRACE OF GOD DOTH NOT JOIN ITSELF WITH THOSE WHO RELISH EARTHLY THINGS

My son, My Grace is precious, it suffereth not itself to be mingled with external things, nor with earthly consolations. Thou oughtest therefore to cast away all the hindrances of grace, if thou desire to receive the inpouring thereof.

Seek for a secret place for thyself, love to dwell alone with thyself, desire the conversation of none; but rather pour out devout prayer unto God, that thou mayest keep a contrite mind and a pure conscience. Esteem thou the whole world as nothing; prefer waiting upon God before all outward things. For thou wilt not be able to wait upon Me, and at the same time to take delight in things transitory. It is fitting that thou remove thyself far away from acquaintance and dear friends,[1] and keep thy mind void of all temporal comfort. So the blessed Apostle Peter beseecheth, that the faithful of Christ would keep themselves in this world *as strangers and pilgrims.*[2]

O how great a confidence shall he have at the hour of death, whom no affection to anything detaineth in the world. But what it is to have a heart so separate from all things, the sickly mind doth not as yet comprehend; nor doth the natural man know the liberty of the spiritual man. Notwithstanding if he would be truly spiritual, he ought to renounce as well those who are far off, as those who are near unto him, and to beware of no man more than of himself. If thou perfectly overcome thyself, thou shalt very easily bring all else under the yoke. The perfect victory is to triumph over ourselves. For he that keepeth himself subject, in such sort that his sensual affections be obedient to reason, and his reason in all things obedient to Me; that person is truly conqueror of himself, and lord of the world.

2. If thou desire to mount unto this height, thou must begin like a man, and lay the axe to the root,[3] that thou mayest pluck up and destroy the hidden inordinate inclination to self, and to all private and earthly good.

By this fault, (that a man too inordinately loveth himself,) everything almost is upheld, which ought from its roots to be overcome. If this evil be once vanquished and subdued, there will presently, ensue great peace and tranquillity. But because few labour to be perfectly dead to themselves, or fully go forth from themselves, therefore in themselves they remain entangled, nor can be lifted up in spirit above themselves.

But he that desireth to walk at liberty[4] with Me, it is necessary that he mortify all his corrupt and inordinate affections, and that he should not with desire cleave to any creature in selfish love.

CHAPTER FIFTY-FOUR

OF THE DIFFERENT MOTIONS OF NATURE AND GRACE

My son, mark diligently the motions of Nature and of Grace; for in a very contrary and subtle manner do they move, and can hardly be distinguished but by him that is spiritual and inwardly enlightened. All men indeed desire that which is good, and pretend somewhat good in their words and deeds; and therefore under the show of good, many are deceived.

2. Nature is crafty, and draweth away many, ensnareth and deceiveth them, and hath always self for her end: but Grace walketh in simplicity, abstaineth from all show of evil, sheltereth not herself under deceits, doeth all things purely for God's sake, in whom also she finally resteth.

Nature is loth to die, or to be kept down, or to be overcome, or to be in subjection, or readily to be subdued: but Grace studieth self-mortification, resisteth sensuality, seeketh to be in subjection, longeth to be defeated, hath no wish to use her own liberty; she loveth to be kept under discipline, and desireth not to rule over any, but ever under God to live, to stand, and to be, and for God's sake she is ready humbly to bow down to every ordinance of man.[1]

Nature striveth for her own advantage, and considereth what profit she may reap by another: Grace considereth not what is profitable and useful unto herself, but rather what may be for the good of many.[2]

Nature willingly receiveth honour and reverence; but Grace faithfully assigneth all honour and glory unto God.

Nature feareth shame and contempt: but Grace rejoiceth *to suffer reproach for the Name of Jesus.*[3]

Nature loveth leisure and bodily rest: Grace cannot be unemployed, but cheerfully embraceth labour.

Nature seeketh to have things that are curious and beautiful, and abhorreth those which are cheap and coarse: but Grace delighteth in what is plain and humble, despiseth not rough things, nor refuseth to be clad in that which is old and patched.

Nature respecteth temporal things, rejoiceth at earthly gains, sorroweth for loss, is irritated by every slight word of injury: but Grace looketh to things eternal, cleaveth not to things temporal,[4] is not disturbed at losses, nor soured with hard words; because she hath placed her treasure and joy in Heaven,[5] where nothing perisheth.

Nature is covetous, doth more willingly receive than give, and loveth to have things private and her own: but Grace is kind and open-hearted, shunneth private interest, is content with a few things, judgeth that *it is more blessed to give than to receive.*[6]

Nature inclineth a man to the creatures, to his own flesh, to vanities, and to rovings about. But Grace draweth unto God and to virtues; renounceth creatures, avoideth the world, hateth the desires of the flesh, restraineth wanderings abroad, blusheth to be seen in public.

Nature is willing to have some outward solace, wherein she may be sensibly delighted: but Grace seeketh consolation in God alone, and to have delight in the highest Good above all visible things.

Nature manageth everything for her own gain and profit, she cannot without payment do anything, but for every kindness she hopeth to obtain either what is equal, or what is better, or at least praise or favour; and is very earnest to have her works and gifts and words much valued: but Grace seeketh no temporal thing, nor desireth any other reward than God alone for her wages, nor asketh more of temporal necessaries, except so far as these may serve her for the obtaining of things eternal.

Nature rejoiceth to have many friends and kinsfolk, she glorieth of noble place and noble birth, smileth on the powerful, fawneth upon the rich, applaudeth those who are like herself: but Grace loveth even her enemies, and is not puffed up with multitude of friends; nor thinketh aught of place or of high birth, unless there shall be the greater virtue. She favoureth the poor rather than the rich, sympathiseth more with the innocent than with the powerful, rejoiceth with the true man, not with the deceitful: she is ever exhorting good men *to strive for the better gifts*;[7] and by virtues to become like to the Son of God.

Nature quickly complaineth of want and of trouble: Grace with constancy endureth need.

Nature turneth all things back to herself, striveth and argueth for herself: but Grace bringeth back all to God, from whence originally they flow; she ascribeth no good to herself, nor doth she arrogantly presume; she contendeth not, nor preferreth her own opinion before others; but in every matter of sense and understanding submitteth herself unto the Eternal wisdom and the Divine judgment.

Nature is eager to know secrets, and to hear news; she liketh to appear abroad, and to make proof of many things by her own senses; she desireth to be acknowledged, and to do things for which she may be praised and admired: but Grace careth not to hear news, nor curious matters, because all this taketh its rise from the old corruption of man; seeing that upon earth there is nothing new, nothing durable. Grace teacheth therefore to restrain the senses, to shun vain self-pleasing and outward show, humbly to hide those things that are worthy of admiration and praise, and from every matter and in every knowledge to seek profitable fruit, and the praise and honour of God. She will not have herself nor hers publicly proclaimed, but desireth that God should be blessed in His gifts, who of mere love bestoweth all things.

3. This Grace is a supernatural light, and a certain special gift of God, and the proper mark of the elect, and pledge of everlasting salvation; it raiseth up a man from earthly things to love the things of Heaven, and from being carnal maketh him a spiritual man.

The more therefore Nature is pressed down and subdued, so much the greater Grace is poured in; and everyday by new visitations the inward man becometh reformed according to the image of God.

→ CHAPTER FIFTY-FIVE ←

OF THE CORRUPTION OF NATURE, AND EFFICACY OF DIVINE GRACE

O Lord my God, who hast created me after Thine own image and likeness,[1] grant me this Grace, which Thou hast shewed to be so great and so necessary to salvation; that I may overcome my most evil nature, which draweth me to sin and to perdition. For I feel in my flesh the law of sin contradicting the law of my mind,[2] and leading me captive to the obeying of sensuality in many things; neither can I resist the passions thereof, unless Thy most holy Grace fervently infused into my heart do assist me.

There is need of Thy Grace, yea, of great grace, that Nature may be overcome, which is *ever prone to evil from her youth.*[3] For through the first man, Adam, Nature being fallen and corrupted by sin, the penalty of this stain hath descended upon all mankind, so that Nature itself, which by Thee was created good and upright, is now represented as the sin and infirmity of corrupted nature; because the inclination thereof left unto itself draweth to evil and to lower things. For the small power which remaineth is as it were a spark lying hid in the ashes. This is Natural Reason itself, encompassed about with great darkness, yet still retaining the discernment of good and evil, the difference between true and false, although it be unable to fulfill all that it approveth, and enjoyeth no longer the full light of the truth, nor soundness of its own affections.

Hence it is, O my God, that *I delight in Thy law after the inward man*,[4] knowing Thy commandment to be *good, just and holy*, proving also that all evil and sin are to be shunned; but *with the flesh I serve the law of sin*, whilst I obey sensuality rather than reason.

Hence it is, that *to will what is good is present with me, but how to perform it I find not.*[5]

Hence it is that I often purpose many good things, but because Grace is wanting to help my infirmity, upon a light resistance I start back and faint.

Hence it cometh to pass that I know the way of perfection, and see clearly enough how I ought to act; but being pressed down with the weight of mine own corruption, I rise not to what is more perfect.

2. O Lord, how entirely needful is Thy Grace for me, to begin anything good, to proceed with it, and to accomplish it. For without it I can do nothing,[6] but in Thee I can do all things, when Thy Grace doth strengthen me.[7]

O Grace truly celestial! Without which our own worthy actions are nothing, nor are any gifts of nature to be esteemed. Neither arts nor riches, neither beauty or strength, neither wit or eloquence, avail before Thee, without Thy Grace, O Lord. For gifts of Nature are common to good and bad, but the peculiar gift of the elect is Grace and Love; and they that are signed therewith, are accounted worthy of everlasting life. So eminent is this Grace, that neither the gift of prophecy, nor the working of miracles, nor any speculation (how high soever) is of any esteem without it. No, not even faith nor hope, or any other virtues, are unto Thee acceptable without Charity and Grace.[8]

3. O most blessed Grace, that makest the poor in spirit rich in virtues, and renderest him who is rich in many goods humble in heart! Come Thou down unto me, come and in the morning fill me with Thy comfort, lest my soul faint for weariness and dryness of mind.

I beseech Thee, O Lord, that I may find Grace in Thy sight; for Thy Grace is sufficient for me,[9] though other things that Nature longeth for be not obtained. Although I be tempted and vexed with many tribulations, yet I will fear no evils,[10] so long as Thy Grace is with me. This alone and of itself is my strength; this alone bringeth counsel and help. This is stronger than all enemies, and wiser than all the company of the wise. Thy Grace is the mistress of truth, the teacher of discipline, the light of the heart, the solace of affliction, the driver-away of sorrow, the expeller of fear, the nurse of devotion, the source and fountain of tears. Without This, what am I but a withered piece of wood, and an unprofitable branch only meet to be cast away![11]

Let Thy Grace therefore, O Lord, always both prevent and follow me, and make me to be continually given to good works, through Jesus Christ Thy Son. Amen.[12]

CHAPTER FIFTY-SIX

THAT WE OUGHT TO DENY OURSELVES AND IMITATE CHRIST BY THE CROSS

My son, the more thou canst go out of thyself, the more wilt thou be able to enter into Me. Even as to desire nothing that is without produceth inward peace, so the forsaking of thyself inwardly, joineth thee unto God.

I wish thee to learn perfect renunciation of thyself in My will, without contradiction or complaint.

Follow thou Me: *I am the Way, the Truth, and the Life.*[1]

Without the Way, there is no going; without the Truth, there is no knowing; without the Life, there is no living. I am the Way, which thou oughtest to follow; the Truth, which thou oughtest to believe; the Life, which thou oughtest to hope for. I am the Way inviolable, the Truth infallible, the Life unending. I am the Way that is straightest, the Truth that is highest, the Life that is true, the Life blessed, the Life uncreated. If thou remain in My way, thou shalt *know the Truth, and the Truth shall make thee free,*[2] and thou shalt lay hold on eternal life.

If thou wilt enter into life, keep the commandments.[3] If thou wilt know the truth, believe Me. *If thou wilt be perfect, sell all.*[4] If thou wilt be My disciple, deny thyself utterly.[5] If thou wilt possess a blessed life, despise this life present. If thou wilt be exalted in Heaven, humble thyself in this world.[6] If thou wilt reign with Me, bear the Cross with Me.[7] For only the servants of the Cross do find the way of blessedness and of true light.

2. O Lord Jesus, forasmuch as Thy way was narrow and despised by the world, grant me grace to imitate Thee, though with the world's

contempt. *For the servant is not greater than his Lord,*[8] *nor the disciple above his Master.*

Let Thy servant be exercised in Thy life, for therein is my salvation and true holiness. Whatsoever I read or hear besides it, doth not refresh me nor delight me to the full.

3. My son, inasmuch as thou knowest and hast read all these things, happy shalt thou be, if thou do them.[9] *He that hath My commandments and keepeth them, he it is that loveth Me*; *and I will love him, and will manifest Myself unto him,*[10] and will make him sit together with Me in the kingdom of My Father.[11]

O Lord Jesu, as Thou hast said and promised, so truly let it be, and let it be mine to win it. I have received the Cross, I have received it from Thy hand; I will bear it, and bear it even unto death, as Thou hast laid it upon me. "Truly a good monk's life is the Cross, but it guides him to Heaven."[12] We have now begun, it is not lawful to go back, neither must we leave it.

4. Come, brethren, go we forward together, Jesus will be with us. For the sake of Jesus we have received this Cross; for the sake of Jesus let us persevere in the Cross. He will be our Helper, who is also our Guide and Forerunner. Behold, our King entereth in before us, and *He will fight for us.*[13] Let us follow manfully, let no man fear any terrors; let us be ready to die valiantly in battle, nor bring such a disgrace on our glory as to flee from the Cross.

CHAPTER FIFTY-SEVEN

THAT A MAN SHOULD NOT BE TOO MUCH DEJECTED, WHEN HE FALLETH INTO SOME DEFECTS

MY SON, PATIENCE AND HUMILITY IN ADVERSITIES ARE MORE PLEASING to Me, than much comfort and devotion when things go well.

Why doth a little matter spoken against thee make thee sad? Although it had been much more, thou oughtest not to have been moved. But now let it pass; it is not the first that hath happened, nor is it anything new; neither shall it be the last, if thou live long.

Thou art manly enough, so long as nothing adverse befalleth thee. Thou canst give good counsel also, and canst strengthen others with thy words; but when sudden tribulation cometh to thy door, thou failest in counsel and in strength. Observe then thy great frailty, of which thou too often hast experience in small occurrences. Notwithstanding it is done for thy good, when these and such like trials happen to thee.

Put it out of thy heart according to thy better knowledge, and if it have touched thee, yet let it not cast thee down, nor long perplex thee. Bear it at least patiently, if thou canst not joyfully. Although thou be unwilling to hear it, and conceivest indignation thereat, yet restrain thyself, and suffer no ill-ordered word to pass out of thy mouth, whereby the little ones may be offended. The storm which is now raised shall quickly be at peace, and inward grief shall be sweetened by the return of Grace. I yet live, saith the Lord, and am ready to help thee,[1] and to give thee more than ordinary consolation, if thou put thy trust in Me, and call devoutly upon Me.

Be of more even mind, and gird thyself to greater endurance. All is not lost, although thou do feel thyself very often afflicted or grievously tempted. Thou art a man, and not God; thou art flesh, not an Angel. How couldst thou continue alway in the same state of virtue, when an Angel in Heaven hath failed in this, as also the first man in Paradise?[2] I am He who lift up the mourners to safety and soundness, and those that know their own weakness I advance to My own Divine Nature.

2. O Lord, blessed be Thy Word, *sweet unto my mouth above honey and the honeycomb.*[3] What should I do in these so great tribulations and straits, unless Thou didst comfort me with Thy holy discourses? What matter is it, what or how much I suffer so as I may at length attain to the haven of safety? Grant me a good end, grant me a happy passage out of this world. Remember me, O my God, and direct me in the right way to Thy kingdom. Amen.

✧ CHAPTER FIFTY-EIGHT ✧

THAT HIGH MATTERS AND GOD'S SECRET JUDGMENTS ARE NOT TO BE NARROWLY ENQUIRED INTO

MY SON, BEWARE THOU DISPUTE NOT OF HIGH MATTERS, NOR OF THE secret judgments of God, why this man is so left, and that man taken into such great favour; why also one is so grievously afflicted, and another so eminently exalted. These things go beyond all reach of man's power, neither doth any reason or disputation avail to search out the judgments of God.

When therefore the Enemy suggesteth these things unto thee, or some curious persons raise the question, let thy answer be that of the Prophet, *Just art Thou, O Lord, and right is Thy judgment.*[1] And again, *The judgments of the Lord are true and righteous altogether.*[2] My judgments are to be feared, not to be discussed; for they are not to be comprehended by the understanding of man.

Neither enquire thou, nor dispute of the merits of the Saints, as to which of them is holier than the other, or which shall be the greater in the Kingdom of Heaven. Such matters oftentimes breed unprofitable strifes and contentions,[3] they also nourish pride and vain-glory; whence arise envies and dissensions, whilst one proudly endeavoureth to put forward one saint, and another another. To wish to know, and to search out such things bring no fruit, but rather are displeasing to the Saints; for I am not the God of dissension, but of peace; which peace consisteth rather in true humility, than in self-exaltation.

Some are drawn by zeal of love towards these Saints or those with fuller affection; nevertheless this is rather human love than divine. I am He who made all the Saints; I gave them Grace; I bestowed on them Glory. I know what everyone hath deserved; I have prevented them with the blessings of my goodness.[4] I foreknew My beloved ones before the ages.[5] I chose them out of the world, they chose not Me first.[6] I called them by grace, I drew them by mercy, I led them safe through sundry temptations. I poured into them glorious consolations, I gave them perseverance, I crowned their patience. I acknowledge both the first and the last; I embrace all with love inestimable. I am to be praised in all My Saints: I am to be blessed above all things, and to be honoured in everyone, whom I have thus gloriously exalted and predestinated,[7] without any merits of their own that went before. He therefore that contemneth one of the least of Mine,[8] honoureth not the greatest; for that I made both the small and the great.[9] And he that disparageth any of the Saints, disparageth Me also, and all others in the Kingdom of Heaven. All are one through the bond of charity; their thought is the same, their will is the same, and all are one in love to each other. But still (which is a far higher thing), they love Me more than they do themselves or any merits of their own. For being ravished above self, and drawn beyond self-love, they go forward with their whole being to love of Me, in whom also they rest with entire fruition. Nothing can turn them back, or press them down; for being full of the eternal Truth, they burn with the fire of unquenchable charity.

Let therefore carnal and natural men who can love nothing but selfish joys, forbear to dispute of the state of God's Saints. Such men add and take away according to their own fancies, not as it pleaseth the eternal Truth. Many are ignorant, especially those who being but little illuminated, can seldom love any with a perfect spiritual love. They are as yet much drawn by a natural affection and human friendship to this man or to that; and according as they behave in lower things, so do they imagine concerning things heavenly. But there is an incomparable distance between the things which the imperfect conceive, and those which men illuminated behold, through revelation from above.

2. Beware therefore, My son, that thou handle not with vain curiosity things which exceed thy knowledge;[10] but rather let this be thy great

business and endeavour, that thou mayest be found even the least in the Kingdom of God. Even if any man should know who was more holy than another, or who was accounted greater in the Kingdom of Heaven; what would this wisdom profit him, unless out of this knowledge he should humble himself in My sight, and then should rise up to give the greater praise to My Name? Far more acceptable to God is he that thinketh of the greatness of his own sins, and the smallness of his virtues, and how far he is from the perfection of Saints, than he who disputeth of their greatness or littleness. It is better to entreat the Saints with devout prayers and tears, and with humility of mind to implore their glorious suffrages, than with vain enquiry to search narrowly into their secret things.

They are well, yea right well contented, if men would but content themselves, and refrain from their vain discourses. They glory not of their own merits, inasmuch as they ascribe no goodness to themselves, but all to Me, since of My infinite love I have given them all things. They are filled with so great love of the divine nature, and with such an overflowing joy, that no glory is wanting unto them, nor can they want aught of happiness. All the Saints, the higher they are in glory, so much the more humble are they in themselves, and the nearer and dearer unto Me. And therefore thou hast it written, That *they did cast their crowns before God, and fell down on their faces before the Lamb, and adored Him that liveth forever and ever.*[11]

3. Many enquire, who is the greatest in the Kingdom of God, who know not whether they shall be meet to be numbered among the least. It is a great thing to be even the least in Heaven, where all are great; for they all shall be called, and shall be, the Sons of God.[12] *The least shall become a thousand,*[13] and *the sinner of an hundred years shall die.*[14] For when the disciples asked who should be greatest in the Kingdom of Heaven, they heard such an answer as this: *Except ye be converted, and become as little children, ye shall not enter into the Kingdom of Heaven; whosoever therefore shall humble himself as this little child, the same is greatest in the Kingdom of Heaven.*[15]

Woe be unto them who disdain to humble themselves willingly with little children; because the low gate of the heavenly Kingdom will not give them entrance.[16] Woe also to the rich, who have here their consolations;[17] for whilst the poor enter into the Kingdom of God, they shall stand lamenting without.

Rejoice ye humble,[18] and be glad ye poor, *for yours is the Kingdom of God,* if at least ye *walk in the Truth.*[19]

✧ CHAPTER FIFTY-NINE ✧

THAT ALL OUR HOPE AND TRUST IS TO BE FIXED IN GOD ALONE

LORD, WHAT IS MY CONFIDENCE WHICH I HAVE IN THIS LIFE? OR WHAT is my greatest comfort out of all things that are seen under Heaven Is it not Thou, O Lord, my God, of whose mercies there is no number? Where hath it ever been well with me without Thee? Or when could it be ill with me, when Thou wert present? I had rather be poor for Thee, than rich without Thee. I rather choose to be a pilgrim on earth with Thee, than without Thee to possess Heaven. Where Thou art, there is Heaven: and where Thou art not, there is death and hell. Thou art all my desire, and therefore after Thee I must needs sigh and call and earnestly pray. In short there is none whom I can fully trust in, none that can more seasonably help me in my necessities, but only Thou, my God. Thou art my hope, Thou my confidence; Thou art my Comforter, and in all things most faithful.

All men seek their own:[1] Thou settest forward my salvation and my profit only, and turnest all things to my good. Although Thou exposest me to divers temptations and adversities, yet Thou orderest all this to my advantage, Who art wont to try Thy beloved ones a thousand ways. In which trial of me Thou oughtest no less to be loved and praised, than if Thou wert filling me full of heavenly consolations. In Thee therefore, O Lord God, I place my whole hope and refuge; on Thee I rest all my tribulation and anguish; for I find all to be weak and inconstant, whatsoever I behold out of Thee.

For many friends will not profit, nor will strong helpers be able to assist, nor prudent counsellors give a profitable answer, nor the books of the learned afford comfort, nor any precious substance deliver, nor any place, however retired and lovely, give shelter, unless Thou Thyself dost stand by, help, strengthen, console, instruct, and guard us. For all things that seem to belong to the possession of peace and felicity, without Thee, are nothing, and do bring in truth no felicity at all. Thou therefore art the perfection of all that is good, the height of life, the depth of all that can be spoken; and to hope in Thee above all things, is the strongest comfort of Thy servants. To Thee therefore do I lift up mine eyes; in Thee my God, the Father of mercies, do I put my trust.

2. Bless and sanctify my soul with Thy heavenly blessing, that it may become Thy holy habitation, and the seat of Thine eternal glory; and let nothing be found in this temple of Thy dignity, which shall offend the eyes of Thy majesty. According to the greatness of Thy goodness and multitude of Thy mercies look upon me,[2] and hear the prayer of Thy poor servant, who is far exiled from Thee in the land of the shadow of death.[3] Protect and keep the soul of me the meanest of Thy servants, amidst so many dangers of this corruptible life, and by Thy grace accompanying me direct it along the way of peace to its native-land of everlasting brightness. Amen.

THE FOURTH BOOK

A DEVOUT EXHORTATION TO THE HOLY COMMUNION

INTRODUCTION

The Voice of Christ

Come unto Me all ye that labour and are heavy laden, and I will refresh you,[1] saith the Lord.

The bread which I will give is My Flesh, for the life of the world.[2]

Take ye and eat; this is My Body which shall be given for you:[3] *Do this for the Commemoration of Me.*[4]

He that eateth My Flesh and drinketh My Blood, dwelleth in Me, and I in him.

The Words which I have spoken unto you are Spirit and Life.[5]

✧ CHAPTER ONE ✧

WITH HOW GREAT REVERENCE CHRIST OUGHT TO BE RECEIVED

THE VOICE OF THE DISCIPLE

These are Thy words, O Christ the eternal Truth, though not uttered all at one time, nor written together in one place. Because, therefore they are Thine and true, they are all thankfully and faithfully to be received by me. Thine they are, and Thou hast uttered them; and they are mine also, because Thou hast spoken them for my salvation. I cheerfully receive them from Thy mouth, that they may be the more deeply implanted in my heart. They arouse me, those words of so much tenderness, so full of sweetness and of love; but mine own offences make me afraid, and an impure conscience driveth me back from the receiving of so great Mysteries. The sweetness of Thy words doth invite me, but the multitude of my sins weigheth me down.

Thou commandest me to come confidently unto Thee, if I would have part with Thee; and to receive the food of immortality, if I desire to obtain everlasting life and glory. *Come unto Me* (sayest Thou), *all ye that labour and are heavy laden, and I will refresh you.*[1] O sweet and loving word in the ear of a sinner, that Thou, my Lord God, shouldest invite the poor and needy to the Communion of Thy most holy Body!

But who am I, Lord, that I should presume to approach unto Thee? Behold the Heaven of Heavens cannot contain Thee,[2] and Thou sayest, *Come ye all unto Me.* What meaneth this most tender condescension, and so loving an invitation? How shall I dare to come, who know not any good in myself, whereupon I may presume? How shall I bring Thee into my house, I that have so often offended Thy most gracious countenance? Angels and Archangels stand in awe of Thee, holy and righteous men do fear Thee, and sayest Thou, *Come ye all unto Me*? Unless Thou, O Lord, didst say this, who would believe it to be true? And unless Thou didst command it, who could attempt to draw near?

Behold, Noah that just man laboured a hundred years in the making of the Ark,[3] that he might be saved with a few; and how can I in one hour's space prepare myself to receive with reverence the Maker of the world?

Moses, Thy great servant, and Thine especial friend, made an ark of incorruptible wood, which also he clothed with the finest gold, that therein he might lay up the tables of the law;[4] and I a corrupted creature, shall I dare so lightly to receive Thee the Maker of the law, and the Giver of life?

Solomon the wisest of the kings of Israel bestowed seven years in building a temple magnifical to the praise of Thy Name.[5] And for eight days he celebrated the feast of dedication thereof; he offered a thousand peace-offerings, and the ark of the covenant he solemnly set in the place prepared for it, with the sound of trumpets, and great joy.[6] And I the most miserable and poorest of men, how shall I bring Thee into my house, I that scarce know how to spend one half hour in true devotion? And would that I could even once spend something like one half hour worthily!

2. O my God, how earnestly did they study to please Thee! Alas, how little is that which I do! How short a time do I spend, when I am disposing myself to receive the Communion! Seldom am I wholly collected; very seldom am I cleansed from all distraction. And yet surely in the life-giving Presence of Thy Godhead no unbecoming thought ought to intrude itself, nor should any creature occupy my heart; for it is not an Angel, but the Lord of the Angels, whom I am about to receive as my Guest.

However, very great is the difference between the ark of the covenant with its relicks, and Thy most pure Body with Its unspeakable virtues; great the difference between those legal sacrifices, figures of things to come, and the True Offering of Thy Body, the fulfilment of all ancient sacrifices. Wherefore then am I not more on fire to seek Thine adorable Presence? Why do I not prepare myself with greater solicitude to receive Thy holy things? Whereas those holy patriarchs and prophets of old, kings also and princes, with the whole people, shewed such zeal of devotion to Thy divine service.

3. The most devout king David[7] danced before the ark of God with all his might, calling to mind the benefits bestowed in time past upon his forefathers. He made instruments of sundry kinds, he set forth psalms, and appointed them to be chanted with joy; he also oftentimes himself played on the harp, being inspired with the grace of the Holy Ghost. He taught the people of Israel to praise God with their whole hearts, and with the voice of melody to bless and praise Him everyday.

If so great devotion was then used, and such celebrating of divine praise was kept up before the ark of the testament; what reverence and devotion ought now to be preserved by me and all Christian people, in the presence of the Sacrament, in receiving the most precious Body of Christ.

4. Many run to divers places to visit the relicks of Saints and are full of admiration at hearing of their deeds, gaze upon the spacious buildings of their temples, and kiss their sacred bones that are wrapped in silks and gold. But behold, Thou art Thyself here present with me on Thine altar, my God, Saint of saints, Creator of man, and Lord of the Angels.

Often in looking upon such memorials people are moved by curiosity, and the novelty of fresh sights, whilst little fruit of amendment is carried home; particularly when they run from place to place so lightly without true contrition. But here, in the Sacrament of the Altar, Thou art wholly present, my God, the Man Christ Jesus; here is reaped an abundant fruit of eternal salvation, as often as Thou art received worthily and with devotion. To this neither levity, nor curiosity, nor sensuality draweth men; nothing but firm faith, devout hope, and sincere charity.

5. O God, the invisible Creator of the world, how wonderfully dost Thou deal with us; how sweetly and graciously dost Thou order all things for Thine elect, to whom Thou offerest Thyself to be received in this Sacrament! For This verily passeth all understanding; This

specially draweth the hearts of the devout, and kindleth their affection. For even Thy true faithful ones, who dispose their whole life to amendment, from this most worthy Sacrament oftentimes gain much grace of devotion, and love of virtue.

6. O admirable and hidden grace of the Sacrament, which only the faithful ones of Christ do know! But the unbelieving and such as are slaves unto sin, cannot have experience thereof. In this Sacrament spiritual grace is conferred, and virtue which was lost is restored in the soul, and the beauty which by sin had been disfigured again returneth. So great sometimes is this Grace, that out of the fulness of devotion here given, not the mind only, but the weak body also feeleth bestowed on itself a fuller strength.

7. Nevertheless our lukewarmness and negligence is exceedingly to be lamented and pitied, that we are not drawn with greater affection to receive Christ; in whom doth consist all the hope of those that are to be saved, and all their merit. For He Himself is our sanctification and redemption;[8] He Himself is the consolation of pilgrims, and the everlasting fruition of Saints. It is therefore exceedingly to be lamented that many do so little consider this saving Mystery, which causeth joy in Heaven, and preserveth the whole world.

Alas for the blindness and hardness of the human heart, that it doth not more consider so unspeakable a Gift; but rather through the daily use thereof sinketh even into disregard of it! For if this most holy Sacrament were celebrated in one place only, and were consecrated by one only priest in the world; with how great desire dost thou think would men be affected to that place, and toward such a priest of God, that they might see the divine Mysteries celebrated? But now many are made priests, and in many places Christ is offered; that the grace and love of God to man may appear so much the greater, the more widely this sacred Communion is spread over the world.

Thanks be unto Thee, O good Jesu, Thou eternal Shepherd, for that Thou hast vouchsafed to refresh us, who are poor and exiles, with Thy precious Body and Blood; and to invite us to the receiving of these Mysteries by a message even from Thine own mouth, saying, *Come unto Me all ye that labour and are heavy laden, and I will refresh you.*

⇢ CHAPTER TWO ⇠

THAT THE GREAT GOODNESS AND LOVE OF GOD IS EXHIBITED TO MAN IN THIS SACRAMENT

THE VOICE OF THE DISCIPLE

In confidence of Thy goodness and great mercy, O Lord, I draw near, sick to the Healer, hungry and thirsty to the Fountain of life, needy to the King of Heaven, a servant to his Lord, a creature to the Creator, desolate to my own tender Comforter.

But whence is this to me, that Thou comest unto me?[1] What am I, that Thou shouldest grant me Thine own self. How dare a sinner appear before Thee? And how is it that Thou dost vouchsafe to come unto a sinner? Thou knowest Thy servant, and art well aware that he hath in him no good thing, for which Thou shouldest grant him this.

I confess therefore mine own vileness, I acknowledge Thy goodness, I praise Thy tender mercy, and give Thee thanks for Thy transcendent love. For Thou doest this for Thine own sake, not for any merits of mine; to the end that Thy goodness may be the better known unto me, Thy love more abundantly heaped upon me, and Thy humility the more eminently set forth. Since therefore this is Thy pleasure, and Thou hast commanded that it should be so, this Thy condescension is also pleasing unto me; and O that my iniquity may not bar the way!

O most sweet and most tender Jesu, how great reverence and thanksgiving, together with perpetual praise, is due unto Thee for the receiving of Thy sacred Body; whose worthiness no one among men is found able to express! But on what shall I think at this Communion, in approaching unto my Lord, whom I am not able duly to honour, and yet whom I desire devoutly to receive? What can I think on better, and more profitable, than utterly to humble myself before Thee, and to exalt above myself Thine infinite goodness? I praise Thee, my God, and exalt Thee forever: I despise myself and cast myself down before Thee, into the deep of mine own vileness.

Behold, Thou art the Holy of holies, and I the scum of sinners! Behold, Thou inclinest Thyself unto me, who am not worthy to look up unto Thee! Behold, Thou comest unto me; it is Thy will to be with me, Thou invitest me to Thy banquet. Thou art willing to give me heavenly food and bread of Angels to eat,[2] which is indeed no other than Thyself the Living Bread, which camest down from Heaven, and givest life unto the world.

Behold, from whence love proceedeth! What condescension shineth forth! How great thanks and praises are due unto Thee for these benefits! O how salutary and profitable was Thy counsel, when Thou didst ordain It! How sweet and pleasant the banquet, when Thou gavest Thyself to be our food! O how admirable is Thy working, O Lord, how mighty is Thy power, how unspeakable Thy truth! For Thou didst speak and all things were made;[3] and this was done which Thou Thyself commandedst. A wondrous thing, worthy of faith, and surpassing man's understanding, that Thou my Lord God, True God and Man, art contained wholly under the form of a little Bread and Wine, and without being consumed art eaten by him that receiveth Thee.

Thou who art the Lord of the universe, and standest in need of none,[4] art pleased to dwell in us by means of Thy Sacrament. Do Thou preserve my heart and body undefiled, that with a cheerful and pure conscience I may be able very frequently to celebrate, and to receive to my everlasting health, Thy Mysteries, which Thou didst consecrate and ordain for Thine own especial honour and for a never-ceasing memorial.

2. Rejoice, O my soul, and give thanks unto God, for so noble a gift, and so marvellous a consolation, left unto thee in this vale of tears. For as often as thou repeatest this Mystery, and receivest the Body of Christ, so often dost thou go over the work of thy redemption, and art made

partaker of all the merits of Christ. For the charity of Christ is never diminished, and the greatness of His propitiation is never exhausted.

Therefore thou oughtest ever to dispose thyself hereunto by a fresh renewing of thy mind, and to weigh with attentive thought the great Mystery of salvation. So great, so new, and so joyful ought it to seem unto thee, when thou celebratest or hearest Mass, as if on this same day Christ first descending into the womb of the Virgin were become man, or hanging on the Cross did this day suffer and die for the salvation of mankind.

CHAPTER THREE

THAT IT IS PROFITABLE TO COMMUNICATE OFTEN

The Voice of the Disciple

Behold, O Lord, I come unto Thee, that it may be well with me through Thy gift, and that I may rejoice in Thy holy feast, which *Thou,* O God, *hast in Thy sweetness prepared for the poor.*[1] Behold in Thee is all whatsoever I can or ought to desire; Thou art my Salvation and my Redemption, my Hope and my Strength, my Honour and Glory.

Rejoice therefore this day the soul of Thy servant; for *unto Thee* O Lord Jesu, *have I lifted up my soul.*[2] I long to receive Thee now with devotion and reverence; I desire to bring Thee into my house, that with Zaccheus I may be counted worthy to be blessed by Thee, and to be numbered amongst the sons of Abraham.[3] My soul desireth to receive Thy Body; my heart longeth to be united with Thee. Give Thyself to me, and it sufficeth; for besides Thee no comfort availeth.

Without Thee I cannot be, and without Thy visitation I have no power to live. And therefore I must needs often draw near unto Thee, and receive Thee for the medicine of my salvation; lest haply I faint in the way, if I be deprived of the heavenly nourishment. For so, most merciful Jesus, Thou once didst say, preaching to the people, and curing divers sicknesses, *I will not send them fasting to their own homes, lest they faint in the way*.[4] Deal thou therefore in like manner now with me, Who hast left thyself in the Sacrament for the comfort of the faithful. For thou art the sweet refection of the soul; and he that eateth Thee worthily, shall be partaker and heir of everlasting glory.

It is indeed necessary for me, who so often fall and sin, so quickly wax dull and faint, that by frequent prayer and confession, and receiving of Thy Holy Body, I renew, cleanse and kindle myself, lest haply, by too long abstaining, I fall away from my holy purpose. *For the imaginations of man are prone unto evil from his youth;*[5] and unless some divine remedy help him, he by and by falleth away to worse things. Holy Communion therefore draweth us back from evil, and maketh us strong in good. For if I be now so often negligent and lukewarm when I communicate or celebrate; what would become of me if I received not this healing, and sought not after so great a help? And although I may not be fit, nor well prepared to celebrate everyday; I will endeavour notwithstanding at due times to receive the divine Mysteries, and to offer myself as partaker of so great a grace. For this is the one chief consolation of the faithful soul, so long as it is absent from Thee in this mortal body; that being mindful of its God, it should often receive its Beloved, with devout mind.

2. O the wonderful condescension of Thy tender mercy towards us, that Thou, O Lord God, the Creator and Life-giver of all Spirits, dost vouchsafe to come unto the soul of the poor, and with Thy whole Godhead and Manhood abundantly to satisfy its famishing hunger!

O happy mind and blessed soul, which hath the privilege of receiving Thee, its Lord God, with devout affection; and in so receiving Thee of being filled with spiritual joy! O how great a Lord it entertaineth! How beloved a Guest it leadeth in! How delightful a Companion it receiveth! How faithful a Friend doth it welcome! How lovely and noble a Spouse doth it embrace! Even Him who is to be loved before all that are beloved, and above all things that can be desired.

O Thou my sweetest, most beloved! Let heaven and earth and all their fair apparel be silent before Thy face; for what praise and beauty soever they have, it is received from Thy bounteous condescension, nor shall they ever attain unto the beauty of Thy Name, of *whose wisdom there is no number.*[6]

→ CHAPTER FOUR ←

THAT MANY BENEFITS ARE BESTOWED UPON THEM THAT COMMUNICATE DEVOUTLY

THE VOICE OF THE DISCIPLE

O Lord my God, do Thou *prevent* Thy servant *with the blessings of Thy sweetness,*[1] that I may be enabled to approach worthily and devoutly to Thy glorious Sacrament.

Stir up my heart toward Thee, and set me free from heavy listlessness: *visit me with Thy salvation,*[2] that I may taste in spirit Thy sweetness, which in this Sacrament as in a fountain plentifully lieth hid.

Enlighten also mine eyes to behold so great a Mystery, and strengthen me with undoubting faith to believe it. For it is Thy work, and no human power; Thy sacred institution, not man's invention. For of himself no man is found able to comprehend and understand these things, which pass even the subtlety of Angels. What portion then of so deep a Mystery shall I, unworthy sinner, dust and ashes, be able to search out and comprehend? O Lord, in the simplicity of my heart, with a good and firm faith, and at Thy commandment, I draw near unto Thee with hope and reverence; and I do truly believe that Thou art here present in this Sacrament, both God and Man.

Thy will therefore is, that I should receive Thee, and that I should unite myself unto Thee in charity. Whereupon I implore Thy mercy, and do crave Thy special grace to be given me, to this end; that I may wholly be dissolved and overflow with love toward Thee, and never hereafter suffer any consolation to enter in, which cometh not from Thee. For this most high and worthy Sacrament is the health both of soul and body, the medicine for all spiritual languor; hereby my vices are cured, my passions bridled, my temptations overcome or diminished; greater grace is infused, virtue begun is increased, faith is confirmed, hope strengthened, and love set on fire and spread abroad.

2. For Thou hast bestowed, and still oftentimes dost bestow, many benefits in this Sacrament upon Thy beloved ones that communicate devoutly, O my God, the Upholder of my soul, the Restorer of human weakness, and the Giver of all inward consolation. For Thou impartest unto them much comfort against every variety of tribulation, and liftest them up from the depth of their own dejected state, to hope in Thy protection; and dost inwardly recreate and enlighten them with a new grace, so that they who at first and before Communion felt themselves full of anxiety and without affection, afterwards, being refreshed with heavenly Meat and Drink, do find themselves changed to the better.

And in such a way of dispensation as this dealest Thou with Thine elect, in order that they may truly acknowledge, and clearly prove, how great infirmity they have of themselves, and what goodness and grace they obtain from Thee. For they of themselves are cold, hard, and undevout; but by Thee they are enabled to become fervent, cheerful, and devout.

For who is there, that approaching humbly unto a fountain of sweetness, doth not carry away from thence some little sweetness? Or who standing near a great fire, receiveth not some small heat therefrom? And Thou art a fountain always full and over-flowing; a fire ever burning and never going out.[3] Wherefore if I am not permitted to draw out of the fulness of the fountain, nor to drink my fill, I will notwithstanding set my lips to the mouth of this heavenly conduit, that I may receive from thence at least some small drop to refresh my thirst, and may not be quite withered up. And though I cannot as yet be altogether heavenly, nor so on fire as the Cherubim and Seraphim, yet notwithstanding I will endeavour to apply myself earnestly to devotion, and to prepare my heart to obtain if it be but some small flame of divine fire, by the humble receiving of this life-giving Sacrament.

But whatsoever is hereunto wanting in me, O Good Jesu, most Holy Saviour, do Thou in my behalf bountifully and graciously supply,

Thou who hast vouchsafed to call us all unto Thee, saying, *Come unto Me all ye that labour and are heavy laden, and I will refresh you.*[4] I indeed labour *in the sweat of my brow,*[5] I am racked with grief of heart, I am burdened with sins, I am troubled with temptations, I am entangled and oppressed with many evil passions; and there is none to help me, none to deliver and save me, but Thou O Lord God my Saviour, to whom I commit myself and all that is mine, that Thou mayest keep watch over me, and bring me safe to life everlasting. Receive me for the honour and glory of Thy Name, Thou who hast prepared Thy Body and Blood to be my meat and drink. Grant O Lord God of my salvation, that by frequenting Thy Mysteries, the zeal of my devotion may increase.

CHAPTER FIVE

OF THE DIGNITY OF THIS SACRAMENT, AND OF THE PRIESTLY ESTATE

THE VOICE OF THE BELOVED

If thou hadst the purity of Angels,[1] and the sanctity of Saint John Baptist, thou wouldst not be worthy either to receive or handle this Sacrament. For it is not due to the deserts of men, that a man should consecrate and handle the Sacrament of Christ, and receive for food the bread of Angels.[2] High is the ministry, and great the dignity of Priests, to whom hath been granted that which is not permitted to Angels. For none but Priests duly ordained in the Church, have power to celebrate, and to consecrate the Body of Christ.

The Priest is indeed the minister of God, using the word of God, by God's command and appointment: nevertheless God is there the principal Author, and invisible Worker; to Whom all that He willeth is subject, and all that He commandeth is obedient.[3] Thou oughtest then to trust God Almighty in this most excellent Sacrament, more than thine own sense, or any visible sign. And therefore with fear and reverence thou must approach to this work.

2. Take heed unto thyself,[4] and see what that is, whereof the ministry hath been delivered unto thee by the laying on of the Bishop's hand.

Behold, thou hast been made a Priest, and consecrated to celebrate; see now that thou offer Sacrifice to God faithfully and devoutly, and at fit time, and shew thyself without reproof. Thou hast not lightened thy burden, but art now bound with a straiter band of discipline, and art obliged to a more perfect degree of sanctity. A Priest ought to be adorned with all virtues, and to give example of good life to others. His conversation[5] is not in the vulgar and common ways of mankind, but with the Angels in Heaven, or with perfect men on earth.

A Priest clad in sacred garments is Christ's Deputy, that with all supplication and humility he may beseech God for himself and for the whole people.[6] He hath both before and behind him the sign of the Lord's Cross, for the continual bringing to mind of the Passion of Christ. He weareth the Cross on the Chasuble before him, that he may diligently look on Christ's footsteps, and earnestly study to follow them. Behind also, he is signed with the Cross, that he may cheerfully endure, for God's sake, any evils inflicted on him by others. He beareth the Cross before him, that he may mourn for his own sins; and behind him, that he may with sympathy and tears lament for the faults of others also, and know that he hath been placed in the midst between God and the sinner.[7] Neither ought he to grow slack in prayer and holy oblation, till he prevail to obtain grace and mercy.

When a Priest doth celebrate he honoureth God; he rejoiceth the Angels, he buildeth up the Church; he helpeth the living, he giveth repose to the departed; and he maketh himself partaker of all good things.

➔ CHAPTER SIX ⬅

AN ENQUIRY CONCERNING SPIRITUAL EXERCISE BEFORE COMMUNION

The Voice of the Disciple

When I weigh Thy worthiness, O Lord, and mine own vileness, I exceedingly tremble, and am confounded within myself. For if I do not draw near, I flee from life; and if I unworthily intrude myself, I incur Thy displeasure. What therefore shall I do, O my God, my Helper and my Counsellor in necessities?

Teach Thou me the right way: appoint me some brief exercise, suitable for Holy Communion. For it is good for me to know how with devotion and reverence I should prepare my heart for Thee, for the receiving of Thy Sacrament to my soul's health; or also for the celebrating of so great and divine a Sacrifice.

CHAPTER SEVEN

OF THOROUGHLY SEARCHING OUR OWN CONSCIENCE, AND OF PURPOSE OF AMENDMENT

The Voice of the Beloved

Above all things, with exceeding humility of heart, and with suppliant reverence, with a full faith, and holy intention to do honour to God, ought God's Priest to come to celebrate, to handle, and to receive this Sacrament.

Examine diligently thy conscience, and to the utmost of thy power purify and make it clear, with true contrition and humble confession; so as thou mayest have no burden, nor know anything that may breed in thee remorse of conscience, and hinder thy free drawing near. Think with displeasure of all thy sins in general, and more particularly bewail and lament thy daily transgressions. And if time allow thee, confess unto God in the secret of thine heart all the wretchednesses of thy evil passions. Groan and lament that thou art yet so carnal and worldly, so unmortified from passions; so full of the motions of concupiscence, so unwatchful over thy outward senses, so often entangled with many vain imaginations: so much inclined to outward things, so negligent in things inward: so lightly moved to laughter and unbridled mirth, so hardly to tears and contrition: so prompt to ease and pleasures of the flesh, so dull to zeal and strictness of life: so curious to hear what is new, and to see what is beautiful, so slack to embrace what is humble and mean: so covetous of abundance, so niggardly in giving, so close in keeping: so inconsiderate in speech, so reluctant to keep silence: so unruly in manners, so fretful in conduct: so eager about food, so deaf to the Word of God: so swift to take rest, so slow to labour: so wakeful after gossiping tales, so drowsy at the sacred Services of the night; so hasty to arrive at the end, so inclined to wandering and inattention: so careless in accomplishing the Hours of prayer, so lukewarm in celebrating, so dry in communicating: so quickly distracted, so seldom thoroughly self-collected: so suddenly moved to anger, so apt to take displeasure against another: so ready to judge, so severe to reprove: so joyful at prosperity, so weak in adversity: so often making many good resolutions, and yet bringing them at last to so poor effect.

These and other thy defects being confessed and bewailed with sorrow and great displeasure at thine own infirmity, make thou a firm resolution to be always amending thy life, and making progress in all that is good.

Then with full resignation and with thy entire will, offer up thyself to the honour of My Name, on the altar of thy heart a perpetual whole burnt offering, even thy body and soul, faithfully committing them unto Me. And thus mayest thou be accounted worthy to draw near to offer this Sacrifice unto God, and to receive the Sacrament of My Body to thy soul's health.

2. For man hath no oblation more worthy, nor any satisfaction greater for the putting away of sins, than to offer himself unto God purely and wholly, together with the oblation of the Body of Christ in the Mass, and in receiving the Communion. And when a man shall have done what lieth in him, and shall be truly penitent, how often soever he shall come to Me for pardon and grace, *as I live,* saith the Lord, *who will not the death of a sinner, but rather that he be converted and live,*[1] I will not remember his sins anymore, but they shall all be forgiven him.

CHAPTER EIGHT

OF THE OBLATION OF CHRIST ON THE CROSS, AND OF RESIGNATION OF OURSELVES

The Voice of the Beloved

As I of Mine own will did offer up Myself unto God the Father for thy sins,[1] My hands stretched out on the cross, and My body stripped bare, so that nothing remained in Me that was not wholly turned into a sacrifice of divine propitiation; in like manner oughtest thou also to offer thyself willingly unto Me everyday in the Mass, as a pure and sacred oblation, with all thy powers and affections, unto the utmost strength of thy soul.

What do I require of thee more, than that thou study to resign thyself entirely unto Me? Whatsoever thou givest besides thyself, I regard not; for I seek not thy gift, but thee.[2] As it would not suffice thee to have all things whatsoever, besides Me; so neither can it please Me, whatsoever thou givest, if thou offer not thyself. Offer up thyself unto Me, and give thyself wholly for God, and thy oblation shall be accepted. Behold, I offered up Myself wholly unto My Father for thee; I gave also My whole Body and Blood for thy food, that I might be wholly thine, and that thou mightest continue Mine to the end. But if thou stand upon thyself, and dost not offer thyself up freely unto My will, the oblation is not complete, neither will there be entire union between us.

Therefore a free-will oblation of thyself into the hands of God ought to go before all thy works, if thou desire to obtain liberty and grace. For this is the cause why so few become illuminated and inwardly free, because they know not how wholly to deny themselves.

My sentence standeth sure, *Unless a man forsake all, he cannot be My disciple.*[3] If thou therefore desire to be My disciple, offer up thyself unto Me with all thine affections.

CHAPTER NINE

THAT WE OUGHT TO OFFER UP OURSELVES AND ALL THAT IS OURS UNTO GOD, AND TO PRAY FOR ALL

The Voice of the Disciple

Thine, O Lord, are all things that are in heaven, and that are in earth.[1] I desire to offer up myself unto Thee, as a freewill oblation, and to continue Thine forever. O Lord, in the simplicity of my heart I offer myself unto Thee this day to be Thy servant forever, in humble submission, and for a sacrifice of perpetual praise. Receive Thou me, with this holy Oblation of Thy precious Body; which I offer unto Thee this day in the presence of Angels invisibly attending; and may this further the salvation of myself and of all Thy people.

2. Lord, I offer unto Thee, on Thy propitiatory altar, all my sins and offences, which I have committed before Thee and Thy holy Angels, from the day wherein I first could sin even to this hour; that Thou mayest consume and burn them, one and all, with the fire of Thy love, and blot out all the stains of my sins, and cleanse my conscience from every offence, and restore to me Thy grace which by sinning I lost, fully forgiving me all, and admitting me mercifully to the kiss of peace.

What can I do in regard of my sins, but humbly confess and bewail them,[2] and unceasingly entreat Thy propitiation? I entreat Thee, hear me with Thy favour, when I stand before Thee my God. All my sins are exceedingly displeasing to me; I will never more commit them; but for them I grieve, and will grieve as long as I live, being ready to practice penance, and to the utmost of my power to make restitution. Forgive me, O God, forgive me my sins for the sake of Thy holy Name; save Thou my soul, which Thou hast redeemed with Thy precious Blood. Behold I commit myself unto Thy mercy, I resign myself into Thy hands. Deal with me according to Thy goodness, not according to my wickedness and iniquity.

3. I offer up also unto Thee all that is good in me, though it be very small and imperfect, in order that Thou mayest amend and sanctify it; that Thou mayest make it grateful and acceptable unto Thee, and always be perfecting it more and more; and bring me also, a slothful and unprofitable wretch, to a blessed and worthy end.

4. Moreover I offer up unto Thee all the pious desires of devout persons, the necessities of parents, friends, brethren, sisters, and of all who are dear unto me, and of those who have done good to myself or to others for Thy love; and who have desired and sought of me to offer prayers and Masses for themselves and for all that are theirs, whether they still live in the flesh, or now have done with this world's labours; that all may feel the present help of Thy grace, the aid of Thy consolation, protection from dangers, deliverance from punishment; and that being rescued from all evils, they may with joy return worthy thanksgivings unto Thee.

5. I offer up also unto Thee my prayers and sacrifices of propitiation, for those especially who have in any matter hurt, grieved, or reviled me, or who have done me any damage or displeasure. For all those also, whom at anytime I have grieved, troubled, burdened, and scandalized, by words or deeds, knowingly or in ignorance; that Thou wouldst grant us all equally pardon for our sins, and for our offences against each other.

Take away from our hearts, O Lord, all suspiciousness, indignation, wrath, and contention, and whatsoever may wound charity, and lessen brotherly love.

Have mercy, O Lord, have mercy on those who crave Thy mercy, give grace unto them that stand in need thereof, and make us such as that we may be worthy to enjoy to the full Thy grace, and go forward to life eternal. Amen.

➔ CHAPTER TEN ⟵

THAT THE HOLY COMMUNION IS NOT LIGHTLY TO BE FORBORNE

THE VOICE OF THE BELOVED

Often oughtest thou to run back to the Fountain of grace and divine mercy, to the Fountain of goodness and of all purity; that thou mayest be healed of thy passions and sins, and obtain to be made more strong and vigilant against all the temptations and deceits of the devil.

The enemy knowing the exceeding great profit and healing which lieth in the Holy Communion, endeavoureth by every means and occasion to the utmost of his power to withdraw and hinder faithful and devout persons from partaking therein. Thus it is that some persons when they are preparing to fit themselves for Holy Communion, suffer the worse insinuations of Satan. For that wicked spirit himself (as it is written in Job) cometh amongst the sons of God,[1] to trouble them according to his accustomed malice, or to render them over-fearful and perplexed, that so he may diminish their affection, or by his assaults take away their faith; to the end they may haply altogether forbear communicating, or come with lukewarmness.

But there is no heed at all to be taken of these his wiles and phantoms, be they never so filthy and hideous; but all his vain imaginations are to be turned back upon his own head. Thou must despise and laugh to scorn the wretched one, nor on account of his assaults, or for the troubles which he raiseth, omit the Holy Communion.

Oftentimes also an over-great solicitude for the obtaining of devotion, and some anxiety or other about the confession of sins, hindereth them. Act according to the counsel of the wise,[2] and lay aside anxiety and scrupulousness; for it hindereth the grace of God, and overthroweth the devotion of the mind.

Do not omit the Holy Communion for every small vexation and trouble, but rather proceed at once to confess thy sins, and cheerfully forgive others all their offences.[3] And if thou hast offended any, humbly crave pardon, and God will readily forgive thee.

2. What availeth it to delay long thy Confession; or to defer the Holy Communion? Make thyself thoroughly clean as soon as possible, spit out with all speed the poison, make haste to receive the healing, and thou shalt find it to be better with thee, than if thou long defer it. If thou omit it today for one cause, perhaps tomorrow another of greater force may occur to thee; and so thou mayest be hindered a long time from Communion, and grow more and more unfit. As quickly as ever thou canst, shake off from thyself thy present heaviness and sloth, for it is of no use to continue long in disquietude, or to be going on long with a troubled mind, and for everyday impediments to withdraw thyself from divine things. Yea, it is most exceedingly hurtful to defer the Communion long, for it usually bringeth on a heavy drowsiness.

Alas, some persons, lukewarm and undisciplined, do willingly delay confession, and desire on this account to defer the Holy Communion, lest they should be obliged to keep a stricter watch over themselves. O how poor is their love, how weak their devotion, who so easily put off the Holy Communion!

How happy is he and how acceptable to God, who so liveth, and in such purity guardeth his conscience, that he is prepared and well-disposed to communicate even everyday, if it were in his power, and he might do it without others taking notice.

If a person do sometimes abstain out of humility, or by reason of some lawful cause preventing him, he is to be commended for his reverence. But if a drowsiness have crept over him, he must stir up himself, and do what lieth in him, and the Lord will assist his desire, because of his goodwill, which is what God doth chiefly regard. But when he is lawfully hindered he will yet always have a goodwill, and a pious intention to communicate; and so shall he not lose the fruit of the Sacrament. For it is in the power of any devout person everyday and every hour profitably and without let to draw near to the spiritual Communion of Christ. And yet on certain days, and at time appointed, he ought to receive sacramentally, with affectionate reverence, the Body of his Redeemer, and rather seek the honour and glory of God, than his own comfort.[4] For he communicateth mystically, and is invisibly refreshed, as often as he devoutly calleth to mind the mystery of the Incarnation and the Passion of Christ, and is inflamed with the love of Him.

He that prepareth not himself, except only when a festival draweth near, or when custom compelleth him thereunto, shall too often be unprepared.

Blessed is he that offereth up himself as a whole burnt offering to the Lord, as often as he doth celebrate or communicate.

Be not too slow nor too quick in celebrating, but keep the good accustomed manner of those with whom thou livest. Thou oughtest not to cause trouble and weariness to others, but to keep the accustomed path, according to the appointment of our fathers; and rather be a servant to the edification of others, than to thine own devotion or affection.

CHAPTER ELEVEN

THAT THE BODY AND BLOOD OF CHRIST AND THE HOLY SCRIPTURES ARE MOST NECESSARY UNTO A FAITHFUL SOUL

The Voice of the Disciple

O most sweet Lord Jesus, how great is the pleasure of the devout soul that feasteth with Thee in Thy banquet; where there is set for her no other food to be eaten but Thyself, her only Beloved, and most to be desired above all the desires of her heart! To me also it would be indeed sweet, in Thy presence to pour forth tears from the very bottom of my heart, and with the grateful Magdalene to wash Thy feet with tears.[1] But where is that devotion? Where that plenteous flowing of holy tears?

Surely in the sight of Thee and Thy holy Angels, my whole heart ought to burn, and to weep for joy. For in this Sacrament I have Thee truly present, though hidden under another shape. For to look upon Thee in Thine own Divine brightness, mine eyes would not be able to endure; nor could even the whole world stand in the splendour of the glory of Thy Majesty. Herein then Thou hast regard to my weakness, that Thou dost hide Thyself under this Sacrament. Him do I really possess and adore, whom the Angels adore in Heaven; I however, for the present and for a while, by faith; but they by sight, and without a veil.

As to me, I ought to be content with the light of true faith, and therein to walk, *till the day* of everlasting brightness *shall dawn*, and *the shadows* of types *flee away*.[2] *But when that which is perfect is come*,[3] the use of Sacraments shall cease; because the Blessed, in their Heavenly

Glory, need not any sacramental healing: for they rejoice without end in the presence of God, beholding His glory *face to face;* and being *transformed from brightness to brightness,*[4] even that of the boundless Godhead, they taste the Word of God made flesh[5] as He was from the beginning, and as He abideth forever.[6]

Whilst I think on these wonders, it becometh heavy and wearisome unto me, even all spiritual comfort whatever; because as long as I behold not my Lord openly in His own glory, I account as nothing all that in this world I see and hear. Thou art my witness, O God, that nothing can comfort me, no creature can give me rest, but only Thou my God, whom I earnestly desire to contemplate everlastingly. But this is not possible, so long as I linger in this mortal life. Therefore I must frame myself to much patience; and submit myself to Thee in every desire. For even Thy Saints, O Lord, who now rejoice with Thee in the kingdom of Heaven, whilst they lived, waited in faith and in great patience for the coming of Thy glory.[7] What *they* believed, *I* believe; what *they* hoped, *I* hope; whither *they* are arrived, by Thy grace I trust *I* shall come. In the mean time I will walk in faith, strengthened by the examples of the Saints. I have also holy books for my comfort and for the looking-glass of my life; and above all these, I have Thy most Holy Body for a singular remedy and refuge.

2. For two things I perceive to be exceedingly necessary for me in this life; without which this miserable life would be intolerable unto me. Whilst I am detained in the prison of this body, I acknowledge myself to stand in need of two things; namely, food and light. Thou hast given therefore unto me in my weakness Thy sacred Body, for the refreshment of my soul and body;[8] and Thou hast set as *a lamp unto my feet*[9] Thy Word. Without these two I should not well be able to live; for the Word of God is the light of my soul, and Thy Sacrament the Bread of life. These also may be called the two tables, set on this side and on that, in the treasure-house of Holy Church.[10] One table is that of the Sacred Altar, having the holy bread, that is, the precious. Body of Christ; the other is that of the Divine Law, containing holy doctrine; teaching men the right faith, and stedfastly leading them onward even to *the things within the veil,*[11] where is the Holy of Holies.

3. Thanks be unto Thee, O Lord Jesu, Thou Light of everlasting Light, for that table of sacred doctrine, which Thou hast prepared for us by Thy servants the Prophets and Apostles and other teachers. Thanks be unto Thee, O Thou Creator and Redeemer of mankind, who, to manifest Thy love to the whole world, hast prepared a great supper,[12] wherein Thou hast set before us to be eaten, not the typical lamb, but Thine own most sacred Body and Blood;[13] making glad all the faithful with this sacred banquet, and refreshing them with the Cup of Salvation,[14] in which are all the delights of Paradise; and the holy Angels do feast with us, but yet with a more happy sweetness.

4. O how great and honourable is the office of Priests! To whom it is given with sacred words to consecrate the Lord of Glory; with their lips to bless, with their hands to hold, with their own mouth to receive, and also to administer to others.

O how clean ought those hands to be, how pure the mouth, how holy the body, how unspotted the heart of the priest, to whom the Author of purity so often draweth near! From the mouth of the Priest, nothing but what is holy, no word but what is good and profitable, ought to proceed; from him who so often receiveth the Sacrament of Christ. Single and chaste ought to be his eyes that are wont to behold the Body of Christ; the hands should be pure and lifted up to Heaven, that use to touch the Creator of Heaven and earth. Unto the Priests more especially it is said in the Law, *Be ye holy, for that I the Lord your God am holy.*[15]

Assist us with Thy grace, O Almighty God, that we who have undertaken the office of the Priesthood, maybe able to wait on Thee worthily and devoutly, in all purity, and with a good conscience. And if we cannot dwell in so great innocency of life as we ought to do, grant to us at the least worthily to lament the ills which we have committed; and in the spirit of humility, and with the full purpose of a goodwill, to serve Thee more earnestly for the time to come.

CHAPTER TWELVE

THAT HE WHO IS ABOUT TO COMMUNICATE IN CHRIST OUGHT TO PREPARE HIMSELF WITH GREAT DILIGENCE

THE VOICE OF THE BELOVED

I am the Lover of purity and the Giver of all holiness. I seek a pure heart, and there is the place of my rest.[1] *Make ready for Me a large upper room furnished,*[2] *and I will keep the Passover at thy house with My disciples.* If thou wilt have me come unto thee, and remain with thee; *purge out the old leaven,*[3] and make clean the habitation of thy heart. Shut out the whole world,[4] and all the throng of sins; sit thou *as it were a sparrow alone upon the house-top,*[5] and think over thy transgressions in the bitterness of thy soul. For everyone that loveth prepareth before the best and fairest place for his beloved; for herein is known the affection of him that entertaineth his beloved.

Know thou notwithstanding, that no merit of any action of thine is able to make this preparation sufficient, although thou shouldest prepare thyself a whole year together, and have nothing else in thy mind. But it is out of My mere goodness and favour that thou art permitted to approach My table; as if a beggar were invited to a rich man's dinner, and he hath no other return to make to him for his benefits, but to humble himself and give him thanks.

Do what lieth in thee, and do it diligently; not for custom, not for necessity; but with fear and reverence and affection, receive the Body of thy beloved Lord God, when He vouchsafeth to come unto thee. I am he that have called thee, I have commanded it to be done, I will supply what is wanting in thee; come thou and receive Me.

2. When I bestow on thee the grace of devotion, give thanks to thy God; not because thou art worthy, but because I have had mercy on thee.

If thou have it not, but rather dost feel thyself dry, be instant in prayer, sigh and knock,[6] and stay not until thou dost attain to receive some crumb or drop of saving grace. Thou hast need of Me, I have no need of thee. Neither comest thou to sanctify Me, but I come to sanctify thee and make thee better. Thou comest that thou mayest be sanctified by Me, and made one with Me; that thou mayest receive new grace, and be kindled anew to amendment of life. See thou neglect not this grace, but prepare with all diligence thy heart, and receive unto thyself thy Beloved.

3. Thou oughtest however not only to prepare thyself to devotion before Communion, but carefully also to preserve thyself therein, after thou hast received the Sacrament. Nor is the careful guard of thyself afterwards less required, than devout preparation before. For a good guard afterwards is the best preparation again for the obtaining of greater grace. For if one giveth himself up at once too much to outward consolations, he is rendered thereby exceedingly indisposed to devotion.

Beware of much talk,[7] remain in some secret place, and enjoy thy God; for thou hast Him, whom all the world cannot take from thee. I am He, to whom thou oughtest wholly to give up thyself, that so thou mayest now live no longer in thyself, but in Me, free from all anxiety of mind.

⇢ CHAPTER THIRTEEN ⇠

THAT THE DEVOUT SOUL OUGHT WITH THE WHOLE HEART TO SEEK UNION WITH CHRIST IN THE SACRAMENT

THE VOICE OF THE DISCIPLE

Who will grant unto me, Lord *to find Thee alone,*[1] and to open unto Thee my whole heart, and enjoy Thee even as my soul desireth; and that henceforth none may look upon me, nor any creature move me, nor have regard to me; but that Thou alone mayest speak unto me, and I to Thee, as the beloved is wont to speak to his beloved, and friend to feast with friend.[2]

This I beg, this I long for, that I may be wholly united unto Thee, and may withdraw my heart from all created things, and by means of Sacred Communion, and the frequent celebrating thereof, may learn more and more to relish things heavenly and eternal. Ah, Lord God, when shall I be wholly made one with Thee, and lost in Thee, and become altogether forgetful of myself? Thou in me, and I in Thee;[3] so also grant that we may both continue together in one. Verily, Thou art *my Beloved, the Choicest amongst thousands,*[4] in whom my soul is well pleased to dwell all the days of her life. Verily, Thou art my Peacemaker, in whom is highest peace and true rest; out of whom is labour and sorrow and infinite misery. *Verily, Thou art a God that hidest Thyself,*[5] and Thy counsel is not with the wicked, but with the humble and the simple is Thy speech.[6]

2. O how sweet is Thy Spirit,[7] O Lord, who to the end Thou mightest shew forth Thy sweetness toward Thy children, dost vouchsafe to

refresh them with the Bread which is full of all sweetness, which cometh down from Heaven.[8]

Surely *there is no other nation so great,*[9] *that hath gods so nigh unto them, as Thou our God art present* to all Thy faithful ones, unto whom for their daily comfort, and for the raising up of their hearts to Heaven, Thou bestowest Thyself to be eaten and enjoyed. *For what other nation is there of such high renown,* as the Christian people?[10] Or what creature under Heaven is there so beloved, as the devout soul, into which God Himself entereth, to nourish her with His glorious Flesh?

O unspeakable grace! O wondrous condescension! O unmeasurable love bestowed on man!

But what return shall I make to the Lord for this grace,[11] for charity so unparalleled? There is nothing else that I am able to present more acceptable, than to offer my heart wholly to my God, and to unite it most inwardly unto Him.

Then shall all my inward parts rejoice, when my soul shall be perfectly made one with God. Then will He say unto me, "If thou art willing to be with Me, I am willing to be with thee." And I will answer Him, "Vouchsafe, O Lord, to remain with me, I will gladly be with Thee. This is my whole desire, that my heart be made one with thee."

⇾ CHAPTER FOURTEEN ⇽

OF THE FERVENT DESIRE OF CERTAIN DEVOUT PERSONS TO RECEIVE THE BODY OF CHRIST

THE VOICE OF THE DISCIPLE

O how great is the abundance of Thy sweetness, O Lord, which Thou hast laid up for them that fear Thee![1]

When I call to mind some devout persons, who approach to Thy Sacrament, O Lord, with the greatest devotion and affection, I am oftentimes confounded and blush within myself, that I come with such lukewarmness, yea coldness, to Thy Altar and the Table of sacred Communion; that I remain so dry, and without affection of heart; that I am not wholly set on fire in Thy presence, O my God, nor so earnestly drawn and affected as many devout persons have been, who out of a vehement desire of the Communion, and a heart-felt love, were unable to restrain themselves from weeping; but with the mouth of their heart and body alike, they from their inmost reins panted after Thee, O God, the Fountain of life, not otherwise availing to allay or satisfy their hunger, but only by receiving Thy Body with all delight and spiritual eagerness.

O the truly burning faith of those, standing forth as a probable evidence of Thy sacred Presence! For they truly know their Lord *in the breaking of bread*,[2] whose heart within them so vehemently burneth, whilst Thou, O blessed Jesu, dost walk with them.

Far from me often is such affection and devotion, such vehement love and fervency.

2. Be thou favourable unto me, O Jesu, good, sweet and gracious Lord, and grant to me Thy poor and needy creature, sometimes at least, in this holy Communion to feel a little of the heartfelt passion of Thy love; that my Faith may become more strong, my Hope in Thy goodness may go forward, and that Charity once perfectly kindled within me, after the tasting of this Heavenly Manna, may never decay.

Thy mercy however is well able to grant me even the grace which I long for, and, in the day of thy good pleasure, to visit me most graciously with the Spirit of fervour. For although I burn not with so great desire as theirs who are so especially devoted unto Thee, yet notwithstanding, by Thy grace, I have a desire for this great and burning desire, praying and longing that I may have my part with all such Thy fervent lovers, and be numbered in their holy company.

➛ CHAPTER FIFTEEN ➛

THAT THE GRACE OF DEVOTION IS OBTAINED BY HUMILITY AND DENIAL OF OURSELVES

THE VOICE OF THE BELOVED

Thou oughtest earnestly to seek the grace of devotion, fervently to ask it, patiently and with confidence to wait for it, gratefully to receive it, humbly to keep it, diligently to work with it; and the term and manner of the heavenly visitation until it come unto thee, to commit unto God.

Thou oughtest especially to humble thyself, when thou feelest inwardly little or no devotion; but not to be too much cast down, nor to grieve inordinately. God often giveth in one short moment, that which He for a long time denied; He giveth sometimes in the end, that which in the beginning of thy prayer He deferred to give. If grace were always presently given, and were at hand even with a wish, weak man could not well bear it. Therefore the grace of devotion is to be waited for, with good hope and humble patience.

Nevertheless, to thyself, and to thine own sins impute it when this grace is not given thee, or when it is secretly taken away. It is sometimes but a small matter that hindereth and hideth grace; at least if anything can be called small, and not rather a weighty matter, which keepeth away so great a good. And if thou remove this, be it great or small, and perfectly overcome it, thou wilt have thy desire. For immediately, as soon as thou givest thyself to God from thy whole heart, and seekest neither this nor that, according to thine own liking or will, but settlest thyself wholly in Him, thou shalt find thyself united and at peace; for nothing can have so sweet a savour, nothing please so well, as the good pleasure of the Divine will.

Whosoever therefore, with a single heart lifteth up his intention to God, and emptieth himself of all inordinate love or disliking of any created thing, he shall be the most fit to receive grace, and meet for the gift of true devotion. For the Lord bestoweth His blessings there, where He findeth the vessels empty. And the more perfectly one forsaketh these low things, and the more he by contempt of himself dieth to himself, so much the more speedily grace cometh, the more plentifully doth it enter in, and the higher doth it lift up the free heart.

2. *Then shall he see, and flow together, and wonder, and his heart shall be enlarged*[1] within him, because the hand of the Lord is with him, and he hath put himself wholly into His hand, even forever and ever. *Behold thus shall the man be blessed*,[2] who seeketh God with his whole heart,[3] and *receiveth not his soul in vain.*[4] This man in receiving the holy Eucharist, obtaineth the great Grace of Divine Union; because it is not to his own devotion and comfort that he hath regard, but above all devotion and comfort to the honour and glory of God.

CHAPTER SIXTEEN

THAT WE OUGHT TO LAY OPEN OUR NECESSITIES TO CHRIST, AND TO CRAVE HIS GRACE

The Voice of the Disciple

O thou most sweet and loving Lord, whom now with all devotion, I desire to receive, Thou knowest mine infirmity and the necessity which I endure; in how great evils and sins I am lying; how often I am weighed down, tempted, disturbed, and defiled. For healing I come to Thee, for consolation and support I implore Thee. I speak to Thee who knowest all things, to whom all my inward thoughts are open, and who alone canst perfectly comfort and help me. Thou knowest what good things I stand in most need of, and how poor I am in virtues. Behold, I stand before Thee poor and naked, calling for grace, and imploring mercy.

2. Refresh Thy hungry beggar, inflame my coldness with the fire of Thy love, enlighten my blindness with the brightness of Thy presence. Turn for me all earthly things into bitterness, all things grievous and contrary into patience, all low and created things into contempt and oblivion. Lift up my heart to Thee in Heaven, and send me not away to wander over the earth.[1] Be Thou alone sweet unto me, from henceforth for evermore; for Thou alone art my meat and drink, my love and my joy, my sweetness and all my good.

O that with Thy Presence Thou wouldest wholly inflame, consume, and transform me into Thyself; that I might be made one Spirit with

Thee,[2] by the grace of inward Union, and by the meltings of ardent love! Suffer me not to go away from Thee hungry and dry, but deal mercifully with me, as oftentimes Thou hast dealt wonderfully with Thy Saints. What marvel is it if I should be wholly on fire from Thee, and of myself fail and come to nothing; since Thou art Fire alway burning and never failing, Love purifying the heart, and enlightening the understanding!

CHAPTER SEVENTEEN

OF FERVENT LOVE, AND VEHEMENT DESIRE TO RECEIVE CHRIST

THE VOICE OF THE DISCIPLE

With deep devotion and burning love, with all affection and fervour of heart, I desire to receive Thee, O Lord; as many Saints and devout persons have desired Thee, in receiving the Holy Communion, who in holiness of life were to Thee most pleasing, and who in devotion also were most fervent. O my God, Love eternal, my whole Good, Happiness which hath no bounds, I desire to receive Thee with the most vehement desire, and the most worthy reverence, that any of the Saints ever had, or was able to feel. And although I be unworthy to possess all those feelings of devotion, nevertheless I offer unto Thee the whole affection of my heart, as if I alone had all those most grateful and burning longings after Thee. Yea, and all that a holy soul can conceive and desire, I do, with the deepest reverence and most inward fervour, offer and present unto Thee. I desire to reserve nothing unto myself, but freely and most cheerfully to sacrifice unto Thee myself and all that is mine.

O Lord my God, my Creator and my Redeemer, I desire to receive Thee this day, with such affection, reverence, praise and honour, with such gratitude, worthiness and love, with such faith, hope and purity, as Thy most holy Mother, the glorious Virgin Mary, received and desired Thee with, when to the Angel who declared unto her glad tidings of the mystery of the Incarnation, she humbly and devoutly answered, *Behold the handmaid of the Lord, be it unto me according to Thy word.*[1] And as Thy blessed forerunner, the most excellent among the Saints, John Baptist, rejoicing in Thy Presence, leaped for joy of the Holy Ghost, whilst he was yet shut up in his mother's womb;[2] and afterwards seeing Jesus walking among men, humbled himself exceedingly, and said with devout affection, *The friend of the bridegroom that standeth and heareth him, rejoiceth greatly because of the bridegroom's voice*;[3] in like manner do I also wish to be on fire with great and holy desires, and to offer myself up to Thee from my whole heart. Wherefore also for myself, and for all such as are commended to me in prayer, I offer and present unto Thee the triumphant joys, the burning affections, the inward ecstacies, the supernatural illuminations and celestial visions of all devout hearts, with all the virtues and praises celebrated, and to be celebrated by all creatures in Heaven and in earth; that by all Thou mayest worthily be praised and glorified forever.

2. Receive, O Lord my God, my wishes and desires of giving Thee infinite praise, and blessing that hath no bounds, which according to the measure of Thine ineffable greatness, are unto Thee most justly due. These I render unto Thee, and long to render everyday and every moment. And with prayers and zeal I invite and beseech all heavenly spirits, and all Thy faithful servants, to render with me thanks and praises unto Thee. Let all people, nations, and languages praise Thee,[4] and magnify Thy holy and most sweet Name with highest exultation and burning devotion. And let all who reverently and devoutly celebrate Thy most high Sacrament, and receive It with full faith, be accounted worthy to find grace and mercy at Thy hands, and pray with humble supplication for me a sinner. And when they shall have attained to their desired devotion, and joyful Union with Thee, and shall have departed from Thy Holy Heavenly Table, well comforted and marvellously refreshed, may they vouchsafe to remember me that am poor and needy.

➔ CHAPTER EIGHTEEN ➔

THAT A MAN SHOULD NOT BE A CURIOUS SEARCHER INTO THE HOLY SACRAMENT, BUT AN HUMBLE FOLLOWER OF CHRIST, SUBMITTING HIS SENSE TO HOLY FAITH

THE VOICE OF THE BELOVED

Thou oughtest to beware of curious and unprofitable searching into this most profound Sacrament, if thou wilt not be plunged into the depths of doubt. *He that is a searcher of My Majesty, shall be overpowered by the glory thereof:*[1] God is able to work more than man can understand. A loving and humble enquiry after the Truth is allowable, if it be ever ready to be taught, and study to walk according to the sound precepts of the Fathers. It is a blessed simplicity which leaveth the difficult ways of questionings, and goeth forward in the plain and firm path of God's commandments.

Many have lost devotion, whilst they sought to search into things too high. Faith is required at thy hands, and a sincere life; not height of understanding, nor the depths of the mysteries of God. If thou dost not understand, nor grasp the things that are beneath thee, how shalt thou comprehend those which are above thee?[2] Submit thyself unto God, and humble thy sense to Faith; and the light of knowledge shall be given thee, in such degree as shall be profitable and necessary for thee.

2. Some are grievously tempted concerning faith and the Holy Sacrament; but this is not to be imputed to themselves, but rather to

the enemy. Be not thou anxious; dispute not with thine own thoughts, nor give any answer to doubts suggested by the devil; but trust the words of God, trust His Saints and Prophets, and the wicked enemy will flee from thee.

Oftentimes it is very profitable that the servant of God endure such things. For the devil tempteth not unbelievers and sinners, whom he hath already secure possession of; but the faithful and devout in various ways he tempteth and disquieteth. Go forward therefore with simple and undoubting faith, and with the reverence of a supplicant draw near to the Sacrament; and whatsoever thou art not able to understand, commit securely to Almighty God.

God deceiveth thee not; he is deceived that trusteth too much to himself. God walketh with the simple,[3] revealeth Himself to the humble, giveth understanding to the little ones, openeth the sense to pure minds, and hideth grace from the curious and proud. Human reason is feeble and may be deceived, but true Faith cannot be deceived.

All reason and natural searching ought to follow Faith, not to go before it, nor to break in upon it. For Faith and Love here specially have the preeminence, and work in hidden ways, in this most holy, most supremely excellent Sacrament. God, who is eternal, and incomprehensible, and of infinite power, doeth things great and unsearchable in Heaven and in earth, and there is no tracing out of His marvellous works. If the works of God were such that they might be easily comprehended by human reason, they could not be justly called marvellous or unspeakable.

ENDNOTES

THE FIRST BOOK

CHAPTER I

[1] S. John viii. 12.
[2] Rev. ii. 17.
[3] Rom. viii. 9.
[4] 1 Cor. xiii. 2.
[5] Eccles. i. 2.
[6] Eccles. i. 8.

CHAPTER II

[1] Eccles. i. 13; Arist. *Metaphys.* I. 1.
[2] S. Augustine, *Confess.* V. 4.
[3] 1 Cor. xiii. 2.
[4] Rom. xii. 16.
[5] Gen. viii. 21.

CHAPTER III

[1] Psalm xciv. 12.
[2] Eccles. iii. 9–11.
[3] Psalm cxv. 5; S. Mark viii. 18.
[4] S. John vii. 23 (Vulgate).
[5] S. Matt. xi. 25; S. Luke x. 21.
[6] S. Matt. xxv.
[7] Eccles. ii. 11.
[8] Tit. i. 10.
[9] Rom. i. 21.
[10] S. Matt. xviii. 4 and xxiii. 11.
[11] Phil. iii. 8.

CHAPTER IV

[1] 1 John iv. 1.
[2] Gen. viii. 21.

[3] James iii. 2.
[4] Prov. xix. 2.
[5] Prov. xvii. 9.
[6] Prov. xii. 15.
[7] Prov. xv. 33.
[8] Eccles. i. 16.

CHAPTER V

[1] Rom. xv. 4.
[2] 1 Cor. ii. 4.
[3] Psalm cxvii. 2; S. Luke xxi. 33.
[4] Rom. ii. 11; x. 12; Col. iii. 11.
[5] Prov. i. 6; Eccles. xii. 9; Ecclus. xxxii. 8–9.

CHAPTER VI

[1] Psalm xxxvii. 11.

CHAPTER VII

[1] Jer. xvii. 5.
[2] Psalm xxxi. 1.
[3] Jer. ix. 23.
[4] 1 Peter v. 5.
[5] Exodus iii. 11.
[6] Job ix. 20.

CHAPTER VIII

[1] Ecclus. viii. 22.
[2] Prov. v. 10.

CHAPTER X

[1] S. Matt. iv. 1; xiv. 23; S. John vi. 15.
[2] S. Matt. vii. 1; Rom. ii. 1.
[3] S. Matt. xxvi. 41.
[4] Psalm cxli. 3.
[5] Acts i. 14; Rom. xv. 5, 6.

CHAPTER XI

[1] S. Matt. iii 10.

CHAPTER XII

[1] S. Luke ii. 14 (Vulgate).
[2] Phil. i. 23 (Vulgate).

CHAPTER XIII

[1] Job vii. 1 (Vulgate).
[2] 1 Peter v. 8.
[3] James i. 13, 14.
[4] Gen. iii.
[5] James i. 6.
[6] Ovid, lib. 1. de Remed. Am. 91.
[7] 1 Cor. x. 13 (Vulgate).
[8] 1 Peter v 6.

CHAPTER XIV

[1] S Matt. vii. 1; Rom. xv. 1.
[2] Eccles. iii. 16.
[3] S. Matt. xii. 25; S. Luke xii. 51.
[4] Jer. xiii. 23.

CHAPTER XV

[1] S. Matt. xviii. 8.
[2] 1 Cor. xiii. 3; S. Luke vii 47.
[3] Phil. ii. 17.
[4] Phil. ii. 21; 1 Cor. xiii. 5.
[5] Psalm xvii. 15; xxiv. 6.

CHAPTER XVI

[1] S. Matt. vi. 13; S. Luke xi. 4.
[2] S. Matt. vi. 10.
[3] 1 Thess. v. 14; Gal. vi. 1.
[4] Gal. vi. 2.
[5] 1 Thess. v. 14; 1 Cor. xii. 25.

CHAPTER XVII

[1] Gal. vi. 1.
[2] S. Luke xvi. 10.
[3] 1 Peter ii. 11.
[4] 1 Cor. iv. 10.
[5] Eccles. i. 17, 18; Ecclus. i. 18.
[6] S. Matt. xx. 26.

CHAPTER XVIII

[1] Heb. xi.
[2] 2 Cor. xi. 26, 27.
[3] S. John xii. 25.
[4] S. Matt. vii. 14.

[5] S. Matt. xix. 29.
[6] 2 Cor. vi. 10.
[7] James iv. 4.
[8] Wisd. v.

CHAPTER XIX

[1] S. Matt. v. 48.
[2] Psalm xxxiii, 13; Heb. iv. 12, 13.
[3] Psalm xv. 2.
[4] Prov. xvi. 9.
[5] Eccles. vii. 20.
[6] Deut. iv.
[7] Job xxxviii. 3.
[8] Rom. viii. 18.
[9] S. Luke xii. 43, 44; S. Matt. xxiv. 46, 47.

CHAPTER XX

[1] Eccles. iii. 1.
[2] Heb. xi. 38.
[3] Seneca, Ep. vii.
[4] S. Matt. v. 1.
[5] Eccles. iii. 7.
[6] Acts xxiii. 1.
[7] Psalm iv. 5 (Vulgate).
[8] S. Matt. vi. 6.
[9] Psalm vi. 6.
[10] 1 John ii. 17.
[11] Prov. xiv. 13.
[12] Prov. xxiii. 31, 32.
[13] Eccles. i. 10.
[14] Eccles. iii. 11.
[15] Psalm cxxi. 1.
[16] S. Matt. vi. 6.

CHAPTER XXI

[1] Prov, xix, 23.
[2] Gal. i. 10.
[3] Psalm lxxvi. 5.
[4] Judges ii. 4; xx. 26; 2 Kings xiii. (perhaps 2 Sam. xii. 17).
[5] Eccles. vii. 1, 2.
[6] S. Matt. xxv. 41.
[7] Psalm lxxx. 5.

CHAPTER XXII

[1] Eccles. vi. 2.
[2] S. Luke xii. 19.

[3] Prov. xix. 1.
[4] Job xiv. 1; Eccles. ii. 17.
[5] Psalm xxv. 17.
[6] Rom. viii. 22.
[7] Rom. viii. 5.
[8] 1 Peter i. 4; Heb. xi. 26.
[9] Rom. xiii. 11; Heb. x. 35.
[10] Psalm xlvi. 12.
[11] Rom. vii. 24; Gen. iii. 17.
[12] Psalm lvii. 1.
[13] 2 Cor. v. 4.
[14] Gen. vi. 5; viii. 21.
[15] 2 Maccab. ix. 11.
[16] Hebrews v. 12.

CHAPTER XXIII

[1] Job ix. 25, 26; xiv. 1, 2; S. Luke xii. 20; Heb. ix. 27.
[2] S. Matt. xxv. 13.
[3] S. Luke xii. 37.
[4] Wisd. iv. 16.
[5] S. Matt. xxiv. 44; xxv. 10.
[6] Eccles. vii. 1.
[7] Heb. ix. 27.
[8] S. Luke xxi. 36.
[9] S. Matt. xxiv. 44; S. Luke xii. 40.
[10] Ecclus. xli. 1.
[11] Isaiah xxx. 5; xxxi. 1; Jer. xvii. 5; xlviii. 7; S. Matt. vi. 20.
[12] 2 Cor. vi. 2.
[13] Rom. vi. 8.
[14] S. Luke xiv. 33.
[15] 1 Cor. ix. 27.
[16] S. Luke xii. 20.
[17] Job xiv. 2.
[18] S. Matt, vi. 20; S. Luke xii. 33; Gal. vi. 8.
[19] S. Luke xvi. 9; Heb. xi.
[20] 1 Pet. ii. 11.
[21] Heb. xiii. 14.

CHAPTER XXIV

[1] Heb. x. 31.
[2] Job ix. 2.
[3] S. Luke xvi. 9.
[4] 2 Cor. vi. 4.
[5] James i. 4.
[6] S. Luke xxiii. 34; Acts vii. 60.

[7] S. Mark ix. 43–49.
[8] Wisd. v. 1.
[9] 1 Cor, iv. 10.
[10] Psalm cvii. 42.
[11] 2 Cor. iv. 17.
[12] Isaiah xxix. 19.
[13] S. Luke xii. 20.
[14] Eccles. i. 2.
[15] Rom. viii. 39.

CHAPTER XXV

[1] 2 Tim. iv. 5.
[2] S. Matt. v. 48.
[3] Rev. xxi. 4; xxii. 3.
[4] Ecclus. ii. 27; Rev. xxi. 4; xxii. 3.
[5] S. Matt. xxv. 23.
[6] Rom. v. 5.
[7] Probably the Author himself.
[8] Rom. xii. 2.
[9] Psalm xxxvii. 3.
[10] S. Matt. vii. 3.
[11] Eph. v. (perhaps iv. 1, 16); 1 Cor. xii. 18; Eccles. iii. 1, Psalm cxxxiii.
[12] Gal. ii. 20; vi. 14.
[13] Rom. xi. 36; 1 Cor. viii. 6; xii. 6; xv. 28.
[14] Ecclus. vii. 36.
[15] Rev. iii. 16.
[16] Ecclus. xix. 1.

THE SECOND BOOK

CHAPTER I

[1] S. Luke xvii, 21.
[2] Joel ii. 12.
[3] Rom. xiv. 17.
[4] Psalm xlv. 13.
[5] S. John xiv. 25.
[6] S. John xii. 34.
[7] Jer. xvii. 5.
[8] 1 Peter v. 7.
[9] Heb. xiii. 14.
[10] Heb. xi. 13.
[11] Phil. iii. 20.
[12] Wisd. v. 9.
[13] Wisd. v. 16.

[14] S. Matt. xii. 24; xvi. 21; S. John xv. 20.
[15] 2 Tim. ii. 5.
[16] S. Bernard, Serm. ad div. 18.
[17] Isaiah liv. 13.
[18] Rom. viii. 28.

CHAPTER II

[1] Rom. viii. 31; 1 Cor. iv. 3.
[2] Psalm xxviii. 7.
[3] James iii. (perhaps iv. 6); Job v. 11.
[4] S. Matt. xi. 25.

CHAPTER III

[1] 1 Cor. xiii. 5.
[2] S. Matt. vii. 3.
[3] Acts i. 7 (perhaps xxii. 3); S. John xxi. 22.
[4] Gal. vi. 2; 1 Cor. xiii. 7.

CHAPTER IV

[1] Rom. i. 20.
[2] Prov. iii. 3, 4; Psalm cxix. 100.

CHAPTER V

[1] Jer. xvii. 5.
[2] Psalm cxli. 4.
[3] S. Matt. vii. 5.
[4] S. Matt. xvi. 26.
[5] 1 Cor. iv. 3; Gal. i. 10.
[6] Eccles. i. 14.

CHAPTER VI

[1] 1 Cor. i. 31.
[2] Wisd. xvii. 11.
[3] Isaiah xlviii. 22.
[4] Micah iii. 11; S. Luke xii. 19.
[5] Rom. viii. (perhaps v. 3); Gal. vi. 14.
[6] S. John v. 44.
[7] 2 Cor. iii. 5.
[8] 1 Sam. xvi. 7.
[9] 2 Cor. x. 18.

CHAPTER VII

[1] Psalm cxix. 1, 2.
[2] Deut. vi. 5; S. Matt. xxii. 37; Cant. ii. 16.

[3] S. Matt. xi. 7.
[4] Isaiah xl. 6.

CHAPTER VIII

[1] S. John xi. 28.
[2] S. Matt. xvi. 26
[3] Rom. viii. 35.
[4] S. Matt. xiii. 44.
[5] S. Luke xii. 21.
[6] Prov. iii. 17.
[7] Gal. vi. 14.
[8] S. Matt. v. 44; S. Luke vi. 27, 28.
[9] Psalm xxxiv. 9.
[10] S. Matt. viii. 26.

CHAPTER IX

[1] Phil. ii. 12.
[2] *Lives of the Saints,* Aug. 10.
[3] Psalm xxx. 6–11.
[4] S. John. iii. 8.
[5] Job vii. 18.
[6] S. Luke ix. 23.
[7] 2 Cor. xii. 2.
[8] Rev. ii. 7.
[9] 1 Peter v. 8.

CHAPTER X

[1] Job v. 7.
[2] S. Luke xiv. 27.
[3] Ecclus. i. 5.
[4] S. Matt. xxii. 21.
[5] S. Luke xiv. 10.

CHAPTER XI

[1] S. Luke ix. 14; xxii. 41, 42.
[2] Phil. ii. 21.
[3] Job i. 9.
[4] Prov. xxxi. 10 (Vulgate).
[5] Cant. viii. 7.
[6] S. Matt. xvi. 24
[7] S. Luke xvii. 10.
[8] Psalm xxv. 16.

CHAPTER XII

[1] S. Matt. xvi. 24.
[2] S. Matt. xxv. 41.
[3] Psalm cxii. 7.
[4] S. Matt. xxiv. 30.
[5] S. Luke xiv. 27.
[6] S. John xix. 17.
[7] Gal. ii. 20; Rom. vi. 8.
[8] 2 Cor. i. 5.
[9] S. Luke xxiv. 26.
[10] Job vii. 1.
[11] 2 Cor. iv. 16.
[12] 2 Cor. iv. 16; xi. 23–30.
[13] 2 Cor. iii. 5.
[14] S. Matt. xx. 23; S. John xviii. 11.
[15] Rom. viii. 18; cp. S. Bernard, Ann. B. V. M. Serm. i.
[16] Rom. v. 3; Gal. vi. 14.
[17] 2 Cor. xii. 4.
[18] Acts ix. 16.
[19] Acts v. 41.
[20] Psalm xliv. 22.
[21] S. Luke ix. 23.
[22] Acts xiv. 22.

THE THIRD BOOK

CHAPTER I

[1] Psalm lxxxv. 8.
[2] 1 Sam. ii. 9.
[3] S. Matt. xiii. 16, 17.
[4] Psalm lxxxv. 8.
[5] Psalm xxxv. 3.

CHAPTER II

[1] 1 Sam. iii. 9.
[2] Psalm cxix. 125.
[3] Deut. xxxii. 2.
[4] Exod. xx. 19.
[5] 1 Cor. iii. 6.
[6] S. John vi. 68.

CHAPTER III

[1] S. John vi. 63.
[2] Psalm xciv. 12, 13.

[3] Heb. i. 1.
[4] Isaiah xxiii. 4.
[5] Rom. i. 16; S. Matt. xxiv. 35.
[6] Rev. ii. 23; S. Matt. v. 6; xxv. 21.
[7] S. John xii. 48.
[8] Gen. xviii. 27; 1 Sam. xviii. 18, 23.
[9] Psalm xxv. 6.
[10] Psalm lxix. 17.
[11] Psalm cxliii. 6.
[12] Psalm cxliii. 10.

CHAPTER IV

[1] Gen. xvii. 1; Wisd. i. 1.
[2] S. John viii. 32.
[3] S. John viii. 36.
[4] 1 Cor. iv. 7.
[5] Ecclus. iii. 21–23; 2 Cor. ii. 17.
[6] Isaiah xxix. 13.
[7] Psalm xxv. 5.
[8] Psalm i. 2.

CHAPTER V

[1] 2 Cor. i. 3.
[2] Psalm xxxii. 7; lix. 16.
[3] S. Matt. xi. 30.
[4] 1 John iv. 7.
[5] Rom. viii. 19.
[6] 1 Cor. xiii. 5.
[7] 1 Cor. x. 33; Phil. ii. 21.
[8] Rom. viii. 35.

CHAPTER VI

[1] Phil. iv 11–13.
[2] S. Matt. iv. 10.
[3] S. Matt. iv 10; xvi. 23.
[4] Psalm xxvii. 1.
[5] Psalm xix. 15; xxvii. 3.
[6] 1 Tim. vi. 12.

CHAPTER VII

[1] Jer. x. 23; Rom. ix. 16.
[2] Obadiah 5.
[3] Psalm xci. 4.
[4] Psalm xvi. 2; xvli. 10.

[5] 1 Thess. v. 6.
[6] Job vii.
[7] Psalm lxxxiv. 10.

CHAPTER VIII

[1] Gen. xviii. 27.
[2] S. John xii. 25.
[3] S. Matt. v. 45.

CHAPTER IX

[1] Ecclus. i. 5.
[2] S. John iv. 14.
[3] S. John i. 16.
[4] 1 Cor. i. 29.
[5] 1 Cor. iv. 7.
[6] S. Matt. xix. 17; S. Luke xviii. 19.

CHAPTER X

[1] Psalm xxxi. 19.
[2] Gen. i. 27; Psalm cxix. 73; S. Luke xv.
[3] Psalm cxvi. 12.
[4] Judges xvi. 15.
[5] 1 Cor. iv. 7.
[6] Psalm xci. 11; Heb. i. 14.
[7] S. Matt. xix. 29.
[8] S. Matt. vii. 14.
[9] S. Matt. xi. 30; 1 John v. 3.

CHAPTER XI

[1] Psalm cviii. 1; S. Matt. vi. 10.
[2] Phil. ii. 21.
[3] Phil. ii. 12.
[4] Rom. viii. 1–13; 2 Cor. iv. 10; x. 3.
[5] 1 Cor. ix. 27.

CHAPTER XII

[1] Heb. x. 36.
[2] Job vii. 1.
[3] James i. 2.
[4] Psalm lxviii. 2.
[5] Ecclus. xviii. 30.
[6] Psalm xxxvii. 4.

CHAPTER XIII

[7] S. Matt. xvi. 24.
[8] S. Luke ii. 7; S. John xiii. 14.
[9] Isaiah li. 23.

CHAPTER XIV

[1] Job xv. 15.
[2] Job iv. 18.
[3] Rev. viii. 10.
[4] Psalm lxxviii. 25.
[5] S. Luke xv. 16.
[6] Isaiah xlv. 9; Rom. ix. 20.
[7] Isaiah xxix. 16; Ecclus. xxiii, 4, 5.
[8] Psalm cxvii. 2.

CHAPTER XV

[1] James iii. (perhaps iv. 15).
[2] Wisd. ix. 10.
[3] Psalm iv. 8 (Vulgate).

CHAPTER XVI

[1] S. Matt. xvi. 26.
[2] Psalm lxxvii. 1, 2.
[3] Wisd. ii. 23.
[4] Phil. iii. 20.
[5] Psalm ciii. 9.

CHAPTER XVII

[1] S. Matt. vi. 30; S. John vi. 20.
[2] 1 Peter v. 7.
[3] Job ii. 10.
[4] Psalm xxiii. 4.
[5] Rev, iii. 5.

CHAPTER XVIII

[1] S. John iii. 13.
[2] Isaiah liii. 4.
[3] S. Luke ii. 7.
[4] S. John v. 30.
[5] S. Matt. vii. 14.
[6] S. John xii. 46.

CHAPTER XIX

[1] Heb. xii. 4.
[2] Heb. xi. 37.
[3] 2 Tim. ii. 3–5.

CHAPTER XX

[1] Psalm xxxii. 5.
[2] Psalm xxv. 18.
[3] Psalm lxix, 14.
[4] 1 John ii. 16.
[5] Job xxx. 7.

CHAPTER XXI

[1] Rom. viii. 19–22.
[2] S. Augustine, Confess, i. 1.
[3] Psalm lv. 6.
[4] Heb. i. 3.
[5] Psalm lxxxvi. 8.

CHAPTER XXII

[1] Psalm csix.
[2] Gen. xxxii. 10.
[3] 1 Cor. i. 27, 28.
[4] Psalm xlv. 16.
[5] 1 Thess. ii. 10.
[6] Acts v. 41.

CHAPTER XXIII

[1] S. Matt. xxvi. 39; S. John v. 30; vi. 38.
[2] 1 Cor. x. 24.
[3] S. Luke xiv. 10.
[4] S. Matt. vi. 10.
[5] S. Matt. v. 48.
[6] Psalm lxxi. 12.
[7] Isaiah xlv. 2, 3.
[8] Psalm cxxii. 7 (Vulgate).
[9] S. Matt. viii. 26.
[10] Psalm xliii. 3.
[11] Gen. i. 2.

CHAPTER XXIV

[1] Ecclus. iii. 23; 1 Tim. v. 13.
[2] S. John xxi. 22.

[3] Gal. vi. 4, 5.
[4] S. Bernard, from Lucan, *Phars.* i. 135.

CHAPTER XXV

[1] S. John xiv. 27.

CHAPTER XXVI

[1] Gen. iii. 17; Rom. vii. 23, 24.
[2] Rom. xii. 21.

CHAPTER XXVII

[1] S. Matt. vi. 22.
[2] Exodus xviii. 18; Mic, iv. 9.
[3] Isaiah xli. 13.
[4] Psalm li. 12.
[5] Eph. iii. 16.
[6] S. Matt. vi. 34.
[7] Eccles. i. 14; ii. 17, 26.
[8] Wisd. ix. 14.
[9] Eph. iv. 14.

CHAPTER XXVIII

[1] 1 Cor. iv. 13.
[2] Amos v. 13.
[3] S. John xvi. 33.

CHAPTER XXIX

[4] Job i, 21; Psalm cxiii. 2.
[5] S. John xii. 27.
[6] Psalm xl. 13.
[7] S. Matt. vi. 10.
[8] Psalm lxxvii. 10 (Vulgate).

CHAPTER XXX

[1] Nahum i. 7.
[2] S. Matt, xi.
[3] S. Matt. xxiii. 3.
[4] S. Matt. viii. 7.
[5] S. Matt. vi. 34.
[6] S. John xiv. 27.
[7] Psalm xci. 2.
[8] James i. 17.
[9] S. John xv. 9.
[10] S. Luke viii. 15.

CHAPTER XXXI

[1] Psalm lv. 6.
[2] S. Matt. vi. 22.
[3] Gen. vi. 12; vii. 21.
[4] S. Matt. vii. 16.

CHAPTER XXXII

[1] S. Matt. xvi. 24; xix. 21.
[2] Rev. iii. 18.
[3] S. Matt. xiii. 46.

CHAPTER XXXIII

[1] Job xiv. 2.
[2] S. Matt. vi. 22.
[3] S. John xii. 9.
[4] S. Matt. vi. 22.

CHAPTER XXXIV

[1] 1 Cor. i. 26; Rom. viii. 5; 1 John ii. 16.
[2] Psalm cxliv. 6.
[3] Rom. vii.
[4] Psalm lxxxix. 9.
[5] Psalm lxviii. 30.
[6] Psalm xxxi. 14.

CHAPTER XXXV

[1] Job vii. 1.
[2] 2 Cor. vi. 7.
[3] Rev. ii. 17.
[4] Rom. viii. 18.
[5] Psalm xxvii. 14.
[6] Psalm xci. 15.

CHAPTER XXXVI

[1] 1 Cor. ix. 22.
[2] 1 Cor. iv. 3.
[3] Col. i. 29.
[4] Acts xxvi.; Phil. i. 14.
[5] Isaiah ii. 12.
[6] 1 Mac. ii, 62, 63.
[7] Rom. ii. 3; 1 Cor. xi. 32.
[8] Heb. xii. 1, 2.
[9] S. Matt. xvi. 27; Rom. ii. 6.

CHAPTER XXXVII

[1] S. Matt. xvi. 24.
[2] S. Matt. xvi. 24.
[3] Psalm cxxxix. 11 (Vulgate).

CHAPTER XXXVIII

[1] Exod. xxxiii. 9.
[2] S. Matt. vi. 6.
[3] Josh. ix. 14.

CHAPTER XXXIX

[1] 1 Pet. v. 8.
[2] S. Matt. xxii. 41.

CHAPTER XL

[1] Psalm viii. 4.
[2] Psalm cii. 12.
[3] Dan. iv. 16, 23, 32.
[4] Hab. iii. 18.
[5] Psalm cxiii. 3; cxv. 1.
[6] 2 Cor. xii. 5.
[7] S. John v. 44.

CHAPTER XLII

[1] 1 Pet. v. 5.

CHAPTER XLIII

[1] 1 Cor. iv. 20.
[2] Psalm xciv. 10.
[3] Zeph. i. 12; 1 Cor. iv. 5.
[4] This may be a personal reference: cp. Bk. I. xxv. 2. But it would be applicable to many of the saints, e.g., S. Francis of Assisi.

CHAPTER XLIV

[1] Gal. vi. 14.

CHAPTER XLV

[1] Psalm lx. 11.
[2] Prov. x. 29.
[3] S. Agatha. See Lives of the Saints, Feb. 5.
[4] Rom. iii. 4.
[5] Mic. vii. 6.
[6] S. Matt. xxiv. 23.

[7] Prov. xxv. 9.
[8] Isaiah xxvi. 3.

CHAPTER XLVI

[1] Psalm xxxvii. 3.
[2] 1 Pet. ii. 19–20.
[3] 1 Cor. iii. 3.
[4] S. Matt. x. 30; S. Luke xii. 7.
[5] Psalm vii. 8.
[6] S. Luke ii. 35.
[7] Prov. xii. 13.
[8] Psalm vii. 9, Rev. ii. 23.
[9] Psalm vii. 12.
[10] 1 Cor. iv. 4.
[11] Psalm cxliii. 2.

CHAPTER XLVII

[1] S. Matt. xx. 7.
[2] Zech. xiv. 7.
[3] Rom. vii. 24.
[4] Psalm cxx. 5.
[5] Wisd. iii. 1–9; v. 16.

CHAPTER XLVIII

[1] Rev. xxi. 2.
[2] 1 Cor. xiii. 12.
[3] From the Antiphon at Lauds in the Parvum Officium B.V.M.
[4] Job vii.
[5] Rom. vii. 24.
[6] Psalm lxxi. 16.
[7] Rom. vii. 24; viii. 23.
[8] Psalm lxxi. 12.
[9] Psalm cxliv. 6.
[10] S. Matt. vi.
[11] S. Matt. xix. 12.

CHAPTER XLIX

[1] Rom. viii. 21.
[2] Job vii. 1.
[3] Exod. iii. 14; S. John viii. 58.
[4] S. Luke xxii. 18.
[5] Josh. i. 7.
[6] Eph. iv. 24.
[7] 1 Sam. x. 6.

[8] Isaiah lxiii. 3.
[9] Phil. i. 20.

CHAPTER L

[1] 1 Cor. iv. 7.
[2] Psalm lxxxviii. 15.
[3] Psalm cxix. 32.
[4] Job xxix. 3.
[5] Psalm xvii. 8.
[6] Job v. 6 (Vulgate).
[7] Psalm cxix. 71.
[8] Psalm lxix. 7.
[9] Tob. xiii. 2; Psalm xviii. 16.
[10] Isaiah xi. 3.
[11] S. Bonaventura, Leg. S. Francisci, cap. 6.

CHAPTER LI

[1] Psalm cxix. 32; 1 Kings iv. 29; Isaiah lx. 5.
[2] Rom. viii. 18.

CHAPTER LII

[1] Rom. ix. 23.
[2] Job ix. 2, 3.
[3] Psalm li.
[4] Job x. 21.
[5] Psalm li. 17.
[6] S. Luke vii. 38.
[7] Psalm li. 17.

CHAPTER LIII

[1] S. Matt. xix. 29.
[2] 1 S. Peter ii. 11.
[3] S. Matt. iii. 10.
[4] Psalm cxix. 45.

CHAPTER LIV

[1] 1 S. Peter ii. 13.
[2] 1 Cor. x. 33.
[3] Acts v. 41.
[4] 2 Cor. iv. 18.
[5] S. Matt. vi. 20.
[6] Acts xx. 35.
[7] 1 Cor. xii. 31.

CHAPTER LV

[1] Gen. i. 26.
[2] Rom. vii. 23.
[3] Gen. viii. 21.
[4] Rom. vii. 22.
[5] Rom. vii. 18.
[6] S. John xv. 5.
[7] Phil. iv. 13.
[8] 1 Cor. xiii. 13.
[9] 2 Cor. xii. 9.
[10] Psalm xxiii. 4.
[11] S. John xv. 6.
[12] Collect for Seventeenth Sunday after Trinity.

CHAPTER LVI

[1] S. John xiv. 6.
[2] S. John viii. 31–32.
[3] S. Matt. xix. 17.
[4] S. Matt. xix. 21.
[5] S. Luke ix. 23.
[6] S. John xii. 25.
[7] S. Luke xiv. 27.
[8] S. Matt. x. 24; S. Luke vi. 40.
[9] S. John xiii. 17.
[10] S. John xiv. 21.
[11] Rev. iii. 21.
[12] An hexameter from Thomas à Kempis' *Cantica spiritualia:Vere vita boni monachi Crux est, sed dux Paradisi.*
[13] 2 Esdras iv. 20.

CHAPTER LVII

[1] Isaiah xlix.
[2] Gen. iii.
[3] Psalm xix. 10; cxix. 103.

CHAPTER LVIII

[1] Psalm cxix. 137.
[2] Psalm xix. 9.
[3] 2 Tim. ii. 14.
[4] Psalm xxi. 4.
[5] Rom. viii. 29.
[6] S. John xv. 16.
[7] Rom. viii. 29, 30.

[8] S. James ii. 1–5.
[9] Wisdom vi. 7.
[10] Ecclus. iii. 21.
[11] Rev. iv. 10.
[12] 1 John iii. 1 (Vulgate).
[13] Isaiah lx. 22.
[14] Isaiah lxv. 20.
[15] S. Matt. xviii. 3.
[16] S. Matt. vii. 14.
[17] S. Luke vi. 24.
[18] S. Matt. v. 3.
[19] 2 John 4.

CHAPTER LIX

[1] Phil. ii. 21.
[2] Psalm li. 2.
[3] Isaiah ix. 2.

THE FOURTH BOOK

INTRODUCTION

[1] S. Matt. xi. 28.
[2] S. John vi. 51.
[3] S. Matt. xxvi. 26.
[4] 1 Cor. xi. 24.
[5] S. John vi. 56, 63.

CHAPTER I

[1] S. Matt. xi. 28.
[2] 1 Kings viii. 27.
[3] Gen. vi. 3.
[4] Exod. xxv. 10–16.
[5] 1 Kings vi. 38.
[6] 2 Kings viii.
[7] 2 Sam. vi. 14; Ecclus. xlvii. 8, 9.
[8] 2 Cor. i. 30.

CHAPTER II

[1] S. Luke i. 43.
[2] Psalm lxxviii. 25; S. John vi. 33.
[3] Gen. i.; Psalm cxlviii. 5.
[4] Psalm xvi. 2.

CHAPTER III

[1] Psalm lxviii. 10.
[2] Psalm lxxxvi. 4.
[3] S. Luke xix. 9.
[4] S. Matt. xv. 32; S. Mark viii. 8.
[5] Gen. viii. 21.
[6] Psalm cxlvii. 5.

CHAPTER IV

[1] Psalm xxi. 3.
[2] Psalm cvi. 4.
[3] Isaiah xii. 3; Lev. vi. 13.
[4] S. Matt. xi. 28.
[5] Gen. ill. 19.

CHAPTER V

[1] S. Matt. xviii. 10.
[2] Psalm lxxviii. 25.
[3] Gen. i.; Psalm xlix. 7; Rom. ix. 20.
[4] 1 Tim iv. 16.
[5] Phil. iii. 20.
[6] Heb. v. 3.
[7] Psalm cvi. 23.

CHAPTER VII

[1] Ezek. xviii. 22, 23.

CHAPTER VIII

[1] Isaiah liii. 5; Heb. ix. 28.
[2] Prov. xxiii. 26.
[3] S. Luke xiv. 33.

CHAPTER IX

[1] Psalm xxiv. 1.
[2] Psalm xxxii. 5.

CHAPTER X

[1] Job i. 6.
[2] Prov. xiii. 1.
[3] S. Matt. v. 24.
[4] 1 Cor. xi. 23–26.

CHAPTER XI

[1] S. Luke vii. 38.
[2] Cant. ii. 17.
[3] 1 Cor. xiii. 10.
[4] 2 Cor. iii. 18.
[5] S. John i. 14.
[6] 1 John i. 1.
[7] Heb. x. 35, 36; xi. 39, 40.
[8] S. John vi. 51.
[9] Psalm cxix. 105.
[10] Psalm xxiii. 5; Heb. ix. 2–4; xiii. 10.
[11] Heb. vi. 19.
[12] S. Luke xiv. 16.
[13] S. John vi. 53–56.
[14] Psalm xxiii, 5; Wisd. xvi. 20, 21.
[15] Levit. xix. 2; xx. 26; 1 Peter i. 16.

CHAPTER XII

[1] Psalm xxiv. 4; S. Matt. v. 8.
[2] S. Mark xiv. 14, 15; S. Luke xxii. 11, 12.
[3] 1 Cor. v. 7.
[4] Exod. xxiv. 18.
[5] Ps. cii. 8.
[6] S. Luke xi. 9.
[7] Prov. x. 19.

CHAPTER XIII

[1] Cant. viii. 1.
[2] Exod. xxxiii, 11; Cant. viii. 12.
[3] S. John xv. 4.
[4] Cant. v. 10.
[5] Isaiah xlv. 15.
[6] Prov. iii. 34.
[7] Wisd. xii. 1.
[8] S. Thomas Aq. on the Magnificat.
[9] Deut. iv. 7.
[10] Deut. iv. 8.
[11] Psalm cxvi. 12.

CHAPTER XIV

[1] Psalm xxxi. 19.
[2] S. Luke xxiv. 32–35.

CHAPTER XV

[1] Isaiah lx. 5.
[2] Psalm cxxviii. 4.
[3] Psalm cxix. 2.
[4] Psalm xxiv. 4.

CHAPTER XVI

[1] Gen. iv. 12–14.
[2] 1 Cor. vi. 17.

CHAPTER XVII

[1] S. Luke i. 38.
[2] S. Luke i. 44.
[3] S. John iii. 29.
[4] Psalm cxvii.

CHAPTER XVIII

[1] Prov. xxv. 27.
[2] S. John iii.
[3] Psalm xix. 7; cxix. 130; S. Matt. xi. 25.

INDEX OF SCRIPTURAL QUOTATIONS

The references given in this index are only to those passages which appear in the original of the Imitation, to have been intended as more or less *direct quotations* from the Vulgate. These have been translated literally, and therefore do not always exactly correspond to the English of the Authorized Version. They have been printed in the text in italics. The other references given at the foot of the pages are to texts which are alluded to rather than quoted, or which are parallel in meaning.

REFERENCES TO OTHER WRITINGS

INDEX

NOTE: *When the number of the section is not given the reference is either to the* first *section, or to the whole chapter.*

D

I

J

K

T

Y

Z

SUGGESTED READING

BIBLES, NELSON. *My Time with God: New Century Version.* Nashville, TN: Nelson Bibles, 2003.

BROTHER LAWRENCE. *Practice of the Presence of God.* Grand Rapids, MI: Revell, Fleming H. Company, 1989.

DE SALES, FRANCIS. *Introduction to the Devout Life.* Preface. Edward Cardinal Egan. New York: Knopf Publishing Group, 2002.

DYER, WAYNE W. *There's a Spiritual Solution to Every Problem.* New York: HarperCollins Publishers, 2001.

EASWARAN, EKNATH. *Seeing with the Eyes of Love: The Imitation of Christ.* Tomales, CA: Nilgiri Press, 1996.

FINLEY, MITCH. *Season of Promises: Praying through Advent with Julian of Norwich, Thomas à Kempis, Caryll Houselander, Thomas Merton, Brother Lawrence, and Max Picard.* Totowa, NJ: Catholic Book Publishing Company, 1995.

HADDON, CELIA. *One Hundred Lamps for the Soul.* London: Hodder & Stoughton, Ltd., 2003.

JOHNSON, LUKE TIMOTHY. *The Real Jesus.* New York: HarperCollins Publishers, 1997.

JONES, CHESLYN, EDWARD S. YARNOLD, AND GEOFFREY WAINWRIGHT, EDS. *The Study of Spirituality.* Oxford: Oxford University Press, 1986.

KIRVAN, JOHN. *Fear Not the Night: Based on the Classic Spirituality of John of the Cross.* Notre Dame, IN: Ave Maria Press, 1997.

KIRVAN, JOHN J. *True Serenity: Based on Thomas à Kempis' The Imitation of Christ.* Notre Dame, IN: Ave Maria Press, 1995.

KOZLOWSKI, JOSEPH PAUL. *Spiritual Direction and Spiritual Directors.* Sugarland, TX: Queenship Publishing Company, 1998.

LANE, TONY. *Exploring Christian Thought.* Nashville, TN: Thomas Nelson, 1996.

LEECH, KENNETH. *True Prayer: An Invitation to Christian Spirituality.* Harrisburg, Morehouse Publishing, 1995.

LEWIS, C. S. *Mere Christianity.* San Francisco: Harper San Francisco, 2001.

MAGILL, FRANK NORTHEN, AND IAN PHILIP MCGREAL, EDS. *Masterpieces of Christian Spirituality: The Essential Guide to the Most Influential Spiritual Writings of the Christian Tradition.* San Francisco, CA: Harper San Francisco, 1988.

ROLHEISER, RONALD. *Holy Longing: The Search for a Christian Spirituality.* New York: Doubleday & Company, Inc., 1999.

WARREN, RICK. *The Purpose-Driven Life.* Grand Rapids, MI: Zondervan, 2002.

ZWEIG, CONNIE. *The Holy Longing: The Hidden Power of Spiritual Yearning.* New York: Tarcher, 2003.

Look for the following titles, available now from The Barnes & Noble Library of Essential Reading.

Visit your Barnes & Noble bookstore, or shop online at *www.bn.com/loer*

NONFICTION

Age of Revolution, The	Winston S. Churchill	0760768595
Alexander	Theodore Ayrault Dodge	0760773491
American Democrat, The	James Fenimore Cooper	0760761981
American Indian Stories	Zitkala-Ša	0760765502
Ancient Greek Historians, The	J. B. Bury	0760776350
Ancient History	George Rawlinson	0760773580
Antichrist, The	Friedrich Nietzsche	0760777705
Autobiography of Benjamin Franklin, The	Benjamin Franklin	0760768617
Autobiography of Charles Darwin	Charles Darwin	0760769087
Babylonian Life and History	E. A. Wallis Budge	0760765499
Beyond the Pleasure Principle	Sigmund Freud	0760774919
Birth of Britain, The	Winston S. Churchill	0760768579
Boots and Saddles	Elizabeth B. Custer	076077370X
Characters and Events of Roman History	Guglielmo Ferrero	0760765928
Chemical History of a Candle, The	Michael Faraday	0760765227
Civil War, The	Julius Caesar	0760768943
Common Law, The	Oliver Wendell Holmes	0760754985
Confessions	Jean-Jacques Rousseau	0760773599
Conquest of Gaul, The	Julius Caesar	0760768951
Consolation of Philosophy, The	Boethius	0760769796
Conversations with Socrates	Xenophon	0760770441

Creative Evolution	Henri Bergson	0760765480
Critique of Judgment	Immanuel Kant	0760762023
Critique of Practical Reason	Immanuel Kant	0760760942
Critique of Pure Reason	Immanuel Kant	0760755949
Dark Night of the Soul, The	St. John of the Cross	0760765871
Democracy and Education	John Dewey	0760765863
Democracy in America	Alexis de Tocqueville	0760752303
Descent of Man and Selection in Relation to Sex, The	Charles Darwin	0760763119
Dialogues concerning Natural Religion	David Hume	0760777713
Discourse on Method	René Descartes	0760756023
Discourses on Livy	Niccolò Machiavelli	0760771731
Dolorous Passion of Our Lord Jesus Christ, The	Anne Catherine Emmerich	0760771715
Early History of Rome, The	Titus Livy	0760770239
Ecce Homo	Friedrich Nietzsche	0760777721
Edison: His Life and Inventions	Frank Lewis Dyer	0760765820
Egyptian Book of the Dead, The	E. A. Wallis Budge	0760768382
Elements, The	Euclid	0760763127
Emile	Jean-Jacques Rousseau	0760773513
Eminent Victorians	Lytton Strachey	0760749930
Encheiridion	Epictetus	0760770204
Enquiry concerning Human Understanding, An	David Hume	0760755922
Essay concerning Human Understanding, An	John Locke	0760760497
Essays, The	Francis Bacon	0760770182
Essence of Christianity, The	Ludwig Feuerbach	076075764X
Ethics and On the Improvement of the Understanding	Benedict de Spinoza	0760768374
Extraordinary Popular Delusions and the Madness of Crowds	Charles Mackay	0760755825
Fall of Troy, The	Quintus of Smyrna	0760768366
Fifteen Decisive Battles of the Western World	Edward Shepherd Creasy	0760754950
Florentine History	Niccolò Machiavelli	0760756015
From Manassas to Appomattox	James Longstreet	0760759200
From Ritual to Romance	Jessie L. Weston	0760773548
Great Democracies, The	Winston S. Churchill	0760768609
Guide for the Perplexed, The	Moses Maimonides	0760757577
Hannibal	Theodore Ayrault Dodge	076076896X
Happy Hunting-Grounds, The	Kermit Roosevelt	0760755817
History of Atlantis, The	Lewis Spence	076077045X

History of the Conquest of Mexico, The	William H. Prescott	0760759227
History of the Conquest of Peru, The	William H. Prescott	076076137X
History of the Donner Party, The	Charles F. McGlashan	0760752427
History of the English Church and People, The	Bede	0760765510
History of Wales, A	J. E. Lloyd	0760752419
How the Other Half Lives	Jacob A. Riis	0760755892
How to Sing	Lilli Lehmann	0760752311
How We Think	John Dewey	0760770387
Hunting the Grisly and Other Sketches	Theodore Roosevelt	0760752338
Imitation of Christ, The	Thomas À. Kempis	0760755914
In His Steps	Charles M. Sheldon	0760755779
Influence of Sea Power upon History, The, 1660–1783	Alfred Thayer Mahan	0760754993
Interesting Narrative of the Life of Olaudah Equiano, The	Olaudah Equiano	0760773505
Interior Castle, The	St. Teresa of Avila	0760770247
Introduction to Logic	Immanuel Kant	0760770409
Introduction to Mathematical Philosophy	Bertrand Russell	0760773408
Introduction to Mathematics	Alfred North Whitehead	076076588X
Investigation of the Laws of Thought, An	George Boole	0760765847
Kingdom of God is Within You, The	Leo Tolstoy	0760765529
Lady's Life in the Rockies, A	Isabella Bird	0760763135
Leonardo da Vinci and a Memory of His Childhood	Sigmund Freud	0760749922
Letters and Saying of Epicurus	Epicurus	0760763283
Leviathan, The	Thomas Hobbes	0760755930
Life of Johnson	James Boswell	0760773483
Lives of the Caesars, The	Suetonius	0760757585
Manners, Customs, and History of the Highlanders of Scotland	Walter Scott	0760758697
Meditations	Marcus Aurelius	076075229X
Memoirs	William T. Sherman	0760773688
Metaphysics	Aristotle	0760773637
Montcalm and Wolfe	Francis Parkman	0760768358
Montessori Method, The	Maria Montessori	0760749957
Mosby's Memoirs	John Singleton Mosby	0760773726

Myths of North American Indians, The	Lewis Spence	0760770433
Napoleon's Art of War	George C. D'Aguilar	0760773564
New World, The	Winston S. Churchill	0760768587
Nicomachean Ethics	Aristotle	0760752362
Notes on Nursing	Florence Nightingale	0760749949
On Liberty	John Stuart Mill	0760755000
On the Nature of Things	Lucretius	076076834X
On War	Carl von Clausewitz	0760755973
Oregon Trail, The	Francis Parkman	076075232X
Outline of History, The: Volume 1	H. G. Wells	0760758662
Outline of History, The: Volume 2	H. G. Wells	0760758670
Passing of the Armies, The	Joshua L. Chamberlain	0760760527
Personal Memoirs of P. H. Sheridan	Philip H. Sheridan	0760773750
Personal Memoirs of U. S. Grant	Ulysses S. Grant	0760749906
Philosophy of History, The	G. W. F. Hegel	0760757631
Plato and Platonism	Walter Pater	0760765472
Political Economy for Beginners	Millicent Garrett Fawcett	0760754977
Politics	Aristotle	0760768935
Poor Richard's Almanack	Benjamin Franklin	0760762015
Pragmatism	William James	0760749965
Praise of Folly, The	Desiderius Erasmus	0760757607
Principia Ethica	G. E. Moore	0760765464
Principle of Relativity	Alfred North Whitehead	0760765219
Principles of Political Economy and Taxation, The	David Ricardo	0760765367
Problems of Philosophy, The	Bertrand Russell	076075604X
Recollections and Letters	Robert E. Lee	0760759197
Relativity	Albert Einstein	0760759219
Rights of Man, The	Thomas Paine	0760755019
Rough Riders, The	Theodore Roosevelt	0760755760
Russia and Its Crisis	Paul Miliukov	0760768633
Science and Method	Henri Poincare	0760755868
Second Treatise of Government, The	John Locke	0760760950
Sense of Beauty, The	George Santayana	0760770425
Shakespearean Tragedy	A. C. Bradley	0760771693
Social Contract, The	Jean-Jacques Rousseau	0760770212
Subjection of Women, The	John Stuart Mill	076077174X
Tenting on the Plains	Elizabeth B. Custer	0760773718
Theory of Moral Sentiments, The	Adam Smith	0760758689
Totem and Taboo	Sigmund Freud	0760765200
Tractatus Logico-Philosophicus	Ludwig Wittgenstein	0760752354

Tragic Sense of Life	Miguel de Unamuno	0760777764
Travels of Marco Polo, The	Marco Polo	0760765898
Treatise Concerning the Principles of Human Knowledge, A	George Berkeley	0760777691
Treatise of Human Nature, A	David Hume	0760771723
Trial and Death of Socrates, The	Plato	0760762007
Up From Slavery	Booker T. Washington	0760752346
Utilitarianism	William James	0760771758
Vindication of the Rights of Woman, A	Mary Wollstonecraft	0760754942
Violin Playing As I Teach It	Leopold Auer	0760749914
Voyage of the *Beagle*, The	Charles Darwin	0760754969
Wealth of Nations, The	Adam Smith	0760757615
Wilderness Hunter, The	Theodore Roosevelt	0760756031
Will to Believe and Human Immortality, The	William James	0760770190
Will to Power, The	Friedrich Nietzsche	0760777772
Worst Journey in the World, The	Aspley Cherry-Garrard	0760757593
You Know Me Al	Ring W. Lardner	0760758336

THE BARNES & NOBLE
LIBRARY OF ESSENTIAL READING

This newly developed series has been established to provide affordable access to books of literary, academic, and historic value—works of both well-known writers and those who deserve to be rediscovered. Selected and introduced by scholars and specialists with an intimate knowledge of the works, these volumes present complete, original texts in a modern, readable typeface—welcoming a new generation of readers to influential and important books of the past. With more than 100 titles already in print and more than 100 forthcoming, the Library of Essential Reading offers an unrivaled variety of thought, scholarship, and entertainment. Best of all, these handsome and durable paperbacks are priced to be exceptionally affordable. For a full list of titles, visit *www.bn.com/loer.*